Canon® EOS Rebel XS/1000D FOR DUMMIES

Cheat Sheet

Camera Road Map

Here's a handy map to the buttons, dials, and other external features on your Rebel XS/1000D. Note that the lens shown is the Canon EF-S 18–55mm IS model sold with the camera; other lenses may not have the same features. Controls marked with an asterisk have multiple functions; for simplicity's sake, I refer to them in this book by the names you see here. See Chapter 1 for details.

Exposure Compensation* AE Lock AF Point Selection

Viewfinder adjustment knob

White Balance*
Metering mode
Autofocus mode

Drive mode Picture Style

Playback Erase

Auto/Manual Focus switch
Image Stabilizer switch
Flash button

Red-eye reduction/self-timer lamp

Shutter button

Main dial

Lens-release button

Depth-of-Field Preview button

Mode dial ISO button

For Dummies: Bestselling Book Series for Beginners

Automatic Exposure Mode Quick Reference

Refer to the table below for a quick explanation of your camera's fully automatic exposure modes. In these modes, you can choose between automatic or manual focusing, but you have little or no control over most other picture-taking settings. See Chapter 2 for details.

Symbol	Exposure Mode	Description
	Full Auto	Completely automatic photography; the camera analyzes the scene and tries to choose settings that produce the best results.
	Portrait	Designed to produce softly focused backgrounds for flattering portraits.
	Landscape	Designed to keep both near and distant subjects in sharp focus.
	Close-Up	Produces softly focused backgrounds especially suitable for close-ups of flowers and other nature subjects.
	Sports	Selects a faster shutter speed to capture moving subjects without blur.
	Night Portrait	Same as Portrait, but combines flash with a slow shutter speed to produce softer lighting and brighter backgrounds. Use a tripod to avoid camera shake.
	No Flash	Same as Full Auto, but with flash disabled.

Advanced Exposure Modes

These five modes, all covered in Chapter 5, give you more control over your camera settings. In P, Tv, Av, and M modes, you can adjust aperture (f-stop) to manipulate depth of field (the zone of sharp focus) and adjust shutter speed to determine whether moving objects appear sharply focused or blurry. In all five modes, you also can tweak color, ISO (light sensitivity), and exposure.

Symbol	Exposure Mode	Description
P	Programmed Autoexposure	The camera selects both the f-stop and shutter speed to ensure proper exposure, but the user can choose from multiple combinations of the two settings.
Tv	Shutter-priority Autoexposure	The user sets shutter speed, and the camera selects the f-stop that will produce a good exposure.
Av	Aperture-priority Autoexposure	The user selects f-stop, and the camera selects the shutter speed that will produce a good exposure.
M	Manual Exposure	The user controls both the shutter speed and f-stop.
A-DEP	Automatic Depth of Field	The camera selects the f-stop needed to keep all objects in the frame in the zone of sharp focus and then selects the shutter speed that will produce a good exposure.

For Dummies: Bestselling Book Series for Beginners

Canon® EOS Rebel XS/1000D

FOR

DUMMIES®

by Julie Adair King

WILEY

Wiley Publishing, Inc.

Canon® EOS Rebel XS/1000D For Dummies®

Published by
Wiley Publishing, Inc.
111 River Street
Hoboken, NJ 07030-5774

www.wiley.com

For general information on our other products and services, please contact our Customer Care Department within the U.S. at 877-762-2974, outside the U.S. at 317-572-3993, or fax 317-572-4002.

For technical support, please visit www.wiley.com/techsupport.

Wiley also publishes its books in a variety of electronic formats. Some content that appears in print may not be available in electronic books.

Library of Congress Control Number: 2008939708

ISBN: 978-0-470-43392-8

Manufactured in the United States of America

10 9 8 7 6 5 4 3 2 1

WILEY

About the Author

Julie Adair King is the author of many books about digital photography and imaging, including the best-selling *Digital Photography For Dummies*. Her most recent titles include *For Dummies* guides to the Canon EOS Digital Rebel XTi/400D and XSi/450D, *Digital Photography Before & After Makeovers*, *Digital Photo Projects For Dummies, Julie King's Everyday Photoshop For Photographers, Julie King's Everyday Photoshop Elements,* and *Shoot Like a Pro!: Digital Photography Techniques.* When not writing, King teaches digital photography at such locations as the Palm Beach Photographic Centre. A graduate of Purdue University, she resides in Indianapolis, Indiana.

Author's Acknowledgments

I am extremely grateful to the team of talented professionals at John Wiley and Sons for all their efforts in putting together this book. Special thanks go to my awesome project editor, Kim Darosett, who is the type of editor that all authors hope for but rarely experience: supportive, skilled, and amazingly calm in the face of any storm, including my not infrequent freakouts.

I also owe much to the rest of the folks in both the editorial and art departments, especially Heidi Unger, Steve Hayes, Andy Cummings, and Mary Bednarek. Thanks, too, to Jonathan Conrad for providing the awesome nighttime shot for Chapter 7, and to agent extraordinaire, Margot Maley Hutchison, for her continuing help and encouragement.

Last but oh, so not least, I am deeply indebted to Canon guru Chuck Westfall for always answering all my questions, even the silly ones; to Scott Heath at Synergy Communications for his help with this book and various other projects; and to technical editor David Hall, whose keen eye and vast experience set me on the right track whenever I mistakenly thought I should go left. Thank you, thank you, for sharing your time and your expertise — the book would not have been the same without it.

Publisher's Acknowledgments

We're proud of this book; please send us your comments through our online registration form located at `http://dummies.custhelp.com`. For other comments, please contact our Customer Care Department within the U.S. at 877-762-2974, outside the U.S. at 317-572-3993, or fax 317-572-4002.

Some of the people who helped bring this book to market include the following:

Acquisitions and Editorial

Project Editor: Kim Darosett

Executive Editor: Steven Hayes

Copy Editor: Heidi Unger

Technical Editor: David Hall

Editorial Manager: Leah Cameron

Editorial Assistant: Amanda Foxworth

Sr. Editorial Assistant: Cherie Case

Cartoons: Rich Tennant
(`www.the5thwave.com`)

Composition Services

Project Coordinator: Erin Smith

Layout and Graphics: Carrie A. Cesavice, Reuben W. Davis, Christin Swinford

Proofreaders: Lynda D'Arcangelo, Amanda Steiner

Indexer: Galen Schroeder

Publishing and Editorial for Technology Dummies

Richard Swadley, Vice President and Executive Group Publisher

Andy Cummings, Vice President and Publisher

Mary Bednarek, Executive Acquisitions Director

Mary C. Corder, Editorial Director

Publishing for Consumer Dummies

Diane Graves Steele, Vice President and Publisher

Composition Services

Gerry Fahey, Vice President of Production Services

Debbie Stailey, Director of Composition Services

Table of Contents

Introduction

*1*n 2003, when Canon introduced the very first sub-$1000 digital SLR camera, the EOS Rebel/300D, it revolutionized the camera scene. For the first time, photography enthusiasts could enjoy the benefits of digital SLR photography without breaking the bank. And even at the then-unheard-of price, the camera delivered exceptional performance and picture quality, earning it rave reviews and multiple industry awards. No wonder it quickly became a best seller.

That tradition of excellence and value lives on in the EOS Rebel XS/1000D. Available for a price well below that of its 2003 ancestor, this baby offers the range of advanced controls that experienced photographers demand plus an assortment of tools designed to help beginners to be successful as well.

If you count yourself among the latter camp, you may have a few questions about how to take advantage of all the features your camera offers, however. For starters, you may not even be sure what SLR means or how it affects your picture taking, let alone have a clue as to all the other techie terms you encounter in your camera manual — *resolution, aperture, white balance, file format,* and so on. And if you're like many people, you may be so overwhelmed by all the controls on your camera that you haven't yet ventured beyond fully automatic picture-taking mode. Which is a shame because it's sort of like buying a Porsche and never actually taking it on the road.

Therein lies the point of *Canon EOS Rebel XS/1000D For Dummies:* Through this book, you can discover not just what each bell and whistle on your camera does, but also when, where, why, and how to put it to best use. Unlike many photography books, this one doesn't require any previous knowledge of photography or digital imaging to make sense of things, either. In classic *For Dummies* style, everything is explained in easy-to-understand language, with lots of illustrations to help clear up any confusion.

In short, what you have in your hands is the paperback version of an in-depth photography workshop tailored specifically to your Canon picture-taking powerhouse. Whether your interests lie in taking family photos, exploring nature and travel photography, or snapping product shots for your business, you'll get the information you need to capture the images you envision.

A Quick Look at What's Ahead

This book is organized into four parts, each devoted to a different aspect of using your camera. Although chapters flow in a sequence that's designed to take you from absolute beginner to experienced user, I've also tried to make each chapter as self-standing as possible so that you can explore the topics that interest you in any order you please.

The following sections offer brief previews of each part. If you're eager to find details on a specific topic, the index shows you exactly where to look.

Part I: Fast Track to Super Snaps

Part I contains four chapters that help you get up and running with your Rebel XS/1000D:

- Chapter 1, "Getting the Lay of the Land," offers a tour of the external controls on your camera, shows you how to navigate camera menus to access internal options, and walks you through initial camera setup and customization steps.

- Chapter 2, "Taking Great Pictures, Automatically," shows you how to get the best results when using the camera's fully automatic exposure modes, including Portrait, Sports, and Landscape modes.

- Chapter 3, "Controlling Picture Quality," introduces you to one setting that's critical whether you shoot in automatic or manual mode: the Quality setting, which affects resolution (pixel count), file format, file size, and picture quality.

- Chapter 4, "Monitor Matters: Picture Playback and Live View Shooting," explains how to review your pictures on the camera monitor, delete unwanted images, and protect your favorites from accidental erasure. In addition, this chapter introduces you to Live View shooting, in which you can use your monitor as a viewfinder.

Part II: Taking Creative Control

Chapters in this part help you unleash the full creative power of your camera by moving into semiautomatic or manual photography modes.

- Chapter 5, "Getting Creative with Exposure and Lighting," covers the all-important topic of exposure, starting with an explanation of three critical exposure controls: aperture, shutter speed, and ISO. This chapter also discusses your camera's advanced exposure modes (P, Tv, Av, M, and A-DEP), explains exposure options such as metering mode and exposure compensation, and offers tips for using the built-in flash.

✔ Chapter 6, "Manipulating Focus and Color," provides help with controlling those aspects of your pictures. Look here for information about your camera's automatic and manual focusing features as well as details about color controls such as white balance and the Picture Style options.

✔ Chapter 7, "Putting It All Together," summarizes all the techniques explained in earlier chapters, providing a quick-reference guide to the camera settings and shooting strategies that produce the best results for specific types of pictures: portraits, action shots, landscape scenes, close-ups, and more.

Part III: Working with Picture Files

This part of the book, as its title implies, discusses the often-confusing aspect of moving your pictures from camera to computer and beyond.

✔ Chapter 8, "Downloading, Organizing, and Archiving Your Photos," guides you through the process of transferring pictures from your camera memory card to your computer's hard drive or other storage device. Just as important, this chapter explains how to organize and safeguard your photo files.

✔ Chapter 9, "Printing and Sharing Your Photos," helps you turn your digital files into "hard copies," covering both retail and do-it-yourself printing options. This chapter also explains how to prepare your pictures for online sharing and, for times when you have the neighbors over, how to display your pictures on a television screen.

Part IV: The Part of Tens

In famous *For Dummies* tradition, the book concludes with two "top ten" lists containing additional bits of information and advice.

✔ Chapter 10, "Ten Fast Photo-Editing Tricks," shows you how to fix less-than-perfect images using the free software provided with your camera. You can find out how to remove red-eye, adjust color and exposure, crop your photo, and more.

✔ Chapter 11, "Ten Special-Purpose Features to Explore on a Rainy Day," presents information about some camera features that, while not found on most "Top Ten Reasons I Bought My Rebel XS/1000D" lists, are nonetheless interesting, useful on occasion, or a bit of both.

Icons and Other Stuff to Note

If this isn't your first For Dummies book, you may be familiar with the large, round icons that decorate its margins. If not, here's your very own icon-decoder ring:

- A Tip icon flags information that will save you time, effort, money, or some other valuable resource, including your sanity.

- When you see this icon, look alive. It indicates a potential danger zone that can result in much wailing and teeth-gnashing if ignored.

- Lots of information in this book is of a technical nature — digital photography is a technical animal, after all. But if I present a detail that is useful mainly for impressing your technology-geek friends, I mark it with this icon.

- I apply this icon either to introduce information that is especially worth storing in your brain's long-term memory or to remind you of a fact that may have been displaced from that memory by some other pressing fact.

Additionally, I need to point out two other details that will help you use this book:

- **Other margin art:** Replicas of some of your camera's buttons, dials, controls, and menu graphics also appear in the margins of some paragraphs. I include these to provide a quick reminder of the appearance of the button or option being discussed.

- **Software menu commands:** In sections that cover software, a series of words connected by an arrow indicates commands that you choose from the program menus. For example, if a step tells you to "Choose File➪Print," click the File menu to unfurl it and then click the Print command on the menu.

- **Camera firmware:** *Firmware* is the internal software that controls many of your camera's operations. This book was written using version 1.0.3 of the firmware, which was the most current at the time of publication.

  Occasionally, Canon releases firmware updates, and it's a good idea to check the Canon Web site (www.canon.com) periodically to find out whether any updates are available. (Chapter 1 tells you how to determine which firmware version your camera is running.) Firmware updates typically don't carry major feature changes — they're mostly used to solve technical glitches in existing features — but if you do download an update, be sure to read the accompanying description of what it accomplishes so that you can adapt my instructions as necessary.

About the Software Shown in This Book

Providing specific instructions for performing photo organizing and editing tasks requires that I feature specific software. In sections that cover file downloading, organizing, printing, and e-mail sharing, I selected Canon EOS Utility along with Canon ZoomBrowser EX (for Windows users) and ImageBrowser (for Mac users). These programs are part of the free software suite that ships with your camera.

Rest assured, though, that the tools used in these programs work very similarly in other programs, so you should be able to easily adapt the steps to whatever software you use. (I recommend that you read your software manual for details, of course.)

Practice, Be Patient, and Have Fun!

To wrap up this preamble, I want to stress that if you initially think that digital photography is too confusing or too technical for you, you're in very good company. *Everyone* finds this stuff a little mind-boggling at first. So take it slowly, experimenting with just one or two new camera settings or techniques at first. Then, each time you go on a photo outing, make it a point to add one or two more shooting skills to your repertoire.

I know that it's hard to believe when you're just starting out, but it really won't be long before everything starts to come together. With some time, patience, and practice, you'll soon wield your camera like a pro, dialing in the necessary settings to capture your creative vision almost instinctively.

So without further ado, I invite you to grab your camera, a cup of whatever it is you prefer to sip while you read, and start exploring the rest of this book. Your Rebel XS/1000D is the perfect partner for your photographic journey, and I thank you for allowing me, through this book, to serve as your tour guide.

Part I
Fast Track to Super Snaps

The 5th Wave

By Rich Tennant

"Try putting a person in the photo with the product you're trying to sell. We generated a lot of interest in our eBay listing once Leo started modeling my hats and scarves."

In this part . . .

Making sense of all the controls on your Rebel XS/1000D isn't something you can do in an afternoon — heck, in a week, or maybe even a month. But that doesn't mean that you can't take great pictures today. By using your camera's point-and-shoot automatic modes, you can capture terrific images with very little effort. All you do is compose the scene, and the camera takes care of almost everything else.

This part shows you how to take best advantage of your camera's automatic features and also addresses some basic setup steps, such as adjusting the viewfinder to your eyesight and getting familiar with the camera menus, buttons, and dials. In addition, chapters in this part explain how to obtain the very best picture quality, whether you shoot in an automatic or manual mode, how to use your camera's picture-playback features, and how to take advantage of Live View shooting.

1

Getting the Lay of the Land

I still remember the day that I bought my first SLR film camera. I was excited to finally move up from my one-button point-and-shoot camera, but I was a little anxious, too. My new pride and joy sported several unfamiliar buttons and dials, and the explanations in the camera manual clearly were written for someone with an engineering degree. And then there was the whole business of attaching the lens to the camera, an entirely new task for me. I saved up my pennies a long time for that camera — what if my inexperience caused me to damage the thing before I even shot my first pictures?

You may be feeling similarly insecure if your Rebel XS/1000D is your first SLR, although some of the buttons on the camera back may look familiar if you've previously used a digital point-and-shoot camera. If your Canon is both your first SLR and first digital camera, you may be doubly intimidated.

Trust me, though, that your camera isn't nearly as complicated as its exterior makes it appear. With a little practice and the help of this chapter, which introduces you to each external control, you'll quickly become as comfortable with your camera's buttons and dials as you are with the ones on your car's dashboard.

This chapter also guides you through the process of mounting and using an SLR lens, working with digital memory cards, and navigating your camera's internal menus. Finally, the end of the chapter walks you through options that enable you to customize many aspects of your camera's basic operation.

Before you start exploring this chapter, be sure that you fully charge your camera battery and then install it into the battery chamber on the bottom of the camera. I'm guessing that you have already taken this step, but if not and you need help, the front part of the camera manual provides details.

Getting Comfortable with Your Lens

One of the biggest differences between a point-and-shoot camera and an SLR *(single-lens reflex)* camera is the lens. With an SLR, you can swap out lenses to suit different photographic needs, going from an extreme close-up lens to a super-long telephoto, for example. In addition, an SLR lens has a movable focusing ring that gives you the option of focusing manually instead of relying on the camera's autofocus mechanism.

Of course, those added capabilities mean that you need a little background information to take full advantage of your lens. To that end, the next three sections explain the process of attaching, removing, and using this critical part of your camera.

Attaching a lens

Your camera can accept two categories of Canon lenses: those with a so-called EF-S design and those with a plain-old EF design.

The EF stands for *electro focus;* the S, for *short back focus.* And no, you don't really need to remember that little detail — but you do need to make sure that if you buy a Canon lens other than the one sold with the camera, it carries either the EF or EF-S specification. (If you want to buy a non-Canon lens, check the lens manufacturer's Web site to find out which lenses work with the Rebel XS/1000D.)

Whatever lens you choose, follow these steps to attach it to the camera body:

1. **Remove the cap that covers the lens mount on the front of the camera.**

2. **Remove the cap that covers the back of the lens.**

3. **Locate the proper lens mounting index on the camera body.**

   A *mounting index* is simply a marker that tells you where to align the lens with the camera body when connecting the two. Your camera has two of these markers, one red and one white, as shown in Figure 1-1.

Which marker you use to align your lens depends on the lens type:

- *Canon EF-S lens:* Align the lens mounting index with the white square on the camera body.

- *Canon EF lens:* Align the lens mounting index with the red dot instead.

If you buy a non-Canon lens, check the lens manual for help with this step.

Figure 1-1: Which index marker you should use depends on the lens type.

4. **Align the mounting index on the lens with the correct one on the camera body.**

The lens also has a mounting index; Figure 1-2 shows the one that appears on the so-called "kit lens" — the EF-S 18–55mm IS (image stabilizer) zoom lens that Canon sells as a unit with the Rebel XS/1000D. If you buy a different lens, the index marker on the lens may be red or some other color, so again, check the lens instruction manual.

Figure 1-2: Place the lens in the lens mount with the mounting indexes aligned.

5. **Keeping the mounting indexes aligned, position the lens on the camera's lens mount.**

   When you do so, grip the lens by its back collar as shown in the figure.

6. **Turn the lens in a clockwise direction until the lens clicks into place.**

   In other words, turn the lens toward the lens-release button (see Figure 1-1), as indicated by the red arrow in Figure 1-2.

Always attach (or switch) lenses in a clean environment to reduce the risk of getting dust, dirt, and other contaminants inside the camera or lens. Changing lenses on a sandy beach, for example, isn't a good idea. For added safety, point the camera body slightly down when performing this maneuver, as shown in the figure; doing so helps prevent any flotsam in the air from being drawn into the camera by gravity. See Chapter 3 for tips on cleaning your lens.

Removing a lens

To detach a lens from the camera body, take these steps:

1. **Locate the lens-release button on the front of the camera.**

   I labeled the button in Figure 1-1.

2. **Grip the rear collar of the lens.**

   In other words, hold onto the stationary part of the lens that's closest to the camera body.

3. **Press the lens-release button while turning the lens away from the lens-release button.**

   You should feel the lens release from the mount at this point. Just lift the lens off the mount to remove it.

4. **Place the rear protective cap onto the back of the lens.**

   If you aren't putting another lens on the camera, cover the lens mount with the protective cap that came with your camera, too.

Using an IS (image stabilizer) lens

The 18–55mm lens sold with the Rebel XS/1000D offers a feature called *image stabilization*. On Canon lenses, this feature is indicated by the initials *IS* in the lens name.

Image stabilization attempts to compensate for small amounts of camera shake that are common when photographers handhold their cameras and use a slow shutter speed, a lens with a long focal length, or both. That camera movement during the exposure can produce blurry images. Although image stabilization can't work miracles, it does enable most people to capture sharper handheld shots in many situations than they otherwise could.

However, when you use a tripod, image stabilization can have detrimental effects because the system may try to adjust for movement that isn't actually occurring. Although this problem shouldn't be an issue with most Canon IS lenses, if you do see blurry images while using a tripod, try setting the Stabilizer On/Off switch (shown in Figure 1-3) to Off. You also can save battery power by turning off image stabilization when you use a tripod. (Note that blurry images can result from causes other than camera shake; see Chapter 6 for help.)

If you use a non-Canon lens, the image stabilization feature may go by another name: *anti-shake, vibration compensation,* and so on. In some cases, the manufacturers may recommend that you leave the system turned on or select a special setting when you use a tripod, so be sure to check the lens manual for information.

Chapter 6 offers more tips on achieving blur-free photos, and it also explains focal length and its impact on your pictures. See Chapter 5 for an explanation of shutter speed.

Focal length indicator

Zoom barrel   Auto/Manual Focus switch

Focusing ring   Image Stabilizer On/Off

Figure 1-3: Set the focusing switch to MF before turning the manual focus ring.

Focusing and zooming the lens

Like any modern camera, digital or film, yours offers autofocusing capabilities, which you can explore in detail in Chapters 2 and 6. But with some subjects, autofocusing can be slow or impossible, which is why your camera also offers manual focusing. The process is quick and easy: You just turn the focusing ring on the lens until your subject comes into focus. To try it out, take these steps:

1. **Locate the AF/MF switch on the side of the lens.**

   Figure 1-3 shows you the switch as it appears on the Rebel XS/1000D kit lens. The switch should be in a similar location on other Canon lenses; if you use a lens from another manufacturer, check the lens instruction manual.

2. **Set the switch to the MF position, as shown in the figure.**

   Don't try to move the focusing ring with the switch set to the AF (autofocus) position; with some lenses, doing so can damage the lens.

3. **While looking through the viewfinder, twist the focusing ring to adjust focus.**

   The focusing ring is at the far end of the lens barrel, as indicated in Figure 1-3.

   If you have trouble focusing, you may be too close to your subject; every lens has a minimum focusing distance. (See Chapter 6 for more tips on focus issues.) You may also need to adjust the viewfinder to accommodate your eyesight; see the next section for details.

On a zoom lens, a movable zoom barrel lies behind the focusing ring, as shown in Figure 1-3. To zoom in or out, just move that zoom barrel forward and backward.

The numbers on the zoom barrel, by the way, represent *focal lengths*. I explain focal lengths in Chapter 6. In the meantime, just note that when the lens is mounted on the camera, the number that's aligned with the white focal-length indicator, labeled in Figure 1-3, represents the current focal length. In Figure 1-3, for example, the focal length is 55mm.

Adjusting the Viewfinder Focus

Perched on the top right edge of the viewfinder is a tiny black knob, officially called the *dioptric adjustment control*. I labeled the knob in Figure 1-4. With this control, you can adjust the magnification of the viewfinder to mesh with your eyesight.

If you don't take this step, scenes that appear out-of-focus through the viewfinder may actually be sharply focused through the lens, and vice versa.

Dioptric adjustment knob   Autofocus point

Figure 1-4: Use the dioptric adjustment control to set the viewfinder focus for your eyesight.

Here's how to make the necessary adjustment:

1. **Remove the lens cap from the front of the lens.**

2. **Look through the viewfinder and concentrate on the focusing screen shown on the right side of Figure 1-4.**

   The *focusing screen* is the collective name assigned to the group of seven autofocus points that appear in the viewfinder — the little squares with the dots inside. I labeled one of the little guys in Figure 1-4.

3. **Rotate the dioptric adjustment knob until the autofocus points appear to be in focus.**

   Don't worry about focusing the actual picture now; just pay attention to the autofocus points.

If your eyesight is such that you can't get the autofocus points to appear sharp by using the dioptric adjustment control, you can buy an additional eyepiece adapter. This accessory, which you pop onto the eyepiece, just enables further adjustment of the viewfinder display. Prices range from about $15–30 depending on the magnification you need. Look for an adapter called an *E-series dioptric adjustment lens*.

Keep in mind, too, that with the XS/1000D, you can opt to use the monitor instead of the viewfinder to frame and preview your shots. This feature is called *Live View* shooting. Because many of the functions connected with Live View shooting are similar to those you use during picture playback, I cover both uses of your monitor together in Chapter 4. Chapters 5 and 6 spell out some additional details of setting exposure and focusing in Live View mode.

Working with Memory Cards

Instead of recording images on film, digital cameras store pictures on *memory cards.* Your Rebel XS/1000D uses a specific type of memory card called an *SD card* (for *Secure Digital*), shown in Figures 1-5 and 1-6. Other card types — CompactFlash, Memory Stick, or any others — aren't compatible with your camera. However, if you use SD cards in your cell phone, portable music player, or other device, you can use the same cards in your camera. Also, your camera can use the new, high-capacity SD cards, which carry the label SDHC, as well as plain-old SD cards.

Safeguarding your memory cards — and the images you store on them — requires just a few precautions:

- ✓ **Inserting a card:** First, be sure that the camera is turned off. Then put the card in the card slot with the label facing the back of the camera, as shown in Figure 1-5. Push the card into the slot until it clicks into place.

- ✓ **Formatting a card:** The first time you use a new memory card, take a few seconds to *format* it by choosing the Format option on Setup Menu 1. This step ensures that the card is properly prepared to record your pictures. See the upcoming section "Setup Menu 1" for details.

- ✓ **Removing a card:** First, check the status of the memory card access light, labeled in Figure 1-5. After making sure that the light is off, indicating that the camera has finished recording your most recent photo, turn the camera off. Open the memory card door, as shown in Figure 1-5. Depress the memory card slightly until you hear a little click and then let go. The card should pop halfway out of the slot, enabling you to grab it by the tail and remove it.

- ✓ **Handling cards:** Don't touch the gold contacts on the back of the card. (See the left card in Figure 1-6.) When cards aren't in use, store them in the protective cases they came in or in a memory card wallet. Keep cards away from extreme heat and cold as well.

Memory card access light

Figure 1-5: Insert the card with the label facing the camera back.

Paws off!   Lock switch

Figure 1-6: Avoid touching the gold contacts on the card.

- ✓ **Locking cards:** The tiny switch on the left side of the card, labeled *lock switch* in Figure 1-6, enables you to lock your card, which prevents any data from being erased or recorded to the card. Press the switch toward the bottom of the card to lock the card contents; press it toward the top of the card to unlock the data.

Exploring External Camera Controls

Scattered across your camera's exterior are a number of buttons, dials, and switches that you use to change picture-taking settings, review and edit your photos, and perform various other operations.

In later chapters, I discuss all of your camera's functions in detail and provide the exact steps to follow to access those functions. This section provides just a basic road map to the external controls plus a quick introduction to each. You may want to put a sticky note or other bookmark on this page so that you can find it for easier reference later. (The cheat sheet at the front of the book offers a similar guide, albeit with less detail.)

With that preamble out of the way, the next three sections break down the external controls found on the top, back, and front-left side of the camera.

Topside controls

Your virtual tour begins on the top-right side of the camera, shown in Figure 1-7. There are six items of note here, as follows:

Figure 1-7: The tiny pictures on the Mode dial represent special automatic shooting modes.

✔ **On/Off switch:** Okay, I'm pretty sure you already figured this one out, but just move the switch to On to fire up the camera and then back to Off to shut it down.

By default, the camera automatically shuts itself off after 30 seconds of inactivity to save battery power. To wake up the camera, just press the shutter button halfway; you don't need to use the On/Off switch. You can adjust the auto shutdown timing via Setup Menu 1, covered later in this chapter.

✔ **Mode dial:** Rotate this dial to select an *exposure mode,* which determines whether the camera operates in fully automatic, semi-automatic, or manual exposure mode. The little pictographs, or icons, on the dial represent *Image Zone modes,* which are automatic settings geared to specific types of photos: action shots, portraits, landscapes, and so on.

Canon uses the term *Basic Zone* to refer collectively to the Image Zone modes and Full Auto mode. (That's the one represented by the greenish rectangle on the Mode dial.) The more advanced modes (P, Tv, Av, M, and A-DEP) get the label *Creative Zone.* I think that having all those zones can be a little confusing, especially because the modes in the Image Zone category are often referred to generically in photography discussions as *creative scene modes* or *creative modes.* So, just to help keep things a little simpler in this book, I use the generic terms *fully automatic exposure modes* to refer to all the Basic Zone modes and *advanced exposure modes* to refer to the Creative Zone modes. And note that none of the *exposure* modes affect focusing; you can use autofocus or manual focus in any of the exposure modes, as outlined earlier in this chapter.

✔ **Main dial:** Just forward of the Mode dial, you see a black dial that has the official name *Main dial.* This dial plays such an important role in choosing camera settings that you'd think it might have a more auspicious name, but Main dial it is.

✔ **ISO button:** You use this button, in conjunction with the Main dial, to adjust the camera's ISO speed, which determines how sensitive the camera is to light. Chapter 5 details this critical exposure setting.

✔ **Shutter button:** You probably already understand the function of this button, too. But check out Chapter 2 to discover the proper shutter-button-pressing technique — you'd be surprised how many people mess up their pictures because they press that button incorrectly.

✔ **Red-Eye Reduction/Self-Timer Lamp:** When you set your flash to Red-Eye Reduction mode, this little lamp emits a brief beam of light prior to the real flash — the idea being that your subjects' pupils will constrict in response to the light, thus lessening the chances of red-eye. If you use the camera's self-timer feature, the lamp blinks to provide you with a visual countdown to the moment at which the picture will be recorded. See Chapter 2 for more details about Red-Eye Reduction flash mode and the self-timer function.

Back-of-the-body controls

Traveling over the top of the camera to its back side, you encounter a smorgasbord of buttons — 13, in fact, not including the viewfinder's dioptric adjustment control, discussed earlier in this chapter. Figure 1-8 gives you a look at the layout of backside controls.

Set button and cross keys

Figure 1-8: Having lots of external buttons makes accessing the camera's functions easier.

 Don't let the abundance of buttons intimidate you. Having all of those external controls actually makes operating your camera easier. On cameras that have only a few external buttons, you have to dig through menus to access the camera features, which is a big pain in the keister. But on your camera, you can access almost every critical shooting setting via the external buttons. That's a convenience you'll come to appreciate after you familiarize yourself with all the camera options.

Also, as you look through this book, you may notice that the margins contain little representations of some buttons to help you locate the one being discussed. So even though I provide the official control names in the following list, don't worry about getting all of those straight right now. The list I provide here is just to get you acquainted with the *possibility* of what you can accomplish with all of these features.

Do note, however, that many of the buttons have multiple names because they serve multiple purposes depending on whether you're taking pictures, reviewing images, or performing some other function. In this book, I refer to these buttons by the first label you see in the following list just to simplify things. For example, I refer to the AF Point Selection/Enlarge button as the AF Point Selection button. Again, though, the margin icons help you know exactly which button I'm describing.

And here's another tip: If the label or icon for a button is blue, it indicates a function related to viewing, printing, or downloading images. Labels that indicate a shooting-related function are either black or white, depending on whether the camera body is silver or black.

With that preamble out of the way, journey with me now over the camera back, starting at the top-right corner and working westward (well, assuming that your lens is pointing north, anyway):

- ✐ **AF Point Selection/Enlarge button:** When you use certain advanced shooting modes, you use this button to specify which of the seven auto-focus points you want the camera to use when establishing focus. Chapter 6 tells you more about this feature. But in Playback mode and in Live View mode, you use the button to magnify the image display (thus the plus sign in the button's magnifying glass icon). See Chapter 4 for help with that function.

- ✐ **AE Lock/FE Lock/Index/Reduce button:** As you can guess from the official name of this button, it serves many purposes. The first two are related to image capture functions: You use the button to lock in the autoexposure (AE) settings and to lock flash exposure (FE). Chapter 5 details both issues. Additionally, during Live View shooting, the button serves as the autofocus and autoexposure trigger, as explained in Chapter 6.

  The button also serves two image-viewing functions: It switches the display to Index mode, enabling you to see multiple image thumbnails at once, and it also reduces the magnification of images when displayed one at a time. Again, Chapter 4 explains all these monitor-related features.

- ✐ **Aperture/Exposure Compensation button:** When you work in M (manual) exposure mode, you press this button and rotate the Main dial to choose the aperture setting, better known as the *f-stop.* In the other advanced exposure modes, you instead use the button and dial to apply *exposure compensation,* a feature that enables you to adjust the exposure selected by the camera's autoexposure mechanism. Chapter 5 discusses both issues.

- **White Balance/Print/Share button:** Press this button to access the camera's *white balance* setting, which is a feature you can use to adjust image colors. This button is also involved when you transfer images to your computer or print pictures directly from the camera. See Chapter 6 for details about white balance; check out Chapters 8 and 9 for information about image transfer and printing, respectively.

- **Set button and cross keys:** Figure 1-8 points out the Set button and the four surrounding buttons, known as *cross keys.* These buttons team up to perform several functions, including choosing options from the camera menus. You use the cross keys to navigate through menus and then press the Set button to select a specific menu setting. (The later section, "Ordering from Camera Menus," has the details.)

In this book, the instruction "Press the left cross key" just means to press the one that sports the left-pointing arrowhead. "Press the up cross key" means to press the one with the up-pointing arrowhead, and so on.

The cross keys and the Set button also have individual responsibilities, as follows:

- *Press the Set button to switch to Live View display.* You must first enable Live View through Setup Menu 2 and select one of the advanced exposure modes (P, Tv, Av, M, or A-DEP). See the end of Chapter 4 for details about using Live View.

- *Press the right cross key to adjust the AF mode.* This option controls the camera's autofocus behavior, as outlined in Chapter 6.

- *Press the left cross key to change the Drive mode.* The Drive mode settings enable you to switch the camera from single-frame shooting to continuous capture or self-timer/remote-control shooting. See Chapter 2 for details.

- *Press the down cross key to change the Picture Style.* Chapter 6 explains Picture Styles, which you can use to adjust color, contrast, and sharpness of your pictures.

- *Press the up cross key to change the exposure metering mode or to use the Jump feature during picture playback.* The *metering mode* determines which area of the frame the camera uses when determining the correct exposure settings. Chapter 5 has details. The Jump feature enables you to "fast forward" through your images during playback; see Chapter 4 for specifics.

You can customize the functions of the Set button; Chapter 11 explains how. But while you're working with this book, stick with the default setup, just described. Otherwise, the instructions I give in the book won't work.

- **Playback button:** Press this button to switch the camera into picture review mode. Chapter 4 details the camera's playback features.

- **Erase button:** Sporting a trash can icon, the universal symbol for delete, this button lets you erase pictures from your memory card. Chapter 4 has specifics. In Live View mode, also covered in Chapter 4, this button is involved in the focusing process.

- **Menu button:** Press this button to access the camera menus. See the next section for details on navigating menus.

- **DISP button:** The Shooting Settings display, covered later in this chapter, appears automatically on the monitor when you first turn on the camera and any time you press the shutter button halfway and then release it. You also can press the DISP button to view the Shooting Settings screen.

  But that's just the start of the DISP button's tricks. If the camera menus are displayed, pressing the button takes you to the Camera Functions display, explained in the upcoming section "Monitoring Critical Camera Settings." In Playback mode and Live View mode, pressing the button changes the picture-display style, as outlined in Chapter 4.

Front-left buttons

On the front-left side of the camera body, you find three more buttons, all labeled in Figure 1-9. One, the lens-release button, is key to taking the lens off the camera body, as discussed earlier in the chapter. The other two buttons work as follows:

- **Flash button:** Press this button to bring the camera's built-in flash out of hiding when you use the advanced shooting modes. (In fully automatic modes, the camera pops up the flash without your help if it decides the flash light is needed.) Chapters 5 and 7 provide tips on flash photography.

Flash button   Lens-release button

Depth-of-Field Preview button

Figure 1-9: Press the Flash button to bring the built-in flash out of hiding.

✔ **Depth-of-Field Preview button:** When you press this button, the image in the viewfinder offers an approximation of the depth of field that will result from your selected aperture setting, or f-stop. *Depth of field* refers to how much of the scene will be in sharp focus. Chapter 6 provides details on depth of field, which is an important aspect of your picture composition. Chapter 5 explains aperture and other exposure settings.

Ordering from Camera Menus

You access many of your camera's features via internal menus, which, conveniently enough, appear when you press the Menu button, located atop the upper-left corner of the camera monitor. Features are grouped into seven main menus, described briefly in Table 1-1.

Table 1-1		Rebel XS/1000D Menus
Symbol	*Open This Menu . . .*	*to Access These Functions*
	Shooting Menu 1	Picture Quality settings, Red-Eye Reduction flash mode, and a few other basic camera settings.
	Shooting Menu 2	Advanced photography options such as flash exposure compensation and automatic exposure bracketing. Menu appears only when you use advanced exposure modes (P, Tv, Av, M, and A-DEP).
	Playback	Viewing, deleting, and marking pictures for printing.
	Setup Menu 1	Basic camera-customization options, such as the file-numbering system.
	Setup Menu 2	More customization options, Live View control, and maintenance functions, such as sensor cleaning. Some options available only in advanced exposure modes.
	Setup Menu 3	Custom Functions and a couple other options; menu appears only in advanced exposure modes.
	My Menu	User-customized menu setup; also available only in advanced exposure modes.

After you press the Menu button, a screen similar to the one shown on the left in Figure 1-10 appears. Along the top of the screen, you see the icons shown in Table 1-1, each representing one of the seven menus. The icon that is highlighted is the active menu; options on that menu automatically appear on the main part of the screen. In the figure, Shooting Menu 1 is active, for example.

Figure 1-10: Use the cross keys to navigate menus; press Set to access available settings.

REMEMBER

Shooting Menu 2, Setup Menu 3, and My Menu do not appear in the menu display when you set the camera Mode dial to Full Auto or any of the other fully automatic exposure modes (Portrait, Landscape, Sports, and so on). You see these menus only when you use the advanced exposure modes (P, Tv, Av, M, and A-DEP). And some menu items on Setup Menu 2 are hidden in the fully automatic exposure modes.

I explain all the important menu options elsewhere in the book; for now, just familiarize yourself with the process of navigating menus and selecting options. Here's the drill:

✔ **To select a different menu:** Press the right or left cross keys or rotate the Main dial to cycle through the available menus.

✔ **To select and adjust a function on the current menu:** Press the up or down cross key to highlight the feature you want to adjust. On the left side of Figure 1-10, the Quality option is highlighted, for example. Next, press the Set button. Settings available for the selected item then appear either right next to the menu item or on a separate screen, as shown on the right side of the figure. Either way, use the up and down cross keys to highlight your preferred setting and then press Set again to lock in your choice.

Monitoring Critical Camera Settings

As you advance in your photography and begin to move beyond the automatic exposure modes, you need a way to keep track of what camera settings are currently active. To that end, your camera offers the Shooting Settings display, shown in Figure 1-11.

Battery status   Shots remaining

Figure 1-11: If you don't like the default Shooting Settings display (left), you can change it to the one shown in this book (right).

Normally, the display appears as shown on the left in Figure 1-11 — white text on a black background. But you can choose from three other color schemes if you prefer. To make things a little easier to read in this book, figures feature the alternative scheme shown on the right in the figure. If you want to experiment with this option, display Setup Menu 1 and highlight the Screen Color option, as shown on the left in Figure 1-12. Press Set to bring up the options shown on the right in the figure. Highlight one of the four choices and press Set to wrap up. (The color scheme you see from here on out in this book is option 2.)

Whatever color scheme you use, the Shooting Settings screen appears automatically when you turn on the camera. Then, when you press the shutter button halfway, which is the first step in taking a picture, the screen disappears. When you let up on the button, the screen reappears. You also can turn the monitor display on and off by pressing the DISP button or the Set button when no menus are active.

Figure 1-12: Visit Setup Menu 1 to change the color scheme of the Shooting Settings screen.

In Figure 1-11, you see an example of the settings that you can monitor in the advanced exposure modes (P, Tv, Av, M, and A-DEP). In fully automatic modes, many of the settings are hidden to make the display simpler. Either way, if what you see looks like a big confusing mess to you now, don't worry. Most of it won't mean anything to you until you make your way through later chapters and explore all of the camera controls.

The figure does label two key points of data that are helpful even in fully automatic modes, though: how many more pictures can fit on your memory card at the current settings and the status of the battery. A "full" battery icon like the one in the figure shows that the battery is fully charged; if the icon appears empty, go look for your battery charger.

In addition to the Shooting Settings display, you can activate the Camera Function Settings display, shown in Figure 1-13. To display this screen, first display the camera menus by pressing the Menu button. Then press the DISP button.

Again, the items listed on the screen in the figure appear in the advanced exposure modes. The following list explains the settings that you can monitor, detailed from top to bottom in the order they appear on the screen.

Figure 1-13: Press the DISP button when the menus are active to view this screen.

- ✏ **Freespace:** This value indicates how much storage space is left on your current camera memory card. How many pictures you can fit into that space depends on the Quality setting you select. Chapter 3 explains this issue.

- ✏ **Color Space:** This value tells you whether the camera is currently capturing images in the sRGB or Adobe RGB color space, an advanced option that you can investigate in Chapter 6.

- ✏ **White Balance Shift/Bracketing:** Add this to the list of advanced color options covered in Chapter 6.

- ✏ **Live View Shooting:** Chapter 4 details this feature, which enables you to use your monitor instead of the viewfinder to compose your shots.

- ✏ **Auto Sensor Cleaning and Red-Eye Reduction flash mode:** (These two functions share a line in the screen.) See "Setup Menu 2," later in this chapter, for more about automatic sensor cleaning; check out Chapter 2 for information about red-eye reduction flash.

- ✏ **Auto Power Off and Auto Rotate Display:** For information on these two settings, which also cohabitate on the Camera Function Settings screen), see the upcoming section, "Setup Menu 1."

- ✏ **Beep:** This setting determines whether the camera beeps at you after certain operations; you can adjust the setting via Shooting Menu 1, as explained later in this chapter.

- ✏ **Date/Time:** The section "Setup Menu 2" also explains how to adjust the date and time.

In the fully automatic exposure modes, the Color Space, White Balance Shift/ Bracketing, and Live View Shooting status information doesn't appear in this screen because you can't use those features unless you switch to an advanced exposure mode.

Of course, with the exception of the free card space value, you also can simply go to the menu that contains the option in question to check its current status. The Shooting Settings display and Camera Function Settings display just give you a quick way to monitor some of the critical functions without hunting through menus.

In addition, if you switch to Live View shooting, you also can display some of the same settings in the monitor preview, along with your image. Chapter 4, which introduces Live View shooting, shows you how to do so.

Decoding Viewfinder Data

When the camera is turned on, you can view critical exposure settings and a few other pieces of information in the viewfinder. Just put your eye to the viewfinder and press the shutter button halfway to activate the viewfinder display. (I'm assuming that Live View mode, in which you use the monitor as viewfinder, is disabled, as it is by default. See Chapter 4 if you want more details about Live View.)

The viewfinder data changes depending on what action you're currently undertaking and what exposure mode you're using. For example, if you set the Mode dial to P (for programmed autoexposure), you see the current f-stop (aperture setting), shutter speed, exposure compensation setting, and ISO setting, as shown in Figure 1-14.

Shutter speed and f-stop   ISO Speed

Exposure compensation amount   Maximum burst frames

Figure 1-14: You also can view some camera information at the bottom of the viewfinder.

The final value (9, in the figure) shows you the number of *maximum burst frames.* This number relates to shooting in the Continuous capture mode, where the camera fires off multiple shots in rapid-fire succession as long as you hold down the shutter button. (Chapter 2 has details on this mode.) Note that although the highest number that the viewfinder can display is 9, the actual number of maximum burst frames may be higher. At any rate, you don't really need to pay attention to the number until it starts dropping toward 0, which indicates that the camera's *memory buffer* (its temporary internal data-storage tank) is filling up. If that happens, just give the camera a moment to catch up with your shutter-button finger.

Rather than give you a full guide to all the possible viewfinder readouts here, which would only boggle your mind and cause lots of unnecessary page-flipping, I detail the relevant viewfinder data as I cover the various photographic topics later in the book.

Reviewing Basic Setup Options

You know how sometimes you visit someone's house and their kitchen cabinets are arranged in a way that doesn't make sense to you? Why are the mugs above the microwave instead of above the coffeepot? And wouldn't it be better if the serving spoons were next to the stove instead of by the dishwasher? That's how I feel about the way that settings that relate to basic camera setup are organized on the camera menus. They surely make sense to *somebody* — namely, I'm guessing, the important somebodies at Canon. But to me, a couple of the basic setup options are out of place, found on menus other than Setup Menus 1, 2, or 3, where you might expect to find them. And Setup Menus 2 and 3 offer some options that are related more to advanced photographic controls than basic camera operation.

Well, I can't rearrange the menus for you any more than I can put those mugs near the coffeemaker, so instead, the following sections describe the options found on the aforementioned trio of Setup Menus, plus two additional options found on Shooting Menu 1.

If you don't yet know how to select options from the menus, see the earlier section, "Ordering from Camera Menus" for help.

In case you haven't noticed, the icons that represent the menus are color coded. Shooting Menus 1 and 2 have red icons; Setup Menus 1, 2, and 3 sport yellow icons; the Playback menu has a blue symbol; and the My Menus icon is green. (Chapter 11 explains the My Menus feature, through which you can create your own, custom menu.)

Setup Menu 1

At the risk of being labeled conventional, I suggest that you start your camera customization by opening this menu, shown in Figure 1-15.

Here's a quick rundown of each menu item:

Figure 1-15: Options on Setup Menu 1 deal mainly with basic camera behavior.

✔ **Auto Power Off:** To help save battery power, your camera automatically powers down after a certain period of inactivity. By default, the shutdown happens after 30 seconds, but you can change the shutdown delay to 1, 2, 4, 8, or 15 minutes. Or you can disable auto shutdown altogether by selecting the Off setting.

✔ **File Numbering:** This option controls how the camera names your picture files. When the option is set to Continuous, as it is by default, the camera numbers your files sequentially, from 0001 to 9999, and places all images in the same folder. The initial folder name is 100Canon; when you reach image 9999, the camera creates a new folder, named 101Canon, for your next 9999 photos. This numbering sequence is retained even if you change memory cards, which helps to ensure that you don't wind up with multiple images that have the same file name.

By contrast, the Auto Reset option automatically starts file numbering at 0001 each time you put in a different memory card. I discourage the use of this option, for the reason already stated.

Whichever of these two options you choose, beware one gotcha: If you swap out memory cards and the new card already contains images, the camera may pick up numbering from the last image on the new card, which throws a monkey wrench into things. To avoid this problem, just format the new card before putting it into the camera. (See the upcoming Format bullet point for details.)

Finally, if you choose Manual Reset, the camera begins a new numbering sequence, starting at 0001, for your next shot. The Continuous mode is then automatically selected for you again.

✔ **Auto Rotate:** If you enable this feature, your picture files include a piece of data that indicates whether the camera was oriented in the vertical or horizontal position when you shot the frame. Then, when you view the picture on the camera monitor or on your computer, the image is automatically rotated to the correct orientation.

To automatically rotate images both in the camera monitor and on your computer monitor, stick with the default setting. In the menu, this setting is represented by On followed by a camera icon and a monitor icon, as shown in Figure 1-15. If you want the rotation to occur just on your computer and not on the camera, select the second On setting, which is marked with the computer monitor symbol but not the camera symbol. To disable rotation for both devices, choose the Off setting.

Note, though, that the camera may record the wrong orientation data for pictures that you take with the camera pointing directly up or down. Also, whether your computer can read the rotation data in the picture file depends on the software you use; the programs bundled with the camera can perform the auto rotation.

✔ **Format:** The first time you insert a new memory card, you should use this option to *format* the card, a maintenance function that wipes out any existing data on the card and prepares it for use by the camera.

If you previously used your card in another device, such as a digital music player, be sure to copy those files to your computer before you format the card.

When you choose the Format option from the menu, you can opt to perform a normal card formatting process or a *low-level formatting*. The latter gives your memory card a deeper level of cleansing than ordinary formatting and thus takes longer to perform. Normally, a regular formatting will do.

✔ **LCD Off/On Btn:** This option gives you three ways to control when the monitor displays and turns off the Shooting Settings screen. At the default setting, named Shutter Btn, the screen appears when you first turn the camera on, disappears when you press the shutter button halfway, and then reappears after you release the shutter button. The screen remains visible until you next press the shutter button or the camera shuts itself off automatically at the time you specify through the Auto Power Off option. (See the first bullet in this list.)

If you select the second option, named Shutter/DISP, the screen disappears when you press the shutter button halfway and does not reappear when you release the button. You then must press the Set or DISP button to view the screen. And if you select the third option, Remains On, the screen does not go away when you press the shutter button halfway; you must press Set or DISP to turn the monitor off.

Because the monitor is one of the biggest drains on battery power, I don't advise using the Remains On setting. And while using this book, I suggest you stick with the default setting so that things work as described in steps and other text.

✔ **Screen Color:** I cover this option earlier, in the section that introduces the Shooting Settings screen, but here's a quick reminder: If you don't like the default background color of the Shooting Settings display, which is white text on a black background, you can choose from three other color schemes via this menu option.

For this book, I use color scheme 2, which produces black text on a white background, which is a little easier to read on the printed page.

Setup Menu 2

 Setup Menu 2, shown in Figure 1-16, offers an additional batch of customization options. But you can take advantage of only the following options in all exposure modes (Full Auto, Manual, Portrait, and so on):

✔ **LCD Brightness:** This option enables you to make the camera monitor brighter or darker. After highlighting the option on the menu, as shown in Figure 1-16, press Set to display a screen similar to what you see in Figure 1-17. The camera displays a picture from your memory card in the main preview area; if the card is empty, you see a black box instead.

Press the right and left cross keys to adjust the brightness setting. Press Set again to return to the menu.

If you take this step, keep in mind that what you see on the display may not be an accurate rendition of the actual exposure of your image. Crank up the monitor brightness, for example, and an underexposed photo may look just fine. So I recommend that you keep the brightness at the default setting, which places the brightness marker at dead center on the little brightness scale, as shown in Figure 1-17. As an alternative, you can display the *histogram,* an exposure guide that I explain in Chapter 4, when reviewing your images.

Figure 1-16: Most options on Setup Menu 2 can be used only in advanced exposure modes.

Figure 1-17: You can adjust the brightness of the camera monitor.

✔ **Date/Time:** When you power up your camera for the very first time, it automatically displays this option and asks you to set the current date and time.

Keeping the date/time accurate is important because that informa- tion is recorded as part of the image file. In your photo browser, you can then see when you shot an image and, equally handy, search for images by the date they were taken. Chapter 8 shows you where to locate the date/time data when browsing your picture files.

✔ **Language:** This option determines the language of any text displayed on the camera monitor. Screens in this book display the English language, but I find it entertaining on occasion to hand my camera to a friend after changing the language to, say, Swedish. I'm a real yokester, yah?

✔ **Video System:** This option is related to viewing your images on a tele- vision, a topic I cover in Chapter 9. Select NTSC if you live in North America or other countries that adhere to the NTSC video standard; select PAL for playback in areas that follow that code of video conduct.

That leaves the following menu options, which you can't access (or access fully) unless you switch to one of the advanced exposure modes (P, Tv, Av, M, or A-DEP):

✔ **Sensor Cleaning:** By default, the camera's sensor-cleaning mechanism activates each time you turn the camera on and off. This process helps keep the image sensor — which is the part of the camera that captures the image — free of dust and other particles that can mar your photos.

In the fully automatic modes, you have the option of turning the feature off, but I can't imagine why you would choose to do so. You can also initiate a cleaning cycle via this menu option at any time.

In the advanced exposure modes, you can access a third option that prepares the camera for manual cleaning of the sensor. I don't recommend this practice; sensors are delicate, and you're really better off taking the camera to a good service center for cleaning.

✔ **Live View Functions:** This part of the menu enables you to enable Live View mode, in which you can preview your shots in the monitor, and to customize a couple of aspects of how the camera behaves in that mode. Chapter 4 explains your options. (By default, Live View shooting is disabled.)

✔ **Flash Control:** Here's where you customize certain aspects of how your flash behaves. Chapter 5 provides details on flash photography.

Setup Menu 3

This menu, shown in Figure 1-18, contains the following offerings, which you can access only in the advanced exposure modes. Again, those modes are P, Tv, Av, M, and A-DEP. Chapter 5 introduces you to each mode.

Figure 1-18: To display Setup Menu 3, you must set the Mode dial to an advanced exposure mode.

✔ **Custom Functions:** Selecting this option opens the door to customizing 12 camera functions, known as Custom Functions in Canon lingo. These functions either relate to advanced exposure options or are otherwise designed for people with some photography experience. Check the index to find out where to locate details about the various functions.

✔ **Clear Settings:** Via this menu option, you can restore the default shooting settings that are used for the advanced exposure modes. You also can reset all the Custom Functions settings to their defaults through this option.

✔ **Firmware Ver.:** This screen tells you the current version of the camera firmware (internal operating software). At the time of publication, the current firmware version was 1.0.3.

 Keeping your camera firmware up-to-date is important, so visit the Canon Web site (www.canon.com) regularly to find out whether your camera sports the latest version. Follow the instructions given on the Web site to download and install updated firmware if needed.

Three more customization options

 Shooting Menu 1, shown in Figure 1-19, offers two more basic setup options — at least, these options fall into that category if you share my logic, which some may consider a frightening prospect. At any rate, these two options work as follows:

Figure 1-19: You can silence the camera via Shooting Menu 1.

✔ **Beep:** By default, your camera beeps at you after certain operations, such as after it sets focus when you shoot in Autofocus mode. If you're doing top-secret surveillance work and need the camera to hush up, set this option to Off.

✔ **Shoot w/o Card:** Setting this option to Off prevents shutter-button release when no memory card is in the camera. If you turn the option on, you can take a picture and then review the results for a few seconds in the camera monitor. The image isn't stored anywhere, however; it's temporary.

If you're wondering about the point of this option, it's designed for use in camera stores, enabling salespeople to demonstrate cameras without having to keep a memory card in every model. Unless that feature somehow suits your purposes, keep this option set to Off.

Why does this camera have two names?

As is the case with some other Canon cameras, yours goes by different names — EOS Rebel XS or EOS 1000D — depending on the part of the world where it's sold.

The *EOS* part, by the way, stands for Electro Optical System, the core technology used in Canon's autofocus SLR (single-lens reflex) cameras. According to Canon, the proper pronunciation is *ee-ohs,* which is also how you pronounce the name *Eos,* the goddess of dawn in Greek mythology.

With apologies to the goddess, I save a little room in this book by shortening the camera name to simply Rebel XS/1000D, which is already long enough.

2

Taking Great Pictures, Automatically

Are you old enough to remember the Certs television commercials from the 1960s and '70s? "It's a candy mint!" declared one actor. "It's a breath mint!" argued another. Then a narrator declared the debate a tie and spoke the famous catchphrase: "It's two, two, two mints in one!"

Well, that's sort of how I see the Rebel XS/1000D. On one hand, it provides a full range of powerful controls, offering just about every feature a serious photographer could want. On the other, it also offers fully automated exposure modes that enable people with absolutely no experience to capture beautiful images. "It's a sophisticated photographic tool!" "It's as easy as 'point and shoot!'" "It's two, two, two cameras in one!"

Now, my guess is that you bought this book for help with your camera's advanced side, so that's what other chapters cover. This chapter, however, is devoted to your camera's simpler side. Even when you shoot in the fully automatic modes, following a few basic guidelines can help you get better results. For example, your camera offers a variety of fully automatic exposure modes, some of which may be new to you. The mode affects the look of your pictures, so this chapter explains those options. I also cover techniques that enable you to get the best performance from your camera's autofocus and autoexposure systems and review the flash options and Drive mode settings available to you in automatic modes.

Getting Good Point-and-Shoot Results

Your camera offers several fully automatic exposure modes, all of which I explain later in this chapter. But in any of those modes, the key to good photos is to follow a specific picture-taking technique.

To try it out, set the Mode dial on top of the camera to Full Auto, as shown in the left image in Figure 2-1. Then set the focusing switch on the lens to the AF (autofocus) position, as shown in the right image in Figure 2-1. (The figure features the lens that is bundled with the Rebel XS/1000D. If you use a different lens, the switch may look and operate differently; check your lens manual for details.)

Auto/Manual Focus switch

Full Auto mode   Image Stabilizer switch

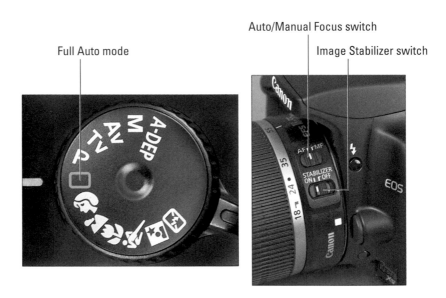

Figure 2-1: Choose these settings for fully automatic exposure and focus.

Unless you are using a tripod, also set the Stabilizer switch to the On setting, as shown in Figure 2-1. This feature helps produce sharper images by compensating for camera movement that can occur when you handhold the camera. Again, if you use a lens other than the kit lens, check your lens manual for details about using its stabilization feature, if provided.

Your camera is now set up to work in the most automatic of automatic modes. Follow these steps to take the picture:

1. **Looking through the viewfinder, frame the image so that your subject appears under an autofocus point.**

   The *autofocus points* are those seven tiny rectangles clustered in the center of the viewfinder, as shown in Figure 2-2.

Figure 2-2: The tiny rectangles in the viewfinder indicate autofocus points.

2. **Press and hold the shutter button halfway down.**

   The camera's autofocus and autoexposure meters begin to do their thing. In dim light, the flash may pop up if the camera thinks additional light is needed. Additionally, the flash may shoot out an *AF-assist beam*, emitting a few rapid pulses of light designed to help the autofocusing mechanism find its target. (The *AF* stands for autofocus.)

   At the same time, the autoexposure meter analyzes the light and selects initial aperture (f-stop) and shutter speed settings, which are two critical exposure controls. These two settings appear in the viewfinder; in Figure 2-2, the shutter speed is 1/250 second and the f-stop is f/5.6. You also see the current ISO setting and the maximum burst rate. (Chapter 5 details shutter speed, f-stops, and ISO; see Chapter 1 for information about the maximum burst rate.)

When focus is established, the camera beeps at you, assuming that you didn't silence its voice via Shooting Menu 1. Additionally, the focus indicator in the viewfinder lights, as shown in Figure 2-3, and the dot inside an autofocus point starts to blink red. That blinking dot indicates which autofocus point the camera used to establish focus. Sometimes multiple dots blink, which simply tells you that all the objects within those autofocus areas are now in focus; for example, in Figure 2-3, all autofocus points except the leftmost one are red.

The autoexposure meter continues monitoring the light up to the time you take the picture, so the f-stop and shutter speed values in the viewfinder may change if the light shifts.

Focus light

Figure 2-3: The green light indicates that the camera has locked focus.

3. Press the shutter button the rest of the way down to record the image.

While the camera sends the image data to the camera memory card, the memory card access lamp lights, as shown in Figure 2-4. Don't turn off the camera or remove the memory card while the lamp is lit, or you may damage both camera and card.

When the recording process is finished, the picture appears briefly on the camera monitor. See Chapter 4 to find out how to adjust or disable the instant review and how to switch to Playback mode and take a longer look at your image.

I need to add a couple important notes about this process, especially related to Step 2:

Memory card access lamp

Figure 2-4: The card access lamp lights while the camera sends the picture data to the card.

 ✔ **Solving autofocus problems:** When you shoot in the fully automatic modes, the camera typically focuses on the closest object. If the camera insists on selecting an autofocus point that isn't appropriate for your subject, the easiest solution is to switch to manual focusing and be done with it. Chapter 1 shows you how. Or you can use the advanced exposure modes, which enable you to select a specific autofocus point. Chapter 6 explains that option plus a few other tips for getting good autofocus results.

 ✔ **Shooting moving subjects:** If the focus indicator doesn't light but you hear a continuous series of beeps, the camera's telling you that it detected motion in the scene. To accommodate that motion, it shifts to an autofocusing mode called AI Servo. (The AI stands for *artificial intelligence.*) In this mode, the camera focuses continually after you press the shutter button halfway. As long as you keep the subject within one of the autofocus points, focus should be correct. See Chapter 6 for more tips about this and other autofocus modes.

 ✔ **Locking exposure:** By default, pressing the shutter button halfway does not lock exposure along with focus. Your camera instead continues metering and adjusting exposure until you fully depress the shutter button. If you want to lock exposure, you must use an advanced exposure mode; see Chapter 5 for help.

 ✔ **Changing the Drive mode setting:** In most of the automatic exposure modes, your camera automatically sets the Drive mode to Single, which records a single image with each press of the shutter button. But in Portrait and Sports modes, the camera instead selects Continuous mode, which records pictures as long as you hold down the shutter button. You can change the Drive mode to a Self-Timer or Remote Control setting for any exposure mode, however. See the end of this chapter for details.

 ✔ **Shooting in Live View mode:** Unfortunately, you can't use Live View mode, which enables you to frame your image using the camera monitor instead of the viewfinder. If you want to take advantage of Live View, you must switch to an advanced exposure mode. Chapter 4 provides a primer on Live View shooting.

More focus factors to consider

When you focus the lens, either in autofocus or manual focus mode, you determine only the point of sharpest focus. The distance to which the sharp-focus zone extends from that point — what photographers call the *depth of field* — depends in part on the *aperture setting,* or *f-stop,* which is an exposure control. Some of your camera's fully automatic exposure modes are designed to choose aperture settings that produce a certain depth of field.

The Portrait setting, for example, uses an aperture setting that shortens the depth of field so that background objects are softly focused — an artistic choice that most people prefer for portraits. On the flip side of the coin, the Landscape setting selects an aperture that produces a large depth of field so that both foreground and background objects appear sharp.

Another exposure-related control, *shutter speed,* plays a focus role when you photograph moving objects. Moving objects appear blurry at slow shutter speeds; at fast shutter speeds, they appear sharply focused. On your camera,

the Sports shooting mode automatically selects a high shutter speed to help you "stop" action, producing blur-free shots of the subject.

A fast shutter speed can also help safeguard against allover blurring that results when the camera is moved during the exposure. The faster the shutter speed, the shorter the exposure time, which reduces the time that you need to keep the camera absolutely still. For a very slow shutter speed, using a tripod is the best way to avoid camera shake.

Keep in mind, too, that the range of f-stops and shutter speeds the camera can select in any of the creative scene modes depends on the lighting conditions. When you're shooting at night, for example, the camera may not be able to select a shutter speed fast enough to stop action even in Sports mode. If you want to manipulate focus and depth of field to a greater extent than the automated exposure modes produce, visit Chapter 6. For an explanation of the role of shutter speed and aperture in exposure, check out Chapter 5.

Using Flash in Automatic Exposure Modes

Your options for using flash depend on which of the fully automatic exposure modes you choose, as follows:

- ✔ **Sports, Landscape, and Flash Off modes:** Flash is disabled for these modes. For the Flash Off mode, that behavior makes sense, of course. But why no flash in the other two modes? Well, Sports mode is designed to enable you to capture moving subjects, and the flash can make that more difficult because it needs time to recycle between shots. On top of that, the maximum shutter speed that's possible with the built-in flash is 1/200 second, which often isn't fast enough to ensure a blur-free subject. Finally, action photos usually aren't taken at a range close enough for the flash to reach the subject, which is also the reason why flash is disabled for Landscape mode.

✔ **Full Auto, Portrait, Close Up, and Night Portrait modes:** In these modes, the camera automatically pops up the built-in flash when needed. You do have the option of setting the flash to either normal or Red-Eye Reduction mode, however. You do so via the Red-Eye On/Off setting on Shooting Menu 1. Select the option, as shown on the left in Figure 2-5, and press the Set button to display the second screen in the figure. Then highlight your choice and press Set again. When you turn the feature off, the flash operates in normal mode.

Figure 2-5: Turn Red-Eye Reduction flash mode on and off via Shooting Menu 1.

In Red-Eye Reduction mode, the Red-Eye Reduction lamp on the front of the camera lights up when you press the shutter button halfway. The purpose of this light is to attempt to shrink the subject's pupils, which helps reduce the chances of red-eye. The flash itself fires when you press the shutter button the rest of the way. See Chapters 5 and 7 for more tips about using your flash.

You can also verify the current flash setting by displaying the Camera Function Settings screen; introduced in Chapter 1. To display this screen, press the Menu button and then press the DISP button. Additionally, the viewfinder displays the following symbols to alert you to the flash status:

 ✔ **Flash On:** A little lightning bolt like the one you see in the margin here and in the highlighted area of Figure 2-6 tells you that the flash is enabled. The viewfinder symbol doesn't indicate whether the Red-Eye Reduction mode is enabled, however.

✔ **Flash Recycling:** If you see the word *Busy* along with the lightning bolt, as shown in Figure 2-6, the flash needs a few moments to recharge. When the flash is ready to go, the *Busy* message disappears.

TIP

✓ **Red-Eye Signal:** After you press the shutter button halfway in Red-Eye Reduction flash mode, a row of vertical bars appears in the center of the viewfinder display, just to the left of the ISO value readout. A few instants later, the bars turn off one by one. For best results, wait until all the bars are off to take the picture. (The delay gives the subject's pupils time to constrict in response to the Red-Eye Reduction lamp.)

Flash status indicators

Figure 2-6: A *Busy* signal means that the flash is recharging.

Exploring Your Automatic Options

You can choose from seven fully automatic exposure modes, all of which you access via the Mode dial on the top of the camera, shown in Figure 2-7.

The next sections provide details on each of these options. For information about the five other settings on the Mode dial, see Chapter 5.

Fully automatic exposure modes

Figure 2-7: You can select from seven fully automatic exposure modes.

Full Auto mode

In this mode, represented on the Mode dial by the rectangle you see in the margin here, the camera selects all settings based on the scene that it detects in front of the lens. Your only job is to lock in focus, using the two-stage autofocus technique I outline at the beginning of the chapter, or by setting the lens to manual focus mode and using the focus ring on the lens, as explained in Chapter 1.

Full Auto mode is great for casual, quick snapshooting. But keep these limitations in mind:

✔ **Picture Style:** Full Auto mode records your photo using the Standard Picture Style setting. The aim of this mode is to produce a crisp, vivid image. You can get more details about how Picture Styles affect your photos in Chapter 6.

✔ **Drive mode:** The camera selects the Single setting automatically, so you record one image for every press of the shutter button. For information on how to change the setting to a Self-Timer or Remote Control mode, see the last section in this chapter.

✔ **Flash:** The camera takes control over whether you can use flash. You can't enable the flash if the camera's autoexposure meter doesn't sense that additional light is needed. Nor can you disable the flash or adjust its intensity, a feature I cover in Chapter 5. You can, however, use Red-Eye Reduction flash mode; see the preceding section for details.

✔ **Autofocusing:** In most cases, the camera focuses the closest object that falls under one of the autofocus points. To focus on a different area, the easiest option is to switch to manual focusing.

If you do stick with autofocus, note that the camera adjusts its autofocusing behavior depending on whether it thinks you're shooting a still or moving subject. For still subjects, the camera locks focus when you depress the shutter halfway. But if the camera senses motion, it continually adjusts focus from the time you depress the shutter button halfway. You must reframe your shot as necessary to keep the subject within one of the seven autofocus points to ensure sharp focus.

See Chapter 6 for additional information on getting good autofocus results.

✔ **Color:** Color decisions are also handled for you automatically. Normally, the camera's color brain does a good job of rendering the scene, but if you do want to tweak color, you must switch to an advanced exposure mode. You can then manipulate color via the white-balance controls and Picture Style options, all covered in Chapter 6.

✔ **Exposure:** You also give up total control over exposure to the camera. Chapter 5 shows you what you're missing.

✔ **Quality:** For the Quality setting, which determines both the image resolution, or pixel count, and the file format, you are limited to settings that use the JPEG file format. Chapter 3 discusses this issue.

I purposely didn't include an example of a photo taken in Full Auto mode because, frankly, the results that this setting create vary widely depending on how well the camera detects whether you're trying to shoot a portrait, landscape, action shot, or whatever. But the bottom line is that Full Auto is a one-size-fits-all approach that may not take best advantage of your camera's capabilities. So if you want to more consistently take great pictures instead of good ones, I encourage you to explore the exposure, focus, and color information found in Part II so that you can abandon this exposure mode in favor of ones that put more photographic decisions in your hands.

Automatic scene modes (a.k.a. Image Zone modes)

In Full Auto mode, the camera tries to figure out what type of picture you want to take by assessing what it sees through the lens. If you don't want to rely on the camera to make that judgment, your camera offers six other fully automatic modes that are specifically designed for taking popular categories of pictures. For example, most people prefer portraits that have softly focused backgrounds. So in Portrait mode, the camera selects settings that can produce that type of background.

These six automatic modes — the ones represented by the little pictographs on the Mode dial — are officially known as Image Zone modes in Canon lingo and in your camera manual. For reasons I state in Chapter 1, I avoid using the whole "zone" moniker system in this book and instead refer to the six Image Zone modes as *fully automatic scene modes*. But if you should seek information about these modes elsewhere, whether online or in your manual, be sure to search for the topic under its official name.

Whatever you call them, all six modes share a few limitations — or benefits, depending on how you look at things:

- **Color:** As with Full Auto mode, you can't tweak color. Some modes manipulate colors in ways that you may or may not appreciate, and you're stuck if you have a color cast problem.

- **Exposure:** The camera takes complete control of exposure, too.

- **Quality:** You can't take advantage of the Raw file format (CR2, on your Canon); you must use the JPEG format. See Chapter 3 to find out which of the JPEG settings is most appropriate for the way you plan to use your pictures.

In the next sections, you can read about the unique features of each of the scene modes.

Portrait mode

Portrait mode attempts to select an aperture (f-stop) setting that results in a short depth of field, which blurs the background and puts the visual emphasis on your subject. Figure 2-8 offers an example. Keep in mind, though, that the short depth of field produced by Portrait mode may result in softer focus on objects set in front of your subject, not just those behind it. Either way, the extent to which the depth of field is reduced depends on the current lighting conditions (which affect the range of f-stops the camera can use), the distance between your subject and those foreground or background objects, and a couple of other factors that I discuss in Chapter 6.

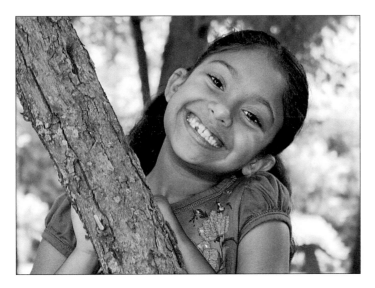

Figure 2-8: Portrait setting produces a softly focused background.

Along with favoring an f-stop that produces a shorter depth of field, the camera selects these settings in Portrait mode:

- **Picture Style:** Logically enough, the camera automatically sets the Picture Style option to Portrait. As detailed in Chapter 6, this Picture Style results in a slightly less sharp image, the idea being to keep skin texture nice and soft. Colors are also adjusted subtly to enhance skin tones.

- **Drive mode:** Contrary to what you may expect, the Drive mode is set to Continuous, which means that the camera records a series of images in rapid succession as long as you hold down the shutter button. This technique can come in especially handy if your portrait subject can't be counted on to remain still for very long — a toddler or pet, for example.

  Should you want to include yourself in the portrait, you can switch the Drive mode setting to a Self-Timer or Remote Control mode. See the end of this chapter for details.

- **Flash:** You have the option of using regular or Red-Eye Reduction mode — but only if the camera decides that you need a flash to properly light the scene.

  For outdoor portraits, this can pose a problem: A flash generally improves outdoor portraits, and if the ambient light is very bright, the camera doesn't give you access to the flash. For an illustration of the difference a flash can make, see Chapter 7. That chapter also contains tips on using flash in nighttime and indoor portraits.

Autofocusing: Portrait mode employs the One-Shot AF (autofocus) mode. This is one of three AF modes available on your camera, all detailed in Chapter 6. In One-Shot mode, the camera locks focus when you press the shutter button halfway. Typically, the camera locks focus on the closest object that falls under one of the seven autofocus points. If your subject moves out of the selected autofocus point, the camera doesn't adjust focus to compensate.

 Keep in mind that you can use Portrait mode any time you want a slightly blurry background, not just for people pictures. Try this mode when shooting statues, still-life arrangements (such as a vase of flowers on a kitchen table), and the like.

Landscape mode

Whereas Portrait mode aims for a very shallow depth of field (small zone of sharp focus), Landscape mode, which is designed for capturing scenic vistas, city skylines, and other large-scale subjects, produces a large depth of field. As a result, objects both close to the camera and at a distance appear sharply focused, as shown in Figure 2-9.

Figure 2-9: Landscape mode produces a large zone of sharp focus and also intensifies blues and greens.

Like Portrait mode, Landscape mode achieves the greater depth of field by manipulating the exposure settings — specifically, the aperture, or f-stop setting. So the extent to which the camera can succeed in keeping everything in sharp focus depends on the available light. To fully understand this issue, see Chapters 5 and 6. And in the meantime, know that you also can extend depth of field by zooming out, if you're using a zoom lens, and moving farther from your subject.

As for other camera settings, Landscape mode results in the following options:

- **Picture Style:** The camera automatically sets the Picture Style option to Landscape, which produces a sharper image, with well-defined "edges" — the borders between areas of contrast or color change. The Picture Style setting also produces more vivid blues and greens, which is what most people prefer from their landscape photos. You can read more about Picture Styles in Chapter 6.

- **Drive mode:** The camera selects the Single option, which records one image for each press of the shutter button. As with the other scene modes, you can switch to a Self-Timer or Remote-Control setting by following the steps laid out at the end of this chapter.

- **Flash:** The built-in flash is disabled, which is typically no big deal: Because of its limited range, a built-in flash is of little use when shooting most landscapes anyway.

- **Autofocusing:** The AF (autofocus) mode is set to One-Shot, which means that focus is locked when you depress the shutter button halfway. (See Chapter 6 for details.) Focus usually is set on the nearest object that falls under one of the seven autofocus points, but remember that because of the large depth of field that the Landscape mode produces, both far and near objects may appear equally sharp, depending on their distance from the lens.

Again, think beyond the Landscape moniker when you look for good ways to put this mode to use: Try it when shooting long-range pictures of animals at the zoo, for example, so that critters both near and far appear sharp.

Close-Up mode

Switching to Close-Up mode doesn't enable you to focus at a closer distance to your subject than normal as it does on some non-SLR cameras. The close-focusing capabilities of your camera depend entirely on the lens you use.

But choosing Close-Up mode does tell the camera to try to select an aperture (f-stop) setting that results in a short depth of field, which blurs background objects so that they don't compete for attention with your main subject. I used this setting to capture the crab apple blossoms in Figure 2-10. As with Portrait mode, though, how much the background blurs varies depending on the distance between your subject and the background as well as on the lighting conditions (which determine the range of f-stops that will produce a good exposure), your camera-to-subject distance, and the lens focal length. (Chapter 6 explains all these issues.)

Other settings selected for you in Close-Up mode are as follows:

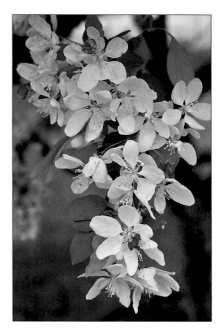

Figure 2-10: Close-Up mode also produces short depth of field.

- ✓ **Picture Style:** Close-Up mode uses the Standard picture style, just like Full Auto. The resulting image features crisp edges and vivid colors.

- ✓ **Drive mode:** The Drive mode is set to Single, so you record one photo each time you fully depress the shutter button. You can, however, select a Self-Timer or Remote Control mode if needed.

- ✓ **Flash:** Flash is enabled when the camera thinks additional light is needed, and it's disabled when the camera decides that the ambient light is sufficient. You can set the flash to Red-Eye Reduction mode, but frankly, you shouldn't be firing the flash at close range to either human or animal subjects — you can hurt their eyes.

- ✓ **Autofocusing:** The AF mode is set to One-Shot mode; again, that simply means that when you depress the shutter button halfway, the camera locks focus, usually on the nearest object that falls under one of the seven autofocus points.

See Chapter 6 for more details about AF modes and other focusing issues. Chapter 7 offers additional tips on close-up photography.

Sports mode

Sports mode results in a number of settings that can help you photograph moving subjects, such as the girl in the swing in Figure 2-11. First, the camera selects a fast shutter speed, which is needed to "stop motion." *Shutter speed* is an exposure control that you can explore in Chapter 5.

Also keep these Sports mode settings in mind:

- ✔ **Picture Style:** The camera automatically sets the Picture Style option to Standard, which is designed to produce sharp images with bold colors.

- ✔ **Drive mode:** To enable rapid-fire image capture, the Drive mode is set to Continuous. This mode enables you to record multiple frames with a single press of the shutter button. You also have the option of switching to a Self-Timer or Remote Control mode. Check out the end of this chapter for details on Drive mode settings.

- ✔ **Flash:** Flash is disabled, which can be a problem in low-light situations, but it also enables you to shoot successive images more quickly because the flash needs a brief period to recycle between shots. In addition, disabling the flash permits a faster shutter speed; when the flash is on, the maximum shutter speed is 1/200 second. (See Chapter 5 for details about flash and shutter speeds.)

Figure 2-11: To capture moving subjects without blur, try Sports mode.

- ✔ **Autofocusing:** The AF mode is set to AI Servo. In this mode, the camera establishes focus initially when you depress the shutter button halfway. But if the subject moves, the camera attempts to refocus.

For this feature to work correctly, you must adjust framing so that your subject remains within one of the autofocus points. You may find it easier to simply switch to manual focusing and twist the focusing ring as needed to track the subject's movement yourself.

The other critical thing to understand about Sports mode is that whether the camera can select a shutter speed fast enough to stop motion depends on the available light and the speed of the subject itself. In Figure 2-11, the camera selected a shutter speed that did, in fact, catch my subject in midswing; although if you look very closely, you can see some slight blurring of the foot near the bottom of the frame.

To fully understand shutter speed, visit Chapter 5. And for more tips on action photography, check out Chapter 7.

Night Portrait mode

As its name implies, Night Portrait mode is designed to deliver a better-looking portrait at night (or in any dimly lit environment). It does so by combining flash with a slow shutter speed. That slow shutter speed produces a longer exposure time, which enables the camera to rely more on ambient light and less on the flash to expose the picture. The result is a brighter background and softer, more even lighting.

I cover the issue of using a slow shutter speed in detail in Chapter 5; Chapter 7 has some additional nighttime photography tips. For now, the important thing to know is that the slower shutter speed means that you probably need a tripod; if you try to handhold the camera, you run the risk of moving the camera during the long exposure, resulting in a blurry image. Enabling the Image Stabilizer (IS) feature of your lens, if available, can help, but for nighttime shooting, even that may not permit successful handheld shooting. Your subjects also must stay perfectly still during the exposure, which can also be a challenge.

If you do try Night Portrait mode, be aware of these other settings that are automatically selected by the camera:

- **Picture Style:** The Standard setting, designed to deliver sharp, bold photos, is selected. See Chapter 6 for more about Picture Styles.

- **Drive mode:** The default setting is Single, but you also can choose a Self-Timer or Remote Control mode. Check out the end of this chapter for details.

- **Flash:** Flash is enabled when the camera thinks more light is needed — which, assuming that you're actually shooting at night, should be most of the time. You can set the flash to Red-Eye Reduction mode if you prefer.

- **Autofocusing:** The AF mode is set to One-Shot, which locks focus when you depress the shutter button halfway.

Flash Off mode

 The Flash Off mode delivers the same results as Full Auto mode but ensures that the flash doesn't fire, even in dim lighting. This mode provides an easy way to ensure that you don't break the rules when shooting in locations that don't permit flash: museums, churches, and so on. But it can also come in handy any time you prefer not to use flash. See Chapters 5 and 7 for information about flash photography.

Changing the Drive Mode

Your camera offers the following Drive mode settings:

 ✓ **Single:** This setting, which is the default for all of the fully automatic modes except Portrait and Sports, records a single image each time you press the shutter button. In other words, this is normal-photography mode.

 ✓ **Continuous:** Sometimes known as *burst mode,* this setting records a continuous series of images as long as you hold down the shutter button. On the Rebel XS/1000D, you can capture as many as three shots per second. Obviously, this mode is great for capturing fast-paced subjects, which is why it's the default setting for Sports mode. It's also selected for Portrait mode, which is a great benefit if your subject is the fidgety type.

 ✓ **Self-Timer/Remote Control:** Want to put yourself in the picture? Select this mode and then press the shutter button and run into the frame. You have about 10 seconds to get yourself in place and pose before the image is recorded.

 I also often use the self-timer function when I want to avoid any possibility of camera shake. The mere motion of pressing the shutter button can cause slight camera movement, which can blur an image. So I put the camera on a tripod and then activate the self-timer function. This enables "hands-free" — and therefore motion-free — picture-taking.

As another alternative, you can purchase the optional remote-control switch sold by Canon. Choose the Self-Timer/Remote Control mode to use that gadget to trigger the shutter release button. (Note that your camera can use only the unit that connects to the camera via cable; wireless remotes aren't compatible with the Rebel XS/1000D.)

 ✓ **2-Second Self-Timer:** This mode works just like the regular self-timer mode, but the capture happens just two seconds after you fully depress the shutter button. Unfortunately, this mode isn't available to you in the fully automatic exposure modes; you can choose this option only in P, Tv, Av, M, or A-DEP modes. I cover it here just so you'll know the option exists.

✔ **Self-Timer Continuous:** With this option, the camera waits 10 seconds after you depress the shutter button and then captures a continuous series of images. You can record as many as 10 continuous images.

To select a Drive mode, press the left cross key. You then see a screen similar to the one in Figure 2-12. However, you see all five Drive mode options *only* in the advanced exposure modes (P, Tv, Av, M, and A-DEP). In the fully automatic modes, you see only the default Drive mode option that the camera uses for your selected exposure mode, plus the Self-Timer/ Remote Control option and the Self-Timer Continuous option.

Figure 2-12: You can access all of these Drive options only in advanced exposure modes.

Either way, press the right or left cross key to highlight your Drive mode of choice. For the Self-Timer Continuous mode, press the up or down cross key to set the number of continuous shots you want the camera to capture, as shown in the figure. Finally, press the Set button to lock in the setting.

Your selected Drive mode remains in force until you change it or switch to an exposure mode for which the selected Drive mode isn't available.

3

Controlling Picture Quality

*A*lmost every review of the Rebel XS/1000D contains glowing reports about the camera's top-notch picture quality. As you've no doubt discovered for yourself, those claims are true, too: This baby can create large, beautiful images.

Getting the maximum output from your camera, however, depends on choosing the right capture settings. Chief among them, and the topic of this chapter, is the appropriately named Quality setting. Found on Shooting Menu 1, this critical control determines two important aspects of your pictures: *resolution,* or pixel count; and *file format,* which refers to the type of computer file the camera uses to store your picture data.

Resolution and file format work together to determine the quality of your photos, so selecting from the eight Quality settings on your camera is an important decision. Why not just dial in the setting that produces the maximum quality level and be done with it, you ask? Well, that's the right choice for some photographers. But because choosing that maximum setting has some disadvantages, you may find that stepping down a notch or two on the quality scale is a better option every now and then.

To help you figure out which Quality setting meets your needs, this chapter explains exactly how resolution and file format affect your pictures. Just in case you're having quality problems related to other issues, though, the first section of the chapter provides a handy quality-defect diagnosis guide.

Diagnosing Quality Problems

When I use the term *picture quality,* I'm not talking about the composition, exposure, or other traditional characteristics of a photograph. Instead, I'm referring to how finely the image is rendered in the digital sense.

Figure 3-1 illustrates the concept: The first example is a high-quality image, with clear details and smooth color transitions. The other examples show five common digital-image defects.

High quality

Pixelation

JPEG artifacts

Noise

Color cast

Lens/sensor dirt

Figure 3-1: Refer to this symptom guide to determine the cause of poor image quality.

Each of these defects is related to a different issue, and only two are affected by the Quality setting on Shooting Menu 1. So if you aren't happy with your image quality, first compare your photos to those in the figure to properly diagnose the problem. Then try these remedies:

✔ **Pixelation:** When an image doesn't have enough *pixels* (the colored tiles used to create digital images), details aren't clear, and curved and diagonal lines appear jagged. The fix is to increase image resolution, which you do via the Quality control. See the upcoming section, "Considering Resolution: Large, Medium, or Small?" for details.

✔ **JPEG artifacts:** The "parquet tile" texture and random color defects that mar the third image in Figure 3-1 can occur in photos captured in the JPEG *(jay-peg)* file format, which is why these flaws are referred to as *JPEG artifacts.* This defect is also related to the Quality setting; see "Understanding File Type (JPEG or Raw)" to find out more.

✔ **Noise:** This defect gives your image a speckled look, as shown in the lower-left example in Figure 3-1. Noise is most often related to a very long exposure time (that is, a very slow shutter speed) or to an exposure control called ISO, which you can explore in Chapter 5. To adjust shutter speed or ISO, you must switch to one of the advanced exposure modes (P, Tv, Av, M, or A-DEP).

✔ **Color cast:** If your colors are seriously out of whack, as shown in the lower-middle example in the figure, try adjusting the camera's white balance setting. Chapter 6 covers this control and other color issues. Note, though, that you also must use an advanced exposure mode to adjust white balance.

✔ **Lens/sensor dirt:** A dirty lens is the first possible cause of the kind of defects you see in the last example in the figure. If cleaning your lens doesn't solve the problem, dust or dirt may have made its way onto the camera's image sensor. See the sidebar "Maintaining a pristine view," later in this chapter, for information on safe lens and sensor cleaning.

When diagnosing image problems, you may want to open the photos in your photo software and zoom in for a close-up inspection. Some defects, especially pixelation and JPEG artifacts, have a similar appearance until you see them at a magnified view.

I should also tell you that I used a little digital enhancement to exaggerate the flaws in my example images to make the symptoms easier to see. With the exception of an unwanted color cast or a big blob of lens or sensor dirt, these defects may not even be noticeable unless you print or view your image at a very large size. And the subject matter of your image may camouflage some flaws; most people probably wouldn't detect a little JPEG artifacting in a photograph of a densely wooded forest, for example.

In other words, don't consider Figure 3-1 as an indication that your Canon is suspect in the image quality department. First, *any* digital camera can produce these defects under the right circumstances. Second, by following the guidelines in this chapter and the others mentioned in the preceding list, you can resolve any quality issues that you may encounter.

Decoding the Quality Options

Your camera's Quality control determines both the image resolution and file format of the pictures you shoot. To access the control, press the Menu button and then display Shooting Menu 1, shown on the left in Figure 3-2. Highlight Quality and press the Set button to display the screen you see on the right in the figure.

Figure 3-2: You set resolution and file format together via the Quality menu.

In Figure 3-2, the right screen displays all the Quality settings available on the Rebel XS/1000D. But see that little replica of the Mode dial on the left side of the screen? When the symbol representing an exposure mode is dimmed, you can't use that mode if you want to access all the settings on the screen. In this case, for example, the graphic tells you that the eight Quality options shown in Figure 3-2 are available only in the P, Tv, Av, M, and A-DEP modes. If you instead set the camera to Full Auto or one of the automatic scene modes, you're limited to the first six settings, as shown in Figure 3-3.

Figure 3-3: You can't capture images in the Raw format if you use a fully automatic exposure mode.

Either way, if you're new to digital photography, the Quality settings won't make much sense to you until you read the rest of this chapter, which explains format and resolution in detail. But even if you are schooled in those topics, you may need some help deciphering the way that the settings are represented on your camera. As you can see from Figures 3-2 and 3-3, the options are presented in rather cryptic fashion, so here's your decoder ring:

- ✔ The first column of settings produce files in the JPEG file format.

- ✔ The little arc-like icons represent the level of JPEG *compression,* which affects picture quality and file size. You get two JPEG options, Fine and Normal. The Fine setting is represented by the smooth arcs; the Normal setting is represented by the stairstepped arcs. Check out the section "JPEG: The imaging (and Web) standard" for details on this issue.

- ✔ Within the JPEG category, you can choose from three resolution settings, represented by L, M, and S *(large, medium,* and *small).* See the next section for information that will help you select the right resolution.

- ✔ The Quality settings in the second column enable you to capture images in the Raw file format. Again, these two options appear only if you set the camera Mode dial to one of the advanced exposure modes. All Raw files are created at the Large resolution setting, giving you the maximum pixel count. One of the two Raw settings also records a JPEG Fine version of the image, also at the maximum resolution. The section "Raw (CR2): The purist's choice" explains the benefits and downsides to using the Raw format.

To select a Quality option, just highlight it and press the Set button. The selected setting then appears next to the Quality item in Shooting Menu 1 and at the bottom of the Shooting Settings display, as shown in Figure 3-4.

Changing the Quality setting also changes the number of pictures that you can store on your memory card. That number appears in the lower-right corner of the display, as labeled in Figure 3-4. See the upcoming sidebar "How many pictures fit on my memory card?" for details.

Which Quality option is best depends on several factors, including how you plan to use your pictures and how much time you care to spend processing your images on your computer. The rest of this chapter explains these and other issues related to the Quality settings.

-2..1..0..1..:2   [ISO] 100

P   [AWB]

□ [S] [⊙] ONE SHOT

[▪▪▪] ▲L (215)

Quality setting   Shots remaining

Figure 3-4: The Quality setting affects the number of pictures remaining.

Considering Resolution: Large, Medium, or Small?

To decide upon a Quality setting, the first decision you need to make is how many *pixels* you want your image to contain. Pixels are the little square tiles from which all digital images are made; the word *pixel* is short for *picture element*. You can see some pixels close up in the right image in Figure 3-5, which shows a greatly magnified view of the eye area of the left image.

Figure 3-5: Pixels are the building blocks of digital photos.

The number of pixels in an image is referred to as *resolution*. Your camera offers you three resolution levels, which are assigned the generic labels Large, Medium, and Small and are represented on the list of Quality settings by the initials L, M, and S. Table 3-1 shows you the pixel count that results from each option. (If you select Raw as your Quality setting, images are always captured at the Large resolution value.)

Table 3-1	The Resolution Side of the Quality Settings	
Symbol	*Setting*	*Pixel Count*
L	Large	3888 x 2592 (10 MP)
M	Medium	2816 x 1880 (5.3 MP)
S	Small	1936 x 1288 (2.5 MP)

In the table, the first pair of numbers shown for each setting represents the image *pixel dimensions* — that is, the number of horizontal pixels and the number of vertical pixels. The values in parentheses indicate the total resolution, which you get by multiplying the horizontal and vertical pixel values. This number is usually stated in *megapixels,* abbreviated MP for short. One megapixel equals 1 million pixels. (I rounded off the megapixel values in the table.)

To figure out how many pixels are enough, you need to understand how resolution affects print quality, display size, and file size. The next sections explain these issues, as well as a few other resolution factoids.

Pixels and print quality

When mulling over resolution options, your first consideration is how large you want to print your photos, because pixel count determines the size at which you can produce a high-quality print. If you don't have enough pixels, your prints may exhibit the defects you see in the pixelation example in Figure 3-1, or worse, you may be able to see the individual pixels, as in the right example in Figure 3-5.

Depending on your photo printer, you typically need anywhere from 200 to 300 pixels per linear inch, or *ppi,* of the print. To produce an 8-by-10-inch print at 200 ppi, for example, you need a pixel count of 1600 x 2000.

Table 3-2 lists the pixel counts needed to produce traditional print sizes at 200 ppi and 300 ppi. But again, the optimum ppi varies depending on the printer — some printers prefer even more than 300 ppi — so check your manual or ask the photo technician at the lab that makes your prints. (And note that ppi is *not* the same thing as *dpi,* which is a measurement of printer resolution. *Dpi* refers to how many dots of color the printer can lay down per inch; most printers use multiple dots to reproduce one pixel.)

Table 3-2	Pixel Requirements for Traditional Print Sizes	
Print Size	*Pixels for 200 ppi*	*Pixels for 300 ppi*
4 x 6 inches	800 x 1200	1200 x 1800
5 x 7 inches	1000 x 1400	1500 x 2100
8 x 10 inches	1600 x 2000	2400 x 3000
11 x 14 inches	2200 x 2800	3300 x 4200

Even though many photo editing programs enable you to add pixels to an existing image, doing so isn't a good idea. For reasons I won't bore you with, adding pixels — known as *resampling* — doesn't enable you to successfully enlarge your photo. In fact, resampling typically makes matters worse. The printing discussion at the start of Chapter 9 includes some example images that illustrate this issue.

Pixels and screen display size

Resolution doesn't affect the quality of images viewed on a monitor, television, or other screen device as it does on printed photos. Instead, it determines the *size* at which the image appears.

This issue is one of the most misunderstood aspects of digital photography, so I explain it thoroughly in Chapter 9. For now, just know that you need *way* fewer pixels for onscreen photos than you do for printed photos. For example, Figure 3-6 shows a 450-x-300-pixel image that I attached to an e-mail message.

Figure 3-6: A 450-x-300-pixel image is plenty large for sharing via e-mail.

For e-mail images, I usually stick with a maximum horizontal pixel count of 450 and a maximum vertical size of 400 pixels, depending on whether the picture is oriented horizontally, as in the figure, or vertically. If your image is much larger, the recipient may not be able to view the entire picture without scrolling the display.

In short, even if you use one of the Small Quality settings on your Rebel XS/1000D, which produces images that contain 1936 x 1288 pixels, you'll have more than enough pixels for most onscreen uses. The only exception might be an image that you want to display via a digital projector that has a very high screen resolution. Again, Chapter 9 details this issue and also shows you how to prepare your pictures for online sharing.

Pixels and file size

Every additional pixel increases the amount of data required to create a digital picture file. So a higher-resolution image has a larger file size than a low-resolution image.

Large files present several problems:

- ✔ You can store fewer images on your memory card, on your computer's hard drive, and on removable storage media such as a CD-ROM.

- ✔ The camera needs more time to process and store the image data on the memory card after you press the shutter button. This extra time can hamper fast-action shooting.

- ✔ When you share photos online, larger files take longer to upload and download.

- ✔ When you edit your photos in your photo software, your computer needs more resources and time to process large files.

To sum up, the tradeoff for a high-resolution image is a large file size. But note that file format, which is the other half of the Quality equation on your Canon, also affects file size. See the section "Understanding File Type (JPEG or Raw)" for more on that topic. The upcoming sidebar "How many pictures fit on my memory card?" provides details on the file-storage issue.

Resolution recommendations

As you can see, resolution is a bit of a sticky wicket. What if you aren't sure how large you want to print your images? What if you want to print your photos *and* share them online?

Personally, I take the "better safe than sorry" route, which leads to the following recommendations about whether to choose Large, Medium, or Small when you select a Quality setting:

- **Always shoot at a resolution suitable for print.** You then can create a low-resolution copy of the image in your photo editor for use online. Chapter 9 shows you how.

  Again, you *can't* go in the opposite direction, adding pixels to a low-resolution original in your photo editor to create a good, large print. Even with the very best software, adding pixels doesn't improve the print quality of a low-resolution image.

- **For everyday snapshots, the Medium setting (5.3 MP) is probably sufficient.** I find that 10 MP, which is what you get from the Large setting, to be overkill for most casual snapshots, which means that you're creating huge files for no good reason. So I stick with Medium unless I'm shooting critical images.

- **Jump up to Large (10 MP) if you plan to crop your photos or make huge prints.** Always use the maximum resolution if you think you may want to crop your photo and enlarge the remaining image. For example, when I shot the left photo in Figure 3-7, I wanted to fill the frame with the butterfly, but I couldn't do so without getting so close that I risked scaring it away. So I kept my distance and took the picture at the Large setting, which enabled me to crop the photo and still have enough pixels left to produce a great print, as you see in the right image.

Figure 3-7: Capture images that you plan to crop and enlarge at the highest possible resolution (Large).

✔ **Reduce resolution if shooting speed is paramount.** If you're shooting action and the shot-to-shot capture time is slower than you'd like — that is, the camera takes too long after you take one shot before it lets you take another — dialing down the resolution may help. Lower resolution produces smaller files, and the smaller the file, the less time the camera needs to record the image to your memory card. Also see Chapter 7 for other tips on action photography.

How many pictures fit on my memory card?

That question is one of the first asked by new camera owners — and it's an important one because you don't want to run out of space on your memory card just as the perfect photographic subject presents itself.

As explained in the discussions in this chapter, image resolution (pixel count) and file format (JPEG or Raw) together determine the size of the picture file which, in turn, determines how many photos fit in a given amount of camera memory.

The table below shows you the approximate size of the files, in megabytes (MB) that are generated at each of the possible resolution/format combinations on your Rebel XS/1000D. (The actual file size of any image also depends on other factors, such as the subject, ISO setting, and Picture Style setting.) In the Image Capacity column, you see approximately how many pictures you can store at the setting on a 1GB (gigabyte) memory card.

Picture Capacity of a 1GB Memory Card			
Symbol	*Quality Setting*	*File Size*	*Image Capacity*
◢ L	Large/Fine	3.8MB	257
◢ L	Large/Normal	2.0MB	491
◢ M	Medium/Fine	2.3MB	430
◢ M	Medium/Normal	1.2MB	815
◢ S	Small/Fine	1.3MB	737
◢ S	Small/Normal	0.7MB	1408
◢ L RAW	Raw+Large/Fine	13.6MB*	71
RAW	Raw	9.8MB	100

Combined size of the two files produced at this setting.

Understanding File Type (JPEG or Raw)

In addition to establishing the resolution of your photos, the Quality setting determines the *file format*. The file format simply refers to the type of image file that the camera produces.

Your Canon offers two file formats, JPEG and Raw, with a couple variations of each. The next sections explain the pros and cons of each setting.

Don't confuse *file format* with the Format option on Setup Menu 1. That option erases all data on your memory card; see Chapter 1 for details.

JPEG: The imaging (and Web) standard

Pronounced *jay-peg,* this format is the default setting on your camera, as it is for most digital cameras. JPEG is popular for two main reasons:

> ✔ **Web compatibility:** All Web browsers and e-mail programs can display JPEG files, so you can share them online immediately after you shoot them.

> ✔ **Small files:** JPEG files are smaller than those produced by the other common format offered by today's digital cameras, known as Camera Raw, or just Raw. And smaller files means that your pictures consume less room on your camera memory card and in your computer's storage tank.

The downside — you knew there had to be one — is that JPEG creates smaller files by applying *lossy compression.* This process actually throws away some image data. Too much compression leads to the defects you see in the JPEG Artifacts example in Figure 3-1, near the start of this chapter.

On your camera, the amount of compression that is applied depends on whether you choose a Quality setting that carries the label Fine or Normal. The difference between the two breaks down as follows:

> ✔ **Fine:** At this setting, represented by the symbol you see in the margin here, very little compression is applied, so you shouldn't see many compression artifacts, if any.

> ✔ **Normal:** Switch to Normal, and the compression amount rises, as does the chance of seeing some artifacting. Notice the jaggedy-ness of the Normal icon, shown in the margin here? That's your reminder that all may not be "smooth" sailing when you choose a Normal setting.

For comparison, Figures 3-8 and 3-9 show you the same subject shot at the Large/Fine and Large/Normal settings, along with the respective file sizes that each option produces. (I captured each image at the same resolution so that file type is the only variable.)

Large/Fine, 3.8MB

Figure 3-8: The Fine setting produces very good image quality and reasonable file sizes.

Large/Normal, 2.0MB

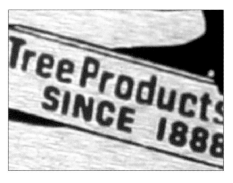

Figure 3-9: Enlarging an image captured at the Normal setting reveals some quality loss.

When you view the left examples in the comparison figures, you may not see much difference between the images. For most printed photos, in fact, compression defects aren't terribly distinct when the print size is small. But when you enlarge your photos, as I did for the right examples in the figures, the exact nature of the quality loss that occurs with JPEG compression becomes clearer.

Know, too, that compression artifacts usually are significantly easier to spot when you view digital images on a computer monitor. (The print process itself softens some of the compression defects.) Artifacting is also usually more visible in areas of flat color than it is in detailed or textured areas.

For my money, the file size benefit you gain when going from Fine to Normal isn't worth the risk of artifacts, especially with the price of camera memory cards getting lower every day. And of all the defects that you can correct in a photo editor, artifacting is perhaps the hardest to accomplish. So if I shoot in the JPEG format, I stick with Fine.

If you don't want *any* risk of artifacting, bypass JPEG altogether and change the file type to Raw, explained next.

Raw (CR2): The purist's choice

The other picture-file type that you can create on your camera is *Camera Raw,* or just *Raw* (as in uncooked) for short.

Each manufacturer has its own flavor of Raw files; Canon's are called CR2 files (or, on some older cameras, CRW). If you use a Windows computer, you see that three-letter designation at the end of your picture filenames.

Raw is popular with advanced, very demanding photographers, for two reasons:

- ✏ **Greater creative control:** With JPEG, internal camera software tweaks your images, making adjustments to color, exposure, and sharpness as needed to produce the results that Canon believes its customers prefer. With Raw, the camera simply records the original, unprocessed image data. The photographer then copies the image file to the computer and uses special software known as a *raw converter* to produce the actual image, making decisions about color, exposure, and so on at that point. The upshot is that "shooting Raw" enables you, not the camera, to have the final say on the visual characteristics of your image.

- ✏ **Best picture quality:** Because Raw doesn't apply the destructive compression associated with JPEG, you don't run the risk of the artifacting that can occur with JPEG.

But of course, as with most things in life, Raw isn't without its disadvantages. To wit:

- ✏ **You must spend time processing your Raw pictures.** Until you process your files in a Raw converter, you can't edit your photos or share them online. Nor can you have them printed at your local drugstore's photo kiosk or your favorite online printer; if you want a hard copy of a Raw image, you must print it yourself, using the Canon software provided with your camera (or a third-party program that offers Raw-printing capabilities). Additionally, some photo browsers can't display Raw images, although again, you can always view your photos using the provided Canon software. Long story short, when you shoot Raw, you add to the time you must spend in front of the computer instead of behind the camera lens. Chapter 8 shows you how to process your Raw files using your Canon software.

✔ **Raw files are larger than JPEGs.** The type of file compression that Raw applies doesn't degrade image quality, but the tradeoff is larger files. In addition, Raw files are always captured at the maximum resolution available on your camera, even if you don't really need all those pixels. For both reasons, Raw files are significantly larger than JPEGs, so they take up more room on your memory card and on your computer's hard drive or other picture-storage device.

Are the disadvantages worth the gain? Only you can decide. But before you make up your mind, compare the Large/Fine JPEG image in Figure 3-8 with its Raw counterpart, shown in Figure 3-10. You may be able to detect some subtle quality differences in the enlarged view, but most people would be hard pressed to distinguish between the two otherwise. And JPEG certainly wins out in terms of convenience, time savings, and smaller file size. (Note that during the Raw conversion process, I tried to use settings that kept the Raw image as close as possible to its JPEG cousin in all aspects but quality. But any variations in exposure, color, and contrast are a result of the conversion process, not of the format per se.)

Raw (CR2), 9.8MB

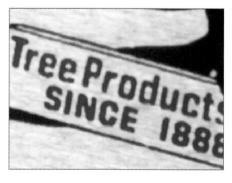

Figure 3-10: The difference between Raw and Large/Fine images typically is noticeable only when images are greatly enlarged.

That said, I *do* shoot in the Raw format when I'm dealing with tricky lighting because doing so gives me more control over the final image exposure. For example, if you use a capable Raw converter, you can specify how bright you want the brightest areas of your photo to appear and how dark you prefer your deepest shadows. With JPEG, the camera makes those decisions, which can potentially limit your flexibility if you try to adjust exposure in your photo editor later.

I also go Raw if I know that I'm going to want huge prints of a subject. But keep in mind: I'm a photography geek, I have all the requisite software, and I don't really have much else to do with my time than process scads of Raw images.

If you do decide to try Raw shooting, you can select from the following two Quality options:

- **RAW:** This setting produces a single Raw file at the maximum resolution (10 megapixels).

- **RAW+Large/Fine:** This setting produces two files: the standard Raw file plus a JPEG file captured at the Large/Fine setting. At first glance, this option sounds great: You can share the JPEG online or get prints made and then process your Raw files when you have time.

  The problem is that, like the Raw file, the JPEG image is captured at the maximum pixel count — which is *too* large for onscreen viewing. That means that you have to edit the JPEG file anyway to trim down the pixel count before online sharing, although you can produce great prints right away. In addition, creating two files for every image eats up substantially more memory card space. I leave it up to you to decide whether the pluses are worth the minuses.

My take: Choose Fine or Raw

At this point, you may be finding all this technical goop a bit much — I recognize that panicked look in your eyes — so allow me to simplify things for you. Until you have time or energy to completely digest all the ramifications of JPEG versus Raw, here's a quick summary of my thoughts on the matter:

- If you require the absolute best image quality and have the time and interest to do the Raw conversion process, shoot Raw. See Chapter 8 for more information on the conversion process.

- If great photo quality is good enough for you, you don't have wads of spare time, or you aren't that comfortable with the computer, stick with one of the Fine settings (Large/Fine, Medium/Fine, or Small/Fine).

- Stay away from JPEG Normal. The tradeoff for smaller files isn't, in my opinion, worth the risk of compression artifacts. As with my recommendations on resolution, this fits the "better safe than sorry" formula: You never know when you may capture a spectacular, enlargement-worthy subject, and it would be a shame to have the photo spoiled by compression defects.

- Finally, remember that the format and resolution together determine the ultimate picture quality. So be sure that you select the Quality setting that offers both the appropriate number of pixels and format for how you plan to use your image. If you capture an image at the Small/Normal setting, for example, and then print the photo at a large size, the combination of a lower pixel count and a higher level of JPEG compression may produce a disappointing picture quality.

Maintaining a pristine view

Often lost in discussions of digital photo defects — compression artifacts, pixelation, and the like — is the impact of plain-old dust and dirt on picture quality. But no matter what camera settings you use, you aren't going to achieve great picture quality with a dirty lens. So make it a practice to clean your lens on a regular basis, using one of the specialized cloths and cleaning solutions made expressly for that purpose.

If you continue to notice random blobs or hair-like defects in your images (refer to the last example in Figure 3-1), you probably have a dirty *image sensor.* That's the part of your camera that does the actual image capture — the digital equivalent of a film negative, if you will. By default, your camera performs an internal sensor cleaning every time you turn it on and off; you can also run the cleaning process at any time you want by opening Setup Menu 2, choosing the Sensor Cleaning option, and then selecting Clean Now.

Especially if you frequently change lenses in a dirty environment, however, this internal cleaning mechanism may not be able to fully remove all specks from the sensor. In that case, you need a more thorough cleaning, which is done by actually opening up the camera and using special sensor-cleaning tools. You can do this job yourself, but . . . I don't recommend it. Image sensors are pretty delicate beings, and you can easily damage it or other parts of your camera if you aren't care-ful. Instead, find a local camera store that offers this service. In my area (central Indiana), sensor cleaning costs about $30 to $50. If you bought your camera at a traditional camera store, the store may even provide free sensor cleaning as a way to keep your business.

One more cleaning tip: Never — and I mean *never* — try to clean any part of your camera using a can of compressed air. Doing so can not only damage the interior of your camera, blowing dust or dirt into areas where it can't be removed, but it can also crack the monitor.

Monitor Matters: Picture Playback and Live View Shooting

*W*ithout question, my favorite thing about digital photography is being able to view my pictures on the camera monitor the instant after I shoot them. No more guessing whether I captured the image I wanted or need to try again; no more wasting money on developing and printing pictures that stink. In fact, this feature alone was reason enough for me to turn my back forever on my closet full of film photography hardware and all the unexposed film remaining from my predigital days.

Of course, with the Rebel XS/1000D, you can use the monitor not only to review your photos, but also to *preview* them. That is, if you turn on Live View shooting, you can use the monitor instead of the viewfinder to compose and focus your shots.

Because both functions of your camera monitor involve some of the same buttons, bells, and whistles, I cover them together in this chapter. In addition, this chapter explains how to delete pictures that you don't like and protect the ones you love from accidental erasure.

For details about still more monitor-related topics, such as accessing camera menus and viewing current shooting settings, check out Chapter 1 if you haven't already done so. Also visit Chapter 9, which covers some additional ways to view your images, including how to create in-camera slide shows and display your photos on a television screen.

Disabling and Adjusting Instant Review

After you take a picture, it automatically appears briefly on the camera monitor. By default, the instant-review period lasts just two seconds. But you can customize this behavior via the Review Time option on Shooting Menu 1, as shown in Figure 4-1.

Figure 4-1: You can extend or disable automatic picture review.

Your choices are as follows:

- ✓ Select one of three specific review periods: 2, 4, or 8 seconds.
- ✓ Select Off to disable the automatic instant review altogether. Turning off the monitor can save battery power, so keep this option in mind if the battery is running low. You can still view your pictures by pressing the Playback button. See the next section for details.
- ✓ Select Hold to display the current image indefinitely — or at least until the camera automatically shuts itself off to save power. (See the Chapter 1 section about Setup Menu 1 to find out about the auto-shutdown feature.)

Viewing Images in Playback Mode

To switch your camera to Playback mode and view the images currently on your memory card, take these steps:

1. **Press the Playback button, labeled in Figure 4-2 and shown in the margin here.**

   The monitor displays the last picture you took along with some shooting data.

   To find out how to interpret the picture data and specify what data you want to see, see the upcoming section "Viewing Picture Data." If you're curious about your options now, though, press the DISP button to cycle through the available data-display formats. (Figure 4-2 shows the image in the mode that displays the least amount of shooting data.)

Playback button

Figure 4-2: Press the Playback button to inspect your photos.

2. **Press the right or left cross key to scroll through your pictures.**

   - Press the right cross key to view images starting with the oldest one on the card.

   - Press the left cross key to view images in reverse order, starting with the most current picture.

   Just keep pressing either key to browse through all of your images.

3. **To return to picture-taking mode, press the Playback button or press the shutter button halfway.**

   The camera exits Playback mode, and the Shooting Settings display appears on the monitor. Chapter 1 introduces you to that display.

These steps assume that the camera is currently set to display a single photo at a time, as shown in Figure 4-2. You can also display multiple images at a time and jump through images 10 or 100 at a time; the next two sections tell all.

Jumping through images

If your memory card contains scads of images, here's a trick you'll love: By using the Jump feature, you can rotate the Main dial to leapfrog through pictures instead of pressing the right or left cross key a bazillion times to get to the picture you want to see. You also can search for the first image shot on a specific date.

This feature works like so:

1. **Press the Playback button to put the camera into Playback mode.**

2. **Press the up cross key.**

   The *jump bar* appears at the bottom of the monitor, as shown in Figure 4-3.

3. **Select a Jump mode by pressing the up or down cross key.**

   The current Jump mode appears on the jump bar. You have four Jump mode options:

   - *Jump 10 Images:* Select this option to advance 10 images at a time.

   - *Jump 100 Images:* Select this option to advance 100 images at a time.

Figure 4-3: The current Jump mode appears on the jump bar.

   - *Jump Shot Date:* If your card contains images shot on different dates, you can jump between dates with this option. For example, if you're looking at the first of 30 pictures taken on June 1, you can jump past all the others from that day to the first image taken on, say, June 5.

   - *Jump 1 Image:* This option, in effect, disables jumping, restricting you to browsing pictures one at a time. More about the point of this option later.

4. **Rotate the Main dial to browse images using the selected Jump mode.**

   How many images you advance with each turn of the dial depends upon the Jump mode you selected.

5. **To exit Jump mode, press the right or left cross key.**

   Now you're back to regular Playback mode, in which each press of the right or left cross key advances through your pictures one at a time. You can return to your selected Jump mode by simply rotating the Main dial at any time.

So what's the point of the Jump 1 Image option, if you can return to one-by-one playback just by pressing the right or left cross key? It's simply provided in case you prefer to use the Main dial to browse your images instead of the cross keys. When you select the option, the Jump bar disappears, and then you can use either the Main dial or the cross keys to navigate your pictures.

You can jump through images only in regular, full-screen Playback mode. The Main dial performs a different function in *index display* mode, in which you can view four or nine image thumbnails at a time. The next section explains this viewing mode.

Viewing multiple images at a time

If you want to quickly review and compare several photos, you can set the camera to *index display* mode and view thumbnails of either four or nine images at a time, as shown in Figure 4-4. Just press the AE Lock button, found on the upper-right corner of the camera back and shown in the margin here. Press once to display four thumbnails at a time; press again to display nine thumbnails.

Note the little blue checkerboard and magnifying glass icons under the button — they're reminders of the function the button serves in Playback mode. The checkerboard indicates the index function, and the minus sign in the magnifying glass tells you that pressing the button reduces the size of the image thumbnail. (The black or silver labels near these buttons indicate a function related to picture-taking.)

Selected photo

Figure 4-4: You can view four or nine thumbnails at once.

Remember these factoids about navigating and viewing your photo collection in index display mode:

- **The highlight box surrounds the currently selected image.** For example, in Figure 4-4, the upper-left photo is selected.

- **Use the cross keys to select a different image.** Press the up cross key to shift the selection box up, the right cross key to move it right, and so on.

- **Rotate the Main dial to scroll through screens of thumbnails.** Rotate right to shift to the next screen; rotate left to go back one screen.

- **Press the AF Point Selection button to reduce the number of thumbnails.** This button lives right next door to the AE Lock button. It, too, has a blue magnifying glass icon, this time with a plus sign in the center to indicate that pressing the button enlarges the thumbnail size. Press once to go from nine thumbnails to four; press again to go from four thumbnails to filling the screen with the selected image. To return to index display mode, press the AE Lock button again.

Rotating vertical pictures

When you take a picture, the camera can record the image *orientation* — that is, whether you held the camera normally, creating a horizontally oriented image, or turned the camera on its side to shoot a vertically oriented photo. This bit of data is simply added into the picture file. Then when you view the picture, the camera reads the data and rotates the image so that it appears upright in the monitor, as shown on the left in Figure 4-5. The image is also rotated automatically when you view it in the photo software that shipped with your camera.

Figure 4-5: You can display vertically oriented pictures in their upright position (left) or sideways (right).

Official photo lingo uses the term *portrait orientation* to refer to vertically oriented pictures and *landscape orientation* to refer to horizontally oriented pictures.

By default, automatic picture rotation is enabled for you. If you want to turn it off, you can do so through the Auto Rotate option on Setup Menu 1, as shown in Figure 4-6. You also can specify that you want the picture to be rotated just on your computer monitor by choosing the second of the two On settings (the one that doesn't sport the little camera icon).

Figure 4-6: Go to Setup Menu 1 to disable or adjust automatic image rotation.

If you do turn off automatic rotation, you can rotate one or more images during playback by taking these steps:

1. **Display the Playback menu and highlight Rotate, as shown in Figure 4-7.**

Figure 4-7: You also can rotate individual images from the Playback menu.

2. **Press the Set button.**

   An image appears on the monitor, as shown on the right in Figure 4-7.

3. **Navigate to the photo that you want to rotate.**

   Just press the right and left cross keys to do so.

4. **Press Set to rotate the image.**

   Press once to rotate the image 90 degrees; press again to rotate 270 degrees; and once more to return to 0 degrees.

5. **Repeat Steps 3 and 4 to rotate additional photos.**

6. **Press Menu to exit Rotate mode and return to the Playback menu.**

You can also rotate images in Index Display mode; just use the cross keys to select the photo that you want to rotate and then press the Set key. Remember, the highlight box indicates the selected photo.

Zooming in for a closer view

By pressing the AF Point Selection button, posing here in the margin, you can more closely inspect a portion of the onscreen image. This feature comes in especially handy for checking small details, such as whether anyone's eyes are closed in a group portrait. Here's the scoop on this feature:

- ✔ **Zoom in.** You can enlarge an image display to a maximum of 10 times its original size. Just keep pressing the AF Point Selection button until you reach the magnification you want.

- ✔ **View another part of the picture.** Whenever the image is magnified, a little thumbnail representing the entire image appears briefly in the lower-right corner of the monitor, as shown in Figure 4-8. The white box indicates the portion of the image that's currently consuming the rest of the monitor space.

  Use the cross keys to scroll the display to view a different portion of the image. Press the up cross key to scroll up, the left cross key to scroll left, and so on.

Figure 4-8: Press the cross keys to scroll the display of the magnified image.

✏ **View more images at the same magnification.** Here's an especially neat trick: While the display is zoomed, you can rotate the Main dial to display the same area of the next photo at the same magnification. So, for example, if you shot that group portrait several times, you can easily check each one for shut-eye problems.

✏ **View magnified images in index display mode.** You can get close-up views of the currently selected thumbnail (the one surrounded by the highlight box) by pressing the AF Point Selection button. Just press the button once or twice to get to full-frame view (depending on whether you're in 4-thumbnail or 9-thumbnail view). Then press again to magnify the selected image.

✏ **Zoom out.** To zoom out to a reduced magnification, press the AE Lock button. Continue holding the button down until you reach the magnification you want.

✏ **Return to full-frame view.** When you're ready to return to the normal magnification level, you don't need to keep pressing the AE Lock button until you're all the way zoomed out. Instead, just press the Playback button, which quickly returns you to the standard view.

Viewing Picture Data

In Playback mode, you can choose from four information-display styles, which determine which shooting data appears along with the image in the monitor.

To cycle through the various modes, just press the DISP button. In single-image Playback mode, you can access all four display styles. When you switch to index mode (viewing four or nine thumbnails at a time) or magnify an image, you can choose from just the first two display modes.

Each display mode provides a different assortment of shooting information along with your image. The next several sections offer a guide to the data you can see in each mode, starting with the most basic and working up to the most complex.

Basic information modes

In the simplest display mode, officially called Single Image display, your photo appears on the monitor as shown in Figure 4-9. Along the top of the screen, you see the following bits of information, labeled in the figure:

✔ **Shutter speed and aperture (f-stop):** Chapter 5 explains these two exposure settings.

✔ **Exposure Compensation value:** This option, also detailed in Chapter 5, enables you to produce a brighter or darker image than the camera's autoexposure meter thinks appropriate. If you applied exposure compensation, the amount appears to the right of the f-stop. If you applied no exposure compensation, this area of the display is empty.

✔ **Protect:** Using the Protect feature, described later in this chapter, you can "lock" an image to prevent it from being erased when you use the camera's Erase function. (Formatting the memory card *does* delete the picture, however, so use caution.) If you protect the photo, a little key icon appears next to the Exposure Compensation value. Otherwise, this part of the display is empty.

✔ **Folder number and last four digits of file number:** See Chapter 1 for information about how the camera assigns folder and file numbers.

Figure 4-9: The most basic Playback mode displays your image with minimal shooting information.

From Single Image mode, press the DISP button again to shift to a mode called Single Image Plus Quality. Now you get two additional pieces of information, as shown in Figure 4-10:

✔ **Quality setting:** This setting, covered in Chapter 3, determines the image resolution (pixel count) and file format (JPEG or Raw).

The Quality symbols are the same ones used to indicate the Quality setting on the camera menus and Shooting Settings screen. Chapter 3 has a chart to help you decode them.

Figure 4-10: Press DISP again to add Quality setting information to the basic display.

> ✔ **Image number/total images:** This pair of values shows you the current image number and the total number of images on the memory card. For example, in Figure 4-10, you're seeing picture 20 out of 29. (Don't confuse the image number with the actual file number; again, the last four digits of the file number appear in the top-right corner of the display, along with the folder number.)

To view more complete details about the camera settings you used to take a picture, switch to Shooting Information display mode or Histogram display mode. The next sections explain how to interpret all the data that appears in these two modes.

Shooting Information display

In the Shooting Information display mode, the camera presents a thumbnail of your image along with scads of shooting data, as shown in Figure 4-11. (*Remember:* Just press the DISP button to cycle through display modes.)

The chart-like thingy on the right side of the screen is an exposure-evaluation tool known as a *histogram.* You can get schooled in reading histograms in the next section.

Figure 4-11: You can view more data in Shooting Information playback mode.

If any areas of the image thumbnail are blinking, though, you don't even need to go that far to know that you may have an exposure problem. Those blinking spots indicate areas that are completely white — known in the photography business as *blown highlights.* Depending on where in the image those areas occur, you may or may not have an exposure problem. For example, if someone's face contains the blinking spots, that someone is overexposed, and you should take steps to correct the problem. But if the blinking occurs in, say, a bright window behind the subject, and the subject itself looks fine, you may choose to just ignore the alert.

To sort out the maze of other data, it helps to break the display down into five rows of information — the row along the top of the screen and the four rows that appear under the image thumbnail and histogram, as follows:

> ✔ **Row 1 data:** Here you see the same data that appears in the two basic display modes, explained in the preceding section.

> ✔ **Row 2 data:** Jump now to the row of symbols just underneath the thumbnail and histogram. Labeled in Figure 4-12, these symbols indicate the following:

Figure 4-12: This row contains additional exposure information.

- *Exposure mode:* This symbol indicates which of the camera's exposure modes you used — Full Auto, P (programmed autoexposure), Portrait, and so on. The symbols mirror what you see on the camera Mode dial. You can find details about all the modes in Chapters 2 and 5.

- *Exposure metering mode:* This symbol represents the metering mode, which determines which part of the frame the camera used when calculating exposure. Chapter 5 explains.

- *Flash Compensation amount:* Here you can see whether you adjusted flash power using the Flash Compensation feature, detailed in Chapter 5.

- *ISO speed:* Chapter 5 also explains this option, which controls the light sensitivity of the camera's image sensor.

✓ **Row 3 data:** Information on this row of the display, labeled in Figure 4-13, is mostly related to color settings. Here's the scoop:

Figure 4-13: Look to this row for details about advanced color settings.

- *White balance setting:* Chapter 6 has details on this option, which helps eliminate any unwanted color casts from your photos. AWB stands for Auto White Balance; see the table in Chapter 6 for a look at what the other symbols you may see here represent.

- *White balance correction:* Adjacent to the White Balance icon, this collection of data tells you whether you applied any adjustment to the white balance setting you used. Chapter 6 explains this advanced color option.

- *Picture Style*: Notice that this symbol looks just like the one on the bottom cross key on the camera back? In both cases, the symbol represents Picture Styles, which enable you to tweak image color, contrast, and sharpness. The *S* you see in Figure 4-13 represents the Standard Picture Style, which is the default applied in most exposure modes. The values to the right of the symbol relate to the four characteristics that you can adjust for each Picture Style. Chapter 6 explains how each Picture Style affects your image.

✔ **Row 4 data:** Shown at the top of Figure 4-14, this row tells you the following tidbits of information:

Figure 4-14: The bottom two rows of the display offer this data.

- *Quality and file size:* For details on the Quality setting and how it affects file size and picture quality, see Chapter 3.

- *Original Decision Data:* The Rebel XS/1000D enables you to tag an image file with a code that indicates that the image is original — meaning that it hasn't been altered in a photo program or otherwise tampered with after it was captured. In order to check the code, you need a separate product called the Original Data Verification Kit, which retails for about $650, unfortunately. If you do enable the feature on the camera, which I explain how to do in Chapter 11, a lock icon appears in this area of the playback screen.

- *Color space:* Your camera can capture images in two *color spaces,* sRGB and Adobe RGB. A *color space* is a definition of the spectrum of colors that an image can contain. You can change color spaces only in advanced exposure modes; Chapter 6 has details about how and why to do so.

✔ **Row 5 data:** Wrapping up the smorgasbord of shooting data, the bottom row of the playback screen holds two more pieces of information:

- *Image number/total images recorded:* Again, this pair of numbers indicates the current image number with respect to the total number of images on the current memory card.

• *Date and time:* These values show you the exact moment that the image was recorded. Of course, you must first set the camera date and time, as Chapter 1 explains.

One note about Figures 4-11 through 4-14: I included all possible symbols, values, and other shooting data just for the purposes of illustration. If any of the data items don't appear on your monitor, it simply means that the feature wasn't enabled when you captured the photo.

Understanding Histogram display mode

When you switch from Shooting Information display mode to the Histogram display mode, you see the data shown in Figure 4-15. Again, you get the thumbnail view of your image, but this time some of the extensive shooting data is replaced by a second histogram.

The next two sections explain what information you can glean from the histograms. See the preceding sections for a map to the other shooting data on the screen.

RGB histogram

Brightness histogram

Figure 4-15: Histogram display mode replaces some shooting data with an RGB histogram.

Interpreting a brightness histogram

One of the most difficult photo problems to correct in a photo editing program is known as *blown highlights* in some circles and *clipped highlights* in others. In plain English, both terms mean that *highlights* — the brightest areas of the image — are so overexposed that areas that should include a variety of light shades are instead totally white. For example, in a cloud image, pixels that should be light to very light gray become white due to overexposure, resulting in a loss of detail in those clouds.

In Shooting Information display mode, areas that fall into this category blink in the image thumbnail. This warning is a great feature because simply viewing the image on the camera monitor isn't always a reliable way to gauge exposure; the relative brightness of the monitor and the ambient light in which you view it affect the appearance of the image onscreen.

For a detailed analysis of the image exposure, check the *Brightness histogram,* which is a little graph that indicates the distribution of shadows, highlights, and *midtones* (areas of medium brightness) in your image, as shown in Figure 4-16.

Photographers use the term *tonal range* to describe this aspect of their pictures. The Brightness histogram appears to the right of the image thumbnail in Shooting Info display mode and in the lower right corner in Histogram display mode.

The horizontal axis of the graph represents the possible picture brightness values, from the darkest shadows on the left to the brightest highlights on the right. And the vertical axis shows you how many pixels fall at a particular brightness value. A spike indicates a heavy concentration of pixels. For example, in Figure 4-16, which shows the histogram for the image in Figure 4-15, the histogram shows a fairly broad range of brightness values, but few pixels at the maximum brightness or shadow values.

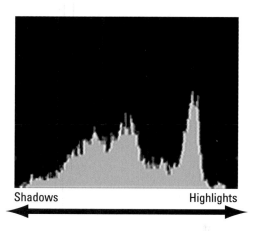

Figure 4-16: The Brightness histogram indicates the tonal range of your image.

Keep in mind that there is no one "perfect" histogram that you should try to achieve. Instead, you need to interpret the histogram with respect to the amount of shadows, highlights, and midtones that comprise your subject. For example, the histogram in Figure 4-15 makes sense for this particular image because the subject itself contains few very white or black areas — hence the lack of pixels at either end of the histogram. You should pay attention, however, if you see a very high concentration of pixels at the far right or left end of the histogram, which can indicate a seriously overexposed or underexposed image, respectively.

Reading an RGB histogram

When you view your images in Histogram display mode, you see two histograms: the Brightness histogram, covered in the preceding section, and an RGB histogram, shown in Figure 4-17.

To make sense of the RGB histogram, you first need to know that digital images are called *RGB images* because

Figure 4-17: The RGB histogram can indicate problems with color saturation.

they are created out of three primary colors of light: red, green, and blue. The RGB histogram shows you the brightness values for each of those primary colors.

By checking the brightness levels of the individual color components, sometimes referred to as color *channels,* you can assess the picture's color saturation levels. If most of the pixels for one or more channels are clustered toward the right end of the histogram, colors may be oversaturated, which destroys detail. On the flip side, a heavy concentration of pixels at the left end of the histogram indicates an image that may be undersaturated.

A savvy RGB histogram reader can also spot color balance issues by looking at the pixel values. But frankly, color-balance problems are fairly easy to notice just by looking at the image itself. And understanding how to translate the histogram data for this purpose requires more knowledge about RGB color theory than I have room to present in this book.

If you are a fan of RGB histograms, however, you may be interested in another possibility: You can swap the standard Brightness histogram that appears in Shooting Information playback mode with the RGB histogram. Just visit the Playback menu, highlight the Histogram option, as shown in Figure 4-18, and press the Set button to display the right screen in the figure. Select RGB instead of Brightness and press the Set button again.

Figure 4-18: You can change the histogram type that appears in Shooting Information playback mode.

For information about manipulating color, see Chapter 6.

Deleting Photos

When you spot a clunker image during your picture review, you can erase it from your memory card in a couple of ways, as outlined in the next three sections.

Erasing single images

To delete photos one at a time, take these steps:

1. **Select the image that you want to delete.**

   If you are viewing images in single-frame mode, just display the image on the monitor. In index display mode, use the cross keys to move the highlight box over the image thumbnail.

2. **Press the Erase button.**

   It's the one with the little trash can icon, as shown in the margin here.

   Two options — Cancel and Erase — appear at the bottom of the screen, as shown in Figure 4-19.

3. **Highlight Erase and then press the Set button.**

   Your picture is zapped into digital oblivion.

Figure 4-19: Highlight Erase and press Set to delete the current image.

If you accidentally erase a picture, don't panic — you *may* be able to restore it by using data-restoration software. One memory card manufacturer, SanDisk, even provides this type of software free on some of its memory cards. You also can buy stand-alone programs such as MediaRecover ($30, www.mediarecover.com) or Lexar Image Rescue (also $30, www.lexar.com). But in order to have a chance at recovering deleted data, you must not take any more pictures or perform any other operations on your camera while the current memory card is in it. If you do, you may overwrite the erased picture data for good and eliminate the possibility of recovering the image.

Erasing all images on your memory card

To dump all the pictures on the memory card, take this approach:

1. **Display the Playback menu and highlight Erase Images, as shown on the left in Figure 4-20.**

Figure 4-20: Use the Erase option on the Playback menu to delete multiple images quickly.

2. **Press the Set button to display the right screen in Figure 4-20.**

3. **Highlight All Images on Card and press the Set button.**

   After you press Set, you see a confirmation screen asking whether you really want to delete all of your pictures. Select OK and press Set to go ahead and dump the photos. (Note, though, that pictures that you have protected, a step discussed two sections from now, are left intact.)

4. **Press Menu to return to the Playback menu.**

   Or press the shutter button halfway to return to shooting pictures.

Erasing selected images

If you want to erase many, but not all, images on your memory card, you can save time by using this deleting option:

1. **On the Playback menu, highlight Erase Images, as shown on the left in Figure 4-21, and press Set.**

   You see the main Erase Images screen, as shown on the right in Figure 4-21.

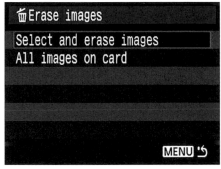

Figure 4-21: You can delete multiple selected images at once.

2. **Highlight Select and Erase Images and press the Set button.**

   You see the current image in the monitor. At the top of the screen, a little check box appears, as shown in Figure 4-22.

3. **Press the up or down cross key to put a check mark in the box and tag the image for deletion.**

   If you change your mind, press the cross key again to remove the check mark.

4. **Press the left or right cross keys to view the next image.**

5. **Keep repeating Steps 3 and 4 until you mark all of the images that you want to trash.**

Figure 4-22: Use the up and down cross keys to check the box for images you want to delete.

 6. **Press the Erase button on the camera back.**

   Your see a confirmation screen asking whether you really want to get rid of the selected images.

7. **Highlight OK and press Set.**

   The selected images are deleted, and you're returned to the Erase Images menu.

8. **Press Menu to return to the Playback menu.**

   Or, to continue shooting, press the shutter button halfway.

Deleting versus formatting: What's the diff?

In Chapter 1, I introduce you to the Format command, which lives on Setup Menu 1 and erases everything on your memory card. What's the difference between erasing photos by formatting and by using the Erase Images option on the Playback menu to delete all your pictures?

Well, in terms of pictures taken with your Canon, none. But if you happen to have stored other data on the card, such as, say, a music file or a picture taken on another type of camera, you need to format the card to erase everything on

it. You can't view those files on the monitor, so you can't use the Erase Images feature to get rid of them.

One final — and important — note: Although using the Protect feature (explained elsewhere in this chapter) prevents the Erase function from erasing a picture, formatting erases all pictures, protected or not. Formatting also ensures that the card is properly prepared to store any new images you may take.

Protecting Photos

You can protect pictures from accidental erasure by giving them *protected status.* After you take this step, the camera doesn't allow you to delete a picture with the Erase Images function.

Formatting your memory card, however, *does* erase even protected pictures. See the nearby sidebar for more about formatting.

The picture protection feature comes in especially handy if you share a camera with other people. You can protect pictures so that those other people know that they shouldn't delete your super-great images to make room on the memory card for their stupid, badly photographed ones. (This step isn't foolproof, though, because anyone can remove the protected status from an image.)

Perhaps more importantly, when you protect a picture, it shows up as a "read-only" file when you transfer it to a computer. Files that have that read-only status can't be altered. Again, anyone with some computer savvy can remove the status, but this feature can keep casual users from messing around with your images after you've downloaded them to your system.

Of course, *you* have to know how to remove the read-only status yourself if you plan on editing your photo in your photo software. (*Hint:* In Canon ZoomBrowser EX, the free Windows-based software that ships with your camera, you can do this by choosing File➪Protect. That command toggles image protection on and off. In ImageBrowser, the Mac version of the Canon software, choose File➪Get Info and then click the Lock box to toggle file-protection on and off.)

Anyway, protecting a picture on the camera is easy. Just take these steps:

1. **Display the Playback menu and highlight Protect Images, as shown on the left in Figure 4-23.**

Figure 4-23: Apply Protect status to prevent accidental erasure of important images.

2. **Press Set.**

   An image appears on the monitor, along with a little key icon in the upper-left corner, as shown on the right in Figure 4-23.

3. **Navigate to the picture that you want to protect.**

   Just press the right or left cross key to scroll through your pictures.

4. **Press Set to lock the picture.**

   Now a second key icon appears with the data at the top of the screen, as shown in Figure 4-24.

5. **To lock more pictures, repeat Steps 3 and 4.**

6. **Press the Menu button to exit the protection process.**

To remove picture protection while the picture card is still in the camera, follow these same steps. When you display the locked picture, just press Set to turn the protection off.

Figure 4-24: The key icon indicates that the picture is protected.

Using Your Monitor as a Viewfinder

If you've used a compact, point-and-shoot digital camera, you may be used to composing your pictures on the camera monitor rather than by looking through the viewfinder. In fact, many compact cameras no longer even offer a viewfinder, which is a real shame, in my opinion. Why? Because when you use the monitor to frame the image, you must hold the camera away from your body, a shooting posture that increases the likelihood of blurry images caused by camera shake. When you use the viewfinder, you can brace the camera against your face, creating a much steadier shooting stance.

Due to some design complexities that I won't bore you with, most digital SLR cameras do not enable you to preview shots on the monitor. Your XS/1000D, however, does offer that feature, known as *Live View* in Canon nomenclature. But using your monitor as a viewfinder on your camera isn't quite as simple as when you use a point-and-shoot, non-SLR model — again, the difference is due to the more involved design of an SLR camera.

Here are the important points to know before you experiment with Live View shooting:

- **Live View is available only in advanced exposure modes.** That is, you must set the Mode dial to P, Tv, Av, M, or A-DEP mode.

- **Manual focusing is recommended.** You can use autofocusing, but manual focusing usually offers faster, more precise results. Chapter 6 covers the autofocusing methods available in Live View mode just the same.

- **You must set some capture settings before switching to Live View mode.** After you enable Live View, you can't adjust the Drive mode (covered in Chapter 2), the Picture Style (Chapter 6), the AF Selection Point, or the AF mode (both covered in Chapter 6). Of course, the latter two options, which relate to autofocusing, don't matter if you're using manual focus.

- **Some other functions are either disabled or limited in Live View mode.** Here's the list of affected features:

  - *Flash limitations:* Flash Exposure lock, covered in Chapter 5, is disabled. In addition, non-Canon flash units will not work in Live View mode.

  - *A-DEP mode:* This mode functions the same as P (programmed autoexposure), meaning that it no longer tries to achieve a depth of field that keeps all objects in the frame in sharp focus. Chapter 5 explains more about these two modes; Chapter 6 details depth of field and its creative impact on your pictures.

- *Continuous shooting:* You can use the Continuous Drive mode, introduced in Chapter 2, but the camera will use the exposure settings chosen for the first frame for all the images.

- *Metering mode:* You cannot use Center-Weighted Average or Partial exposure metering; the camera always uses Evaluative metering in Live View mode. Chapter 5 explains metering modes.

- *Custom Functions 9, 10, and 11:* You can't enable mirror lock-up (Custom Function 9) in Live View mode. Also, any custom settings that you apply to the shutter button and AE Lock button through Custom Function 10 don't work. Finally, the Set button is used to switch Live View on and off, so it can't perform any of the functions that you may assign via Custom Function 11. (See Chapter 11 for details on all these Custom Functions.)

✔ **Using Live View for an extended period of time can increase image noise.** When you work in Live View mode for a long time, the camera's innards heat up, and that extra heat can create the right electronic conditions for *noise,* a defect that gives your pictures a speckled look.

Shooting at a high ISO speed or selecting a very slow shutter speed can also produce noise. To avoid compounding the risk of noise when you use Live View, set up your shot and then give the camera a brief cooldown by turning off Live View for a few minutes. You can then return to Live View mode and capture the image. See Chapter 5 for more information about the other two potential causes of noise.

✔ **You must be extra careful to keep the camera steady during the image capture.** Just as with a point-and-shoot camera, holding the camera out in front of you to capture the image can cause slight camera shake that can blur your image. But with an SLR, the risk is greater because of the added weight of the camera and lens. And if you use a so-called *long lens* — a telephoto or zoom lens that extends to a long focal length — the potential for camera shake is compounded. So for best results, mount the camera on a tripod when you use Live View.

Live View also has the same two other disadvantages that you get when you frame with the monitor on a point-and-shoot camera: First, any time you use the camera monitor, whether it's for composing a shot or reviewing your images, you put extra strain on the battery. So keep an eye on the battery status icon to avoid running out of juice at a critical moment. Second, the monitor display can wash out in bright sunlight, making it difficult to use for composing outdoor shots.

This laundry list of caveats doesn't mean that I'm advising you not to use Live View, however — just that you shouldn't envision it as a full-time alternative to your viewfinder. Rather, think of it as a special-purpose tool that can help in shooting situations where framing with the viewfinder is cumbersome.

I find Live View most helpful for still-life, tabletop photography, especially in cases that require a lot of careful arrangement of the scene. For example, I have a shooting table that's about waist high. Normally, I put my camera on a tripod, come up with an initial layout of the objects I want to photograph, set up my lights, and then check the scene through the viewfinder. Then there's a period of refining the object placement, the lighting, and so on. If I'm shooting from a high angle, requiring the camera to be positioned above the table and pointing downward, I have to stand on my tiptoes or get a stepladder to check things out through the viewfinder between each compositional or lighting change. At lower angles, where the camera is tabletop height or below, I have to either bend over or kneel to look through the viewfinder, causing no end of later aches and pains to back and knees. With Live View, I can alleviate much of that bothersome routine (and pain) because I can usually see how things look in the monitor no matter what the camera position.

With that lengthy preamble out of the way, the next few sections show you how to enable Live View and provide a brief introduction to the process of Live View shooting. Also see Chapter 5 for details about monitoring and adjusting exposure in Live View mode; check out Chapter 6 for Live View autofocusing options.

Enabling Live View

Before you can use Live View, you must take these steps:

1. **Set the Mode dial to P, Tv, Av, M, or A-DEP.**

   You can use Live View only in these exposure modes. Chapter 5 explains them all; for now, choose P (programmed autoexposure) if you're not familiar with the other modes and you just want to experiment with Live View.

2. **Press the Menu button and display Setup Menu 2.**

3. **Highlight Live View Function Settings, as shown in Figure 4-25.**

Figure 4-25: You must enable Live View through Setup Menu 2.

4. **Press the Set button.**

   You see the screen shown on the left in Figure 4-26.

Figure 4-26: Select Enable and press the Set button.

5. Select Live View Shoot and press the Set button again.

Now you see the screen shown on the right in Figure 4-26.

6. Select Enable and press Set.

7. Adjust the metering timing (optional).

By default, the exposure meter shuts itself off after 16 seconds when you work in Live View mode to conserve battery power. You can adjust this timing through the Metering Timer option, shown on the left in Figure 4-26. Highlight the option, press Set, and then select a time option. Your choices range from 4 seconds to 30 minutes. Press Set once more after making your selection. (Chapter 5 talks more about the purpose of the exposure meter.)

8. Press the Menu button to return to Setup Menu 2.

 After you enable Live View shooting, just press Set to toggle the monitor preview on and off. Note, though, that turning the monitor preview off does not officially disable Live View mode; you must revisit the Live View Shoot option on Setup Menu 2 to do that. (Don't forget that while Live View is enabled, you lose access to certain other camera features; see the preceding section for details.)

Taking a shot in Live View mode

After you enable Live View, follow this approach to focus and record your shot:

1. Check the setting on the Mode dial on top of the camera.

Remember, you must set the dial to P, Tv, Av, M, or A-DEP to use Live View. (Again, if you're just experimenting, select P.)

2. Set the focus switch on your lens to MF (for manual focus).

You can use autofocusing in Live View mode, but focusing manually is easier, faster, and may be more precise. If you do want to use autofocus, Chapter 6 spells out how to do so; you can set up the camera for two types of Live View autofocusing, each of which works a little differently.

Note that if you use a lens other than the kit lens sold with the Rebel XS/1000D, the switch that shifts you to manual focus may sport a label other than MF. Consult the lens manual for specifics.

3. If the camera is mounted on a tripod, turn off the Image Stabilizer feature.

As explained in Chapter 1, image stabilization isn't necessary when you shoot with a tripod. And because it consumes extra battery power, turning it off is a good idea for Live View tripod shooting with most lenses. However, check your lens manual just to be sure: Some lens manufacturers vary in their recommendations on this issue.

4. Press the Set button to switch from normal viewfinder operation to the Live View preview.

Now you see your scene in the monitor, as shown in Figure 4-27. At the bottom of the screen, you see data similar to what is displayed in the viewfinder during normal shooting: shutter speed and aperture (f-stop), the exposure meter, the number of shots remaining on the camera memory card, and the ISO speed setting.

Focusing frame

Also note the rectangle in the center of the screen, labeled *Focusing frame* in Figure 4-27. That frame is provided as a way for you to verify focus, as detailed in Steps 5 and 6.

Figure 4-27: Place the center square over the point where you want to establish focus.

You can display other information by pressing the DISP button; see the next section for a look at your options.

5. Frame the shot as desired.

6. **Press the cross keys to move the focusing frame over the spot where you want to focus.**

   Or, to put the focusing frame smack in the middle of the screen, press the Erase button (the one that sports the trash can symbol).

7. **Turn the lens focusing ring to set initial focus.**

   On the kit lens, the focus ring is at the far end of the lens. (See Chapter 1 if you need help.)

8. **Press the AF Point Selection button to magnify the view and refine focus if needed.**

   By pressing the button, you magnify the area within the focusing frame. Your first press of the button magnifies the view by five, as shown on the left in Figure 4-28. The second press zooms you to ten times magnification, as shown on the right.

Magnified area

Figure 4-28: Magnify the preview to double-check focus.

In the lower-right corner of the monitor, you see a label showing the current magnification level. Underneath that label, the box inside the small rectangle indicates the portion of the overall frame that you're viewing. If needed, you can reposition the focusing frame to check another part of the image by using the cross keys.

Adjust the focusing ring as needed to achieve just the right focusing distance. When you're happy with the focus, press the AF Point Selection button once more to return to full-frame view.

9. **Press the shutter button halfway to initiate exposure metering.**

   If needed, you can adjust exposure in P, Av, and Tv modes by using Exposure Compensation, a feature covered in Chapter 5. In Manual (M) exposure mode, you can adjust shutter speed and f-stop as usual. Again, Chapter 5 spells out the details.

10. **Depress the shutter button fully to take the shot.**

   You see your just-captured image on the monitor for a few seconds as usual. Then the Live View preview returns, and you're ready to take the next shot.

11. **To exit the Live View preview, press the Set button.**

   You're returned to the standard Shooting Settings screen. You can then return to framing your images through the viewfinder.

Customizing the Live View display

You can alter a couple of aspects of the monitor display for Live View shooting, as follows:

✔ **Display an alignment grid.** When you're doing the kind of work for which Live View is best suited, such as taking product shots or capturing other still-life subjects, the exact placement of objects in the frame can sometimes be important. To assist you in that regard, the camera can display a grid on the monitor, as shown in Figure 4-29.

Figure 4-29: For help aligning objects in the frame, display the grid.

To display the grid, visit Setup Menu 2, highlight Live View Function Settings, and press the Set button. Then highlight Grid Display, as shown on the left in Figure 4-30, press the Set button, highlight On as shown on the right in the figure, and press Set again. Repeat the process and choose Off to lose the grid.

✔ **Display shooting information.** By pressing the DISP button, you can superimpose a few additional bits of shooting information on the scene, as shown in Figure 4-31. For the most part, the icons you see here are the same as when you view shooting information in Playback mode, a topic discussed earlier in this chapter. Here's a brief review:

Figure 4-30: Enable the grid via the Live View Function Settings option on Setup Menu 2.

- *Drive mode:* The icon you see in the figure represents the Single Drive mode, in which you capture one image for each press of the shutter button. See the end of Chapter 2 for information about other Drive mode options.

Figure 4-31: Press DISP to view more camera settings on the screen.

- *White balance setting:* The initials AWB, shown in the figure, represent Auto White Balance. To see what icons for other settings look like and find out what white balance does in the first place, visit Chapter 6.

- *Picture Style:* Chapter 6 also details Picture Styles, which affect picture color, contrast, and sharpness.

- *Quality:* This icon tells you the selected Quality setting, which Chapter 3 explains.

- *Exp.SIM:* This symbol, which stands for *exposure simulation,* indicates whether the image brightness you see on the monitor is simulating the actual exposure you will record. If the symbol blinks or is dimmed, as in the figure, the camera can't provide an accurate exposure preview, which can occur if the ambient light is either very bright or very dim. Exposure simulation is also disabled when you use flash in Live View mode.

- *AE (autoexposure) lock and flash status:* The asterisk tells you that autoexposure lock is in force; a steady flash symbol tells you that the flash is ready to fire. Neither symbol appears if you don't use these features for your shot. See Chapter 5 for information about both features.

- *Shutter speed and aperture (f-stop):* See Chapter 5 for help understanding these options, too.

- *Exposure meter:* Yep, here's another exposure feature covered in Chapter 5.

- *Flash Compensation:* If you enabled Flash Compensation to adjust the flash power, this symbol appears. Otherwise, the area of the screen is empty. Chapter 5 covers this feature as well.

- *Shots remaining:* This number tells you how many pictures will fit on the memory card at your current Quality setting.

- *ISO speed:* This setting controls the camera's sensitivity to light; see Chapter 5 for information.

- *Battery status:* A full battery icon like the one in Figure 4-31 says you're good to go.

✔ **Display a brightness histogram.** After pressing DISP once to reveal all the icons shown in Figure 4-31, press again to add a brightness histogram to the mix, as shown in Figure 4-32. See the section "Interpreting a brightness histogram," earlier in this chapter, to find out what the histogram can tell you.

When you use flash, the histogram is dimmed (and what you can see isn't accurate because it doesn't reflect the exposure as it will be when the flash is used).

If you switch to autofocusing in Live View mode, what you see on the monitor differs slightly than what you see in the figures in this chapter. For details about using autofocus with Live View, visit Chapter 6.

Brightness histogram

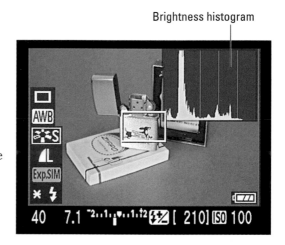

Figure 4-32: Press DISP again to add a histogram to the display.

Part II
Taking Creative Control

Av, M, and A-DEP). In these modes, you can make your own decisions about the exposure, focus, and color characteristics of your photo, which is key to capturing an image as you see it in your mind's eye. And don't think that you have to be a genius or spend years to be successful — adding just a few simple techniques to your photographic repertoire can make a huge difference in how happy you are with the pictures you take.

The first two chapters in this part explain everything you need to know to do just that, providing some necessary photography fundamentals and details about using the advanced exposure modes. Following that, Chapter 7 helps you draw together all the information presented earlier in the book, summarizing the best camera settings and other tactics to use when capturing portraits, action shots, landscapes, and close-up shots.

Getting Creative with Exposure and Lighting

In This Chapter

▶ Exploring advanced exposure modes: P, Tv, Av, M, or A-DEP?

▶ Understanding the basics of exposure

▶ Getting a grip on aperture, shutter speed, and ISO

▶ Choosing an exposure metering mode

▶ Tweaking autoexposure with exposure compensation

▶ Experimenting with exposure Custom Functions

▶ Using flash in the advanced exposure modes

▶ Adjusting flash output

*B*y using the fully automatic modes covered in Chapter 2, you can take great pictures with your Rebel XS/1000D. But to really exploit your camera's capabilities — and, more important, to exploit *your* creative capabilities — you need to explore your camera's five advanced exposure modes, represented on the Mode dial by the letters P, Tv, Av, M, and A-DEP.

This chapter explains everything you need to know to start taking advantage of these five modes. First, you get an introduction to the critical exposure controls known as *aperture, shutter speed,* and *ISO.* Adjusting these settings enables you to not only fine-tune image exposure but also affect other aspects of your image, such as *depth of field* (the zone of sharp focus) and motion blur. In addition, this chapter explains other advanced exposure features, such as exposure compensation and metering modes, and discusses the flash options available to you in the advanced exposure modes.

If you're worried that this stuff is too complicated for you, by the way, don't be. Even in these advanced exposure modes, the camera provides you with enough feedback that you're never truly flying without a net. Between the in-camera support and the information in this chapter, you can easily master aperture, shutter speed, and all the other exposure features — an important step in making the shift from picture-taker to photographer.

Kicking Your Camera into Advanced Gear

The first step to taking the exposure reins is to set your camera's Mode dial to one of the five shooting modes highlighted in Figure 5-1: P, Tv, Av, M, or A-DEP. You also need to shoot in one of these modes to use certain other camera features, such as manual white balancing, a color feature that you can explore in Chapter 6.

Each of the five modes offers a different level of control over two critical exposure settings, *aperture* and *shutter speed*. Later in this chapter, I explain these controls fully, but here's a quick introduction:

Advanced exposure modes

Figure 5-1: You can control exposure and other picture properties only in P, Tv, Av, M, and A-DEP modes.

- **P (programmed auto exposure):** In this mode, the camera selects both the aperture and shutter speed for you. But you can choose from different combinations of the two, which gives you creative flexibility not possible in the fully automatic modes discussed in Chapter 2.

- **Tv (shutter-priority autoexposure):** In this mode, you select a shutter speed, and the camera chooses the aperture setting that produces a good exposure. Why *Tv?* Well, shutter speed controls exposure time; *Tv* stands for *time value*.

- **Av (aperture-priority autoexposure):** The opposite of shutter-priority autoexposure, this mode asks you to select the aperture setting — thus *Av,* for *aperture value*. The camera then selects the appropriate shutter speed to properly expose the picture.

- **A-DEP (auto depth of field):** *Depth of field* refers to the extent to which objects at a distance from your subject appear sharply focused. One way to control depth of field is to adjust the aperture setting. In this exposure mode, the camera assesses the distance between the lens and major objects in the frame and tries to choose an aperture setting that keeps all those objects within the zone of sharp focus. Then the camera sets the shutter speed appropriate for the aperture it selected.

Although this mode is a nice feature for photographers not yet schooled in manipulating depth of field, it provides the least amount of photographic control of all the advanced exposure modes because you're stuck with whatever aperture and shutter speed the camera selects. In addition, when you use flash or enable Live View shooting, you lose the automatic depth-of-field feature, and A-DEP mode works just like P mode — but without giving you the benefit of being able to select from different combinations of aperture and shutter speed. So after you digest the depth-of-field discussion in Chapter 6, I suggest that you practice using Av mode instead, where you can select the aperture yourself.

✐ **M (manual exposure):** In this mode, you specify both shutter speed and aperture. But even in manual mode, the camera assists you by displaying a meter that tells you whether your exposure settings are on target.

Again, I realize that the descriptions of these modes won't make much sense to you if you aren't already schooled in the basics of exposure. If you are and you just want to know the specifics of using these modes on your camera, flip to "Setting ISO, f-stop, and Shutter Speed," later in this chapter. Otherwise, the next several sections provide you with the fundamentals you need to make good use of the advanced modes.

Introducing the Exposure Trio: Aperture, Shutter Speed, and ISO

Any photograph, whether taken with a film or digital camera, is created by focusing light through a lens onto a light-sensitive recording medium. In a film camera, the film negative serves as that medium; in a digital camera, it's the image sensor, which is an array of light-responsive computer chips.

Between the lens and the sensor are two barriers, known as the *aperture* and *shutter,* which together control how much light makes its way to the sensor. The actual design and arrangement of the aperture, shutter, and sensor vary depending on the camera, but Figure 5-2 offers an illustration of the basic concept.

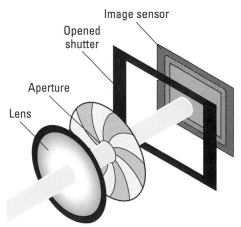

Figure 5-2: The aperture size and shutter speed determine how much light strikes the image sensor.

The aperture and shutter, along with a third feature known as *ISO,* determine *exposure* — what most of us would describe as the picture's overall brightness and contrast. This three-part exposure formula works as follows:

- **Aperture (controls amount of light):** The *aperture* is an adjustable hole in a diaphragm set just behind the lens. By changing the size of the aperture, you control the size of the light beam that can enter the camera. Aperture settings are stated as *f-stop numbers,* or simply *f-stops,* and are expressed with the letter *f* followed by a number: f/2, f/5.6, f/16, and so on. The lower the f-stop number, the larger the aperture, as illustrated by Figure 5-3.

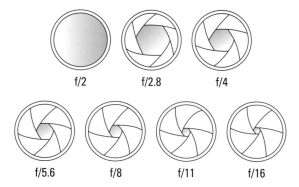

f/2   f/2.8   f/4

f/5.6   f/8   f/11   f/16

Figure 5-3: The smaller the f-stop number, the larger the aperture.

The range of possible f-stops depends on your lens and, if you use a zoom lens, on the zoom position (focal length) of the lens. For the kit lens sold with the Rebel XS/1000D, you can select apertures from f/3.5–f/22 when zoomed all the way out to the shortest focal length (18mm). When you zoom in to the maximum focal length (55mm), the aperture range is f/5.6–f/36. (See Chapter 6 for a discussion of focal lengths.)

- **Shutter speed (controls duration of light):** Set behind the aperture, the shutter works something like, er, the shutters on a window. When you aren't taking pictures, the camera's shutter stays closed, preventing light from striking the image sensor. When you press the shutter button, the shutter opens briefly to allow light that passes through the aperture to hit the image sensor.

  The length of time that the shutter is open is called the *shutter speed* and is measured in seconds: 1/60 second, 1/250 second, 2 seconds, and so on. Shutter speeds on the Rebel XS/1000D range from 30 seconds to 1/4000 second when you shoot without flash. Should you want a shutter speed longer than 30 seconds, manual (M) exposure mode also provides a feature called *bulb* exposure. At this setting, the shutter stays open indefinitely as long as you press the shutter button down.

If you do use a flash, the fastest available shutter speed is 1/200 second; the slowest ranges from 1/60 second to 30 seconds, depending on the exposure mode. See the section "Understanding your camera's approach to flash," later in this chapter, for details.

✒ **ISO (controls light sensitivity):** ISO, which is a digital function rather than a mechanical structure on the camera, enables you to adjust how responsive the image sensor is to light. The term ISO is a holdover from film days, when an international standards organization rated each film stock according to light sensitivity: ISO 100, ISO 200, ISO 400, ISO 800, and so on. Film or digital, a higher ISO rating means greater light sensitivity, which means that less light is needed to produce the image, enabling you to use a smaller aperture, faster shutter speed, or both.

On your camera, you can select ISO settings ranging from 100 to 1600 when you shoot in the advanced exposure modes. For the fully automatic modes, you're limited to ISO speeds from 100 to 800, and the camera chooses the setting for you automatically.

Distilled to its essence, the image-exposure formula is just this simple:

✒ Aperture and shutter speed together determine the quantity of light that strikes the image sensor.

✒ ISO determines how much the sensor reacts to that light.

The tricky part of the equation is that aperture, shutter speed, and ISO settings affect your pictures in ways that go *beyond* exposure. You need to be aware of these side effects, explained in the next section, to determine which combination of the three exposure settings will work best for your picture.

Understanding exposure-setting side effects

As illustrated by the images in Figure 5-4, you can create the same exposure with different combinations of aperture, shutter speed, and ISO. And although the figure shows you only two variations of settings, your choices are pretty much endless — you're limited only by the aperture range allowed by the lens and the shutter speeds and ISO settings offered by the camera.

f/13, 1/25 second, ISO 200   f/5.6, 1/125 second, ISO 200

Figure 5-4: Aperture and shutter speed affect depth of field and motion blur.

But the settings you select impact your image beyond mere exposure, as follows:

- **Aperture affects depth of field.** The aperture setting, or f-stop, affects *depth of field*. I introduce this concept in Chapter 2, but here's a quick recap: With a shallow depth of field, your subject appears more sharply focused than faraway objects; with a large depth of field, the sharp-focus zone spreads over a greater distance.

  As you reduce the aperture size — or *stop down the aperture,* in photo lingo — by choosing a higher f-stop number, you increase depth of field. As an example, notice that the background in the first image in Figure 5-4, taken at f/13, appears noticeably sharper than in the right example, taken at f/5.6. Aperture is just one contributor to depth of field, however; see Chapter 6 for the complete story.

- **Shutter speed affects motion blur.** At a slow shutter speed, moving objects appear blurry, whereas a fast shutter speed captures motion cleanly. Compare the fountain spray in the photos in Figure 5-4, for example. At a shutter speed of 1/125 second (right photo), the water droplets appear much more sharply focused than at 1/25 second (left). At the slower shutter speed, the water blurs, giving it a misty look. How high a shutter speed you need to freeze action depends on the speed of your subject, of course.

If your picture suffers from overall image blur like you see in Figure 5-5, where even stationary objects appear out of focus, the camera itself moved during the exposure. As you increase the exposure time (by selecting a slower shutter speed), you increase the risk of this problem because you have to keep the camera still longer. Most people enter the camera-shake zone at speeds slower than about 1/50 second, although some people have steadier hands than others. Turning on image stabilization, available on some lenses, helps raise the odds of sharp handheld shots at slower shutter speeds. (On the kit lens, turn the Stabilizer switch on the side of the lens to On to enable this feature.)

My abilities vary depending on the day and my caffeine intake; I was able to snap the first example in Figure 5-4 at 1/25 second, but frankly, that was a lucky accident as I usually can't handhold at speeds that slow, even with image stabilization. At the 1/5 second shutter speed used in Figure 5-5, camera shake was almost inevitable.

To avoid this issue, use a tripod or otherwise steady the camera. (If you're not using the kit lens, check the lens manual to find out whether you should turn off image stabilization for tripod shooting.) See Chapter 6 for tips on solving other focus problems and Chapter 7 for more help with action photography.

f/29, 1/5 second, ISO 200

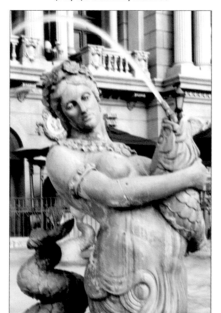

Figure 5-5: Slow shutter speeds increase the risk of all-over blur caused by camera shake.

✎ **ISO affects image noise.** As ISO increases, making the image sensor more reactive to light, you increase the risk of producing a defect called noise. This defect looks like sprinkles of sand and is similar in appearance to film grain, a defect that often mars pictures taken with high ISO film.

Ideally, you should always use the lowest ISO setting on your camera — ISO 100 — to ensure top image quality. But sometimes, the lighting conditions simply don't permit you to do so and still use the aperture and shutter speeds you need.

As an example, I shot the floral close-ups in Figure 5-6 on a windy day. Because the flower was moving quite a bit in the breeze, I knew I needed a fast shutter to capture it without blur. I opened the aperture to f/5.6, which was the maximum on the lens I was using, to allow as much light as possible into the camera. Even so, I needed a shutter speed of 1/125 second to expose the picture at ISO 100 — and that shutter speed wasn't fast enough to catch the swaying flower without blur, as shown on the left in Figure 5-6. By raising the ISO to 400, I was able to use a shutter speed of 1/500 second, which captured the flower cleanly, as shown on the right. Note that the slight softening of focus you see in the center of the flower is due not to motion blur but to the short depth of field created by my open aperture and close proximity to the flower, which also reduces depth of field. (Again, Chapter 6 explores all the ways you can manipulate depth of field.)

ISO 100, f/5.6, 1/125 second   ISO 400, f/5.6, 1/500 second

Figure 5-6: Raising the ISO enabled me to increase the shutter speed and avoid motion blur.

Fortunately, you usually don't encounter serious noise with the Rebel XS/1000D until you really crank up the ISO. You'd have to look pretty close to detect much noise in the ISO 400 image in Figure 5-6, for example. In fact, you may be able to get away with ISO 800 if you keep the print or display size of the picture small — as with other image defects, noise becomes more apparent as you enlarge the photo. Noise also is more problematic in areas of flat color. When you bump ISO all the way up to 1600, however, expect to see at least some noise even at small picture sizes.

Just to give you a better look at how ISO affects noise, Figure 5-7 offers magnified views of an area of my ISO 100 and 400 photos, plus additional shots captured at ISO 200, 800, and 1600.

One more important note about noise: A long exposure time — say, 1 second or more — also can produce this defect. Your camera offers built-in noise-reduction filters that aim to compensate for both high ISO noise and long-exposure noise; see the sidebar "Dampening noise" elsewhere in this chapter for details.

Figure 5-7: Noise becomes more visible as you enlarge your images.

Long story short, understanding how aperture, shutter speed, and ISO affect your image enables you to have much more creative input over the look of your photographs — and, in the case of ISO, to also control the quality of your images. (Chapter 3 discusses other factors that affect image quality.)

Doing the exposure balancing act

As you change any of the three exposure settings — aperture, shutter speed, and ISO — one or both of the others must also shift in order to maintain the same image brightness. If you want a faster shutter speed, for example, you have to compensate with either a larger aperture, to allow in more light during the shorter exposure, or a higher ISO setting, to make the camera more sensitive to the light, or both. And as the preceding section explains, changing these settings impacts your image in ways beyond exposure. So when you boost that shutter speed, you have to decide whether you prefer the shorter depth of field that comes with a larger aperture or the increased risk of noise that accompanies a higher ISO. Figure 5-8 offers an illustration to help you envision this balancing act.

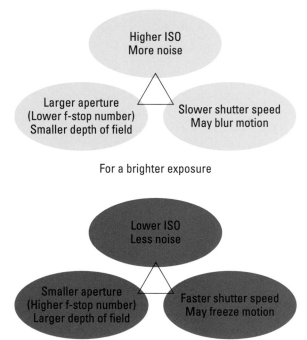

Figure 5-8: When adjusting exposure, remember the side effects produced by different aperture, shutter speed, and ISO settings.

Putting the f (stop) in focus

One way to remember the relationship between f-stop and depth of field, or the distance over which focus remains sharp, is simply to think of the f as standing for *focus*: The higher the f-stop number, the larger the zone of sharp *focus*.

Please *don't* share this tip with photography elites, who will roll their eyes and inform you that the f in f-stop most certainly does *not* stand for focus but for the ratio between the aperture size and lens focal length — as if *that's* helpful to know if you aren't an optical engineer. (Chapter 6 explains focal length, which *is* helpful to know.)

All photographers have their own approaches to finding the right combination of aperture, shutter speed, and ISO, and you'll no doubt develop your own system as you become more practiced at using the advanced exposure modes. In the meantime, here's how I handle things:

- ✔ I always use the lowest possible ISO setting unless the lighting conditions are so poor that I can't use the aperture and shutter speed I want without raising the ISO.

- ✔ If my subject is moving (or might move, as with a squiggly toddler or antsy pet), I give shutter speed the next highest priority in my exposure decision. I might choose a fast shutter speed to ensure a blur-free photo or, on the flip side, select a slow shutter to intentionally blur that moving object, an effect that can create a heightened sense of motion. When shooting waterfalls, for example, I use a slow shutter to give the water a blurry, misty look.

- ✔ For images of non-moving subjects, I make aperture a priority over shutter speed, setting the aperture according to the depth of field I have in mind. For portraits, for example, I use a wide-open aperture (low f-stop number) so that I get a short depth of field, creating a nice, soft background for my subject.

Keeping all this straight is a little overwhelming at first, but the more you work with your camera, the more the whole exposure equation will make sense to you. You can find tips for choosing exposure settings for specific types of pictures in Chapter 7; keep moving through this chapter for details on how to monitor and adjust aperture, shutter speed, and ISO settings.

Monitoring Exposure Settings

When you press the shutter button halfway, the current f-stop, shutter speed, and ISO speed appear in both the viewfinder display, as shown in Figure 5-9, and in the Shooting Settings display, as shown in Figure 5-10. In Live View mode, the exposure data appears at the bottom of the monitor and takes a form similar to what you see in the viewfinder. (The upcoming sidebar provides information about exposure-related aspects of shooting in Live View mode.)

In the viewfinder and on the monitor in Live View mode, shutter speeds are presented as whole numbers, even if the shutter speed is set to a fraction of a second. For example, for a shutter speed of 1/500 second, you see just the number 500 in the display, as shown in Figure 5-9. When the shutter speed slows to 1 second or more, you see quote marks after the number in both displays — 1" indicates a shutter speed of 1 second, 4" means 4 seconds, and so on.

Shutter speed · f-stop · Meter · ISO

Figure 5-9: The shutter speed, f-stop, and ISO speed appear in the viewfinder.

The viewfinder, Shooting Settings display, and Live View display also offer an *exposure meter,* labeled in Figures 5-9 and 5-10. This little graphic serves two different purposes, depending on which of the advanced exposure modes you're using:

Figure 5-10: You also can view the settings in the Shooting Settings display.

✏ In manual (M) exposure mode, the meter acts in its traditional role, which is to indicate whether your current settings will properly expose the image. Figure 5-11 gives you three examples. When the exposure indicator aligns with the center point, as in the middle example, the current settings will produce a proper exposure. If the indicator moves to the left of center, toward the minus side of the scale, as in the left example in the figure, the camera is alerting you that the image will be underexposed. If the indicator moves to the right of center, as in the right example, the image will be overexposed. The farther the indicator moves toward the plus or minus sign, the greater the potential exposure problem.

✏ In the other modes (P, Tv, Av, and A-DEP), the meter displays the current *Exposure Compensation* setting. Exposure compensation is a feature that enables you to tell the camera to produce a brighter or darker exposure than its autoexposure brain thinks is correct. When the exposure indicator is at 0, as in Figures 5-9 and 5-10, no compensation is being applied. See the upcoming section "Overriding Autoexposure Results with Exposure Compensation" for details.

Underexposed	Correct exposure	Overexposed

Exposure indicator

Figure 5-11: In manual mode, the meter indicates whether exposure settings are on target.

Because the meter is designated as an exposure compensation guide when you shoot in the P, Tv, Av, and A-DEP modes, the camera alerts you to exposure problems in those modes as follows:

- **Av mode (aperture-priority autoexposure):** The shutter speed value blinks to let you know that the camera can't select a shutter speed that will produce a good exposure at the aperture you selected. You need to choose a different f-stop or adjust ISO.

- **Tv mode (shutter-priority autoexposure):** The aperture value blinks instead of the shutter speed. That's your notification that the camera can't open or stop down the aperture enough to expose the image at your selected shutter speed. Your options are to change the shutter speed or ISO.

- **P mode (programmed autoexposure):** In P mode, both the aperture and shutter speed values blink if the camera can't select a combination that will properly expose the image. Your only recourse is to either adjust the lighting or change the ISO setting.

- **A-DEP mode (auto depth of field):** Either the aperture or shutter speed value may blink. If the shutter speed value blinks 30" (for 30 seconds) or 4000 (for 1/4000 second), the light is too dark or too bright, respectively, for the camera to expose the image properly at any combination of aperture and shutter speed. To compensate for dim lighting, you can raise the ISO or add flash. In too-bright light, lower the ISO if possible — otherwise, find a way to shade the subject or relocate it.

  If the aperture setting blinks, the exposure will be okay, but the f-stop won't produce the depth of field needed to keep everything in the frame in sharp focus. (See Chapter 6 for complete details on depth of field and the A-DEP mode.)

One more word of advice: Keep in mind that the camera's take on exposure may not always be the one you want to follow. First, the camera's exposure decisions are based on the current *exposure metering mode*. As covered next, you can choose three different metering modes, and each one calculates exposure on a different area of the frame. Second, you may want to purposely choose exposure settings that leave parts of the image very dark or parts very light for creative reasons. In other words, the meter and the blinking alerts are guides, not dictators.

REMEMBER

Exposure and Live View shooting

Your camera's Live View mode, detailed at the end of Chapter 4, enables you to use your monitor instead of the viewfinder to compose your images. If you do switch to Live View mode, keep these exposure-related tips in mind:

✔ Your camera strap sports a little rubber viewfinder cover that you should place over the viewfinder when you're shooting in Live View mode. Otherwise, light can seep in through the viewfinder and affect exposure.

✔ Several exposure-related functions are disabled in Live View mode. You can't use Flash Exposure lock; you're limited to Evaluative metering mode; and you can't adjust the function of the AE Lock (autoexposure lock) button. All three features are explained elsewhere in this chapter. In addition, the A-DEP exposure mode works the same as P mode during Live View shooting.

✔ Image noise may be increased if you engage Live View shooting for a long period of time. This issue is related to the fact that Live View causes the camera to heat up more than usual; you can help matters by composing the shot, powering off the camera for a few minutes, and then turning it back on to take the picture.

✔ You can display certain exposure settings, as shown in the figure here, as well as a histogram along with your image in the monitor. Chapter 4 tells you how and explains histograms.

✔ If the Exposure Simulation symbol on the monitor is white, the image brightness will be approximately the same as what you see on the monitor. But if the symbol blinks or is dimmed, don't rely on the monitor for an exposure preview. In extreme lighting conditions, the camera may not be able to simulate exposure properly. And if you use flash, exposure simulation is automatically disabled.

Exposure Simulation

AE Lock/Flash ready

Shutter speed/f-stop

Exposure meter

ISO

Choosing an Exposure Metering Mode

The *metering mode* determines which part of the frame the camera analyzes to calculate the proper exposure. Your Rebel XS/1000D offers three metering modes, described in the following list and represented in the Shooting Settings display by the icons you see in the margins:

✔ **Evaluative metering:** The camera analyzes the entire frame and then selects an exposure that's designed to produce a balanced exposure.

✔ **Partial metering:** The camera bases exposure only on the light that covers approximately the center 10 percent of the frame.

✔ **Center-Weighted Average metering:** The camera bases exposure on the entire frame but puts extra emphasis — or *weight* — on the center.

In most cases, Evaluative metering does a good job of calculating exposure. But it can get thrown off when a dark subject is set against a bright background or vice versa. As an example, in the left image in Figure 5-12, the amount of bright background caused the camera to select an exposure that left the statue too dark. So I switched to Partial metering, which properly exposed the statue.

Of course, if your background is very bright and the subject is very dark, the exposure that does the best job on the subject typically overexposes the background. Sadly, there is no way around this issue; you just have to decide which part of the picture is the most critical and base exposure on that area.

Evaluative   Partial

Figure 5-12: In Evaluative mode, the camera underexposed the statue; switching to Partial metering produced a better result.

You can verify which metering mode is currently active by checking the Shooting Settings display. The left image in Figure 5-13 shows you where to find the metering mode icon.

Metering mode icon

Figure 5-13: Press the up cross key to access your metering mode options.

 You're restricted to Evaluative metering in the fully automatic exposure modes. In the advanced exposure modes, you can specify a metering mode as long as you don't enable Live View shooting, which also limits you to Evaluative metering. To set the metering mode, follow these steps:

1. **Press the up cross key.**

   The key is marked with the same little icon that represents Evaluative metering mode. The monitor then displays the screen you see on the right in Figure 5-13.

2. **Press the up or down cross key to highlight your choice.**

3. **Press the Set button.**

   Your selected metering mode remains in force until you change it.

 In theory, the best practice is to always check the metering mode before you shoot and choose the one that best matches your exposure goals. But in practice, that's a bit of a pain, not just in terms of having to adjust yet one more capture setting but in terms of having to *remember* to adjust one more capture setting.

So here's my advice: Until you're really comfortable with all the other controls on your camera, just stick with the default setting, which is Evaluative metering. That mode produces good results in most situations, and, after all, you can see in the monitor whether you disagree with how the camera metered or exposed the image and simply reshoot after adjusting the exposure settings to your liking. This option, in my mind, makes the whole metering mode issue a lot less critical than it is when you shoot with film.

Setting ISO, f-stop, and Shutter Speed

If you want to control ISO, aperture (f-stop), or shutter speed, you must set the camera to one of the five advanced exposure modes. Formally called Creative Zone modes in Canon nomenclature, these modes include programmed autoexposure (P), shutter-priority autoexposure (Tv), aperture-priority autoexposure (Av), manual exposure (M), and auto depth of field (A-DEP).

I explain each of these modes at the start of the chapter. The next sections provide specifics (finally, you say) on how to adjust ISO, aperture, and shutter speed in all five modes.

Controlling ISO

As explained at the start of this chapter, your camera's ISO setting controls how sensitive the image sensor is to light. At higher ISO values, you need less light to expose an image.

Remember the downside to raising ISO however: The higher the ISO, the greater the possibility of noisy images. See Figure 5-7 for a reminder of what that defect looks like.

In the fully automatic exposure modes, the camera selects an ISO from 100 to 800, depending on the available light. You have no control over ISO in those exposure modes.

In the advanced exposure modes, you have the following ISO choices:

- **Auto:** You can still rely on the camera to adjust ISO for you in the advanced exposure modes if you prefer. The same parameters apply as for the fully automatic exposure modes; that is, the camera chooses an ISO setting from 100 to 800, depending on the available light. However, if you set the Mode dial to M, for manual exposure mode, or enable the flash, ISO is always set to 400.

- **Specific ISO speeds:** You can choose from ISO 100, 200, 400, 800, or 1600.

The current ISO is displayed in the upper-right corner of the Shooting Settings display, as shown on the left in Figure 5-14. You can also monitor the ISO in the viewfinder display and in the Live View display.

To adjust the setting, press the ISO button, located just behind the Main dial, on top of the camera. You then see the screen shown on the right in the figure. Use the cross keys or rotate the Main dial to highlight your choice. Then press the Set button.

Figure 5-14: Press the ISO button on top of the camera to access the ISO setting.

In Auto ISO mode, the Shooting Settings display and Live View display initially show Auto as the ISO value, as you would expect. But if you press the shutter button halfway, which initiates exposure metering, the value changes to show you the ISO setting the camera has selected for you. You also see the selected value in the viewfinder rather than the word Auto.

Adjusting aperture and shutter speed

You can adjust aperture and shutter speed only in P, Tv, Av, and M exposure modes. In A-DEP mode, the camera forces you to use its selected exposure settings. (You can, however, tweak the exposure by using the exposure-compensation feature discussed in the next section.)

To see the current exposure settings, start by pressing the shutter button halfway. The following activities then take place:

- ✔ The exposure meter comes to life. If autofocus is enabled, focus is also set at this point.

- ✔ The current aperture and shutter speed appear in the viewfinder and Shooting Settings display. In Live View mode, the settings appear under the image preview on the monitor.

- ✔ In manual exposure mode, the exposure meter also lets you know whether the current settings will expose the image properly. In the other advanced exposure modes — Tv, Av, P, and A-DEP — the camera indicates an exposure problem not with the meter, but by flashing either the shutter speed or f-stop value. (See the section "Monitoring Exposure Settings," earlier in this chapter, for details.)

Dampening noise

Noise, the digital defect that gives your pictures a speckled look (refer to Figure 5-7), can occur for two reasons: a high ISO speed and a long exposure time.

The Rebel XS/1000D offers two noise-removal filters, one designed to help eradicate ISO-related noise and another to dampen the type of noise that occurs during long exposures. Both filters are provided through Custom Functions, however, which means that you can access them only in the advanced exposure modes.

To enable High ISO noise reduction, visit Setup Menu 3, select Custom Functions, press Set, and then use the right or left cross key to select Custom Function 4, as shown in the left figure here. (The Custom Function number appears in the upper-right corner of the screen.) Press Set to activate the options, highlight On, and press Set again.

For long-exposure noise reduction, select Custom Function 3 and press Set. You then can choose from these settings, shown in the right figure below. The options work as follows:

- *Off:* No noise reduction is applied. This is the default setting.

- *Auto*: Noise reduction is applied when you use a shutter speed of 1 second or longer, but only if the camera detects the type of noise that's caused by long exposures.

- *On*: Noise reduction is always applied at exposures of 1 second or longer.

Before you enable noise reduction, be aware that doing so has a few disadvantages. First, the filter is applied after you take the picture, as the camera processes the image data and records it to your memory card. The time needed to apply the filter is about the same as the original exposure time, which slows down your shooting speed.

Second, noise-reduction filters work primarily by applying a slight blur to the image. Don't expect this process to totally eliminate noise, and do expect some resulting image softness. You may be able to get better results by using the blur tools or noise-removal filters found in many photo editors because then you can blur just the parts of the image where noise is most noticeable — usually in areas of flat color or little detail, such as skies.

Finally, if you enable ISO noise reduction, you lose the option of continuous shooting (enabled through the Drive mode setting, covered in Chapter 2) and White Balance Bracketing (an advanced color feature you can explore in Chapter 6).

The technique you use to change the exposure settings depends on the exposure mode, as outlined in the following list:

- **P (programmed auto):** In this mode, the camera initially displays its recommended combination of aperture and shutter speed. To select a different combination, rotate the Main dial.

    - To select a lower f-stop number (larger aperture) and faster shutter speed, rotate the dial to the right.

    - To select a higher f-stop number (smaller aperture) and slower shutter speed, rotate the dial to the left.

- **Tv (shutter-priority autoexposure):** Rotate the Main dial to the right for a faster shutter speed; nudge it to the left for a slower speed. As you change the shutter speed, the camera automatically adjusts the aperture as needed to maintain the proper exposure.

    Remember that as the aperture shifts, so does depth of field — so even though you're working in shutter-priority mode, keep an eye on the f-stop, too, if depth of field is important to your photo. Also note that in extreme lighting conditions, the camera may not be able to adjust the aperture enough to produce a good exposure at your current shutter speed — again, possible aperture settings depend on your lens. So you may need to compromise on shutter speed (or, in dim lighting, raise the ISO).

- **Av (aperture-priority autoexposure):** Rotate the Main dial to the right to stop down the aperture to a higher f-stop number. Rotate the dial to the left to open the aperture to a lower f-stop number. As you do, the camera automatically adjusts the shutter speed to maintain the exposure.

    If you're handholding the camera, be careful that the shutter speed doesn't drop so low when you stop down the aperture that you run the risk of camera shake. And if your scene contains moving objects, make sure that when you dial in your preferred f-stop, the shutter speed that the camera selects is fast enough to stop action (or slow enough to blur it, if that's your creative goal).

- **M (manual exposure):** In this mode, you select both aperture and shutter speed, like so:

    - *To adjust shutter speed:* Rotate the Main dial to the right for a faster shutter speed; rotate left for a slower shutter.

    - *To adjust aperture:* Press and hold the Exposure Compensation button, shown in Figure 5-15, as you rotate the Main dial.

        See the *Av* label next to the button? That's your cue as to the aperture-related function of the button — *Av* stands for *aperture value.*

        Rotate the dial to the right for a higher f-stop (smaller aperture); rotate left to select a lower f-stop. Don't let up on the button as you rotate the Main dial — if you do, you instead adjust the shutter speed.

Aperture setting   Exposure Compensation button

Figure 5-15: To set aperture in M mode, press the Exposure Compensation button as you rotate the Main dial.

 In M, Tv, and Av modes, the setting currently available for adjustment appears in the Shooting Settings display in purple, with little arrows at each side. Your camera manual refers to this display as the Main dial pointer, and it's provided as a reminder that you use the Main dial to change the setting. For example, in M (manual exposure) mode, the shutter speed appears purple until you hold down the Exposure Compensation button, at which point the marker shifts to the aperture (f-stop) value, as shown in Figure 5-15.

Keep in mind that when you use P, Tv, Av, and A-DEP modes, the settings that the camera selects are based on what it thinks is the proper exposure. If you don't agree with the camera, you have two options: You can switch to manual exposure mode and simply dial in the aperture and shutter speed that deliver the exposure you want; or if you want to stay in P, Tv, Av, or A-DEP mode, you can tweak the autoexposure settings by using the feature explained in the very next section.

Overriding Autoexposure Results with Exposure Compensation

When you set your camera to the P, Tv, Av, or A-DEP exposure modes, you can enjoy the benefits of autoexposure support but still retain some control over the final, overall exposure. If you think that the image the camera produced is too dark or too light, you can use a feature known as *exposure compensation,* which is sometimes also called *EV compensation.* (The *EV* stands for *exposure value.*)

Whatever you call it, this feature enables you to tell the camera to produce a darker or lighter exposure than what its autoexposure mechanism thinks is appropriate. Best of all, this feature is probably one of the easiest on the whole camera to understand. Here's all there is to it:

- Exposure compensation settings are stated in terms of EV values, as in +2.0 EV. Possible values range from +2.0 EV to –2.0 EV.

- A setting of EV 0.0 results in no exposure adjustment.

- For a brighter image, you raise the EV value. The higher you go, the brighter the image becomes.

- For a darker image, you lower the EV value. The picture becomes progressively darker with each step down the EV scale.

Each full number on the EV scale represents an exposure shift of one *full stop*. In plain English, that means that if you change the exposure compensation setting from EV 0.0 to EV –1.0, the camera adjusts either the aperture or shutter speed to allow half as much light into the camera as you would get at the current setting. If you instead raise the value to EV +1.0, the settings are adjusted to double the light.

By default, the exposure is adjusted in 1/3 stop increments. In other words, you can shift from EV 0.0 to EV +0.3, +0.7, +1.0, and so on. But you can change the adjustment to 1/2-stop increments if you want to shift the exposure in larger jumps — from EV 0.0 to EV +0.5, +1.0, and so on. To do so, display Setup Menu 3, highlight Custom Functions, and press Set. Then select Custom Function 1, press Set, and press the up or down cross key to change the setting. Press Set again to lock in the new setting. If you make this change, the meter will appear slightly different in the Shooting Settings display and Live View display than you see it in this book. (There will be only one intermediate notch between each number on the meter instead of the usual two.) The viewfinder meter does not change, but the exposure indicator bar appears as a double line if you set the exposure compensation value to a half-step value (+0.5, +1.5, and so on).

Exposure compensation is especially helpful when your subject and background are significantly different in brightness. As an example, take a look at the first image in Figure 5-16. Because of the very bright sky in the background, the camera chose an exposure that left the palm tree too dark.

One way to cope with this situation is to adjust the exposure metering mode, as discussed earlier in this chapter. I took the images in Figure 5-16 in Evaluative mode, for example, which meters exposure on the entire frame. Switching to Partial metering might have done the trick, but frankly, I find it easier to use exposure compensation than to fool with metering mode adjustments in most situations. So I left the metering mode alone and just amped the exposure compensation setting to EV +1.0, which produced the brighter exposure on the right.

EV 0.0   EV +1.0

Figure 5-16: For a brighter exposure than the autoexposure mechanism chooses, dial in a positive exposure compensation value.

To apply exposure compensation, take these steps:

1. **Hold down the Exposure Compensation button.**

   You can see the button in the margin here; it's the same one you use to adjust the f-stop when you shoot in manual exposure mode. (Refer to Figure 5-15.)

   If the Shooting Settings display is active, the exposure meter becomes highlighted, as shown in Figure 5-17. Again, the purple highlight and the two pointers at the edges of the highlighted area are there to remind you that you can now adjust the setting with the Main dial. If you're looking through the viewfinder or shooting in Live View mode, the meter appears as usual.

Exposure Compensation setting

Figure 5-17: In autoexposure modes, the meter indicates the exposure compensation setting.

2. **While keeping the button pressed, rotate the Main dial to change the exposure compensation value.**

   As you rotate the dial, the exposure indicator moves right or left along the exposure meter.

   - Rotate the dial to the left to lower the value and produce a darker exposure. In Figure 5-17, for example, I dialed in a setting of EV –1.0.

   - Rotate the dial to the right to raise the value and produce a brighter exposure.

   - To return to no adjustment, rotate the dial until the exposure indicator is back at the center position on the meter.

3. **Release the Exposure Compensation button after you select the value you want to use.**

How the camera arrives at the brighter or darker image you request depends on the exposure mode:

- In Av (aperture-priority) mode, the camera adjusts the shutter speed but leaves your selected f-stop in force. Be sure to check the resulting shutter speed to make sure that it isn't so slow that camera shake or blur from moving objects is problematic.

- In Tv (shutter-priority) mode, the opposite occurs: The camera opens or stops down the aperture, leaving your selected shutter speed alone.

- In P (programmed autoexposure) and A-DEP mode, the camera decides whether to adjust aperture, shutter speed, or both to accommodate the exposure compensation setting.

These explanations assume that you have a specific ISO setting selected rather than Auto ISO; if you do use Auto ISO, the camera may adjust that value instead.

Keep in mind, too, that the camera can adjust the aperture only so much, according to the aperture range of your lens. The range of shutter speeds is limited by the camera itself. So if you reach the ends of those ranges, you either have to compromise on shutter speed or aperture or adjust ISO.

One final, and critical point about exposure compensation: When you power off the camera, it doesn't return you to a neutral setting (EV 0.0). The setting you last used remains in force for the P, Tv, Av, and A-DEP exposure modes until you change it.

Disabling Auto Lighting Optimization

When you shoot in any of the fully automatic exposure modes, the camera automatically checks each picture for two potential exposure problems: a too-dark subject and a lack of contrast. If it detects either, it automatically applies a subtle corrective tweak as it records the picture to the memory card. Canon calls this feature Auto Lighting Optimization.

In general, Auto Lighting Optimization is a good thing, which is why the feature is also applied by default in the advanced exposure modes if you shoot in the JPEG format. (Chapter 3 explains JPEG and the other available format, Raw.) However, if you don't want the camera making these adjustments, you can turn off the feature. You might want to do so if you're purposely trying to shoot a backlit subject in silhouette, for example, or your artistic goal is a low-contrast image.

In addition, the correction filter that's applied by Auto Lighting Optimization can make some other exposure-adjustment features less effective. So turn it off if you don't get the results you expect when you're using the following features:

- ✔ Exposure compensation, discussed earlier in this chapter
- ✔ Flash compensation, discussed later in this chapter
- ✔ Automatic exposure bracketing, also discussed later in this chapter

To disable Auto Lighting Optimization, visit Setup Menu 3, select Custom Functions, and press Set. Then press the right or left cross keys to hunt down Custom Function 5, press Set, and highlight Disable, as shown in Figure 5-18. Press Set again to finish the job.

Figure 5-18: You can disable automatic exposure correction via Custom Function 5.

Note that for all Custom Functions, the option that appears in blue text is the one that's active.

Locking Autoexposure Settings

To help ensure a proper exposure, your camera continually meters the light until the moment you depress the shutter button fully to shoot the picture. In autoexposure modes — that is, any mode but M — it also keeps adjusting exposure settings as needed.

For most situations, this approach works great, resulting in the right settings for the light that's striking your subject at the moment you capture the image. But on occasion, you may want to lock in a certain combination of exposure settings. Here's one such scenario: Suppose that you're shooting several images of a large landscape that you want to join together into a panorama in your photo editor. Unless the lighting is even across the entire landscape, the camera's autoexposure brain will select different exposure settings for each shot, depending on which part of the scene is currently in the frame. That can lead to weird breaks in the brightness and contrast of the image when you seam the image together. And if it's the f-stop that's adjusted, which is what could happen in P or Tv exposure modes, you may notice shifts in depth of field as well because the aperture setting affects that aspect of your pictures.

The easiest way to lock in exposure settings is to switch to M (manual) exposure mode and use the same f-stop, shutter speed, and ISO settings for each shot. In Manual mode, the camera never overrides your exposure decisions; they're locked until you change them.

But if you prefer to stay in P, Tv, or Av mode, you can lock in the current autoexposure settings. Here's how:

1. **Press the shutter button halfway.**

   If you're using autofocusing, focus is locked at this point.

2. **Press the AE Lock button, highlighted in Figure 5-19.**

   The *AE* stands for *autoexposure*.

   Exposure is now locked and remains locked for four seconds, even if you release the AE Lock button and the shutter button. To remind you that AE Lock is in force, the camera displays a little asterisk in the viewfinder and on the monitor in Live View mode. If you need to relock exposure, just press the AE Lock button again.

Note that if your goal is to use the same exposure settings for multiple shots, you must keep the AE Lock button pressed during the entire series of pictures. Every time you let up on the button and press it again, you lock exposure anew based on the light currently in the frame.

AE Lock button

Figure 5-19: You can lock the current autoexposure settings by pressing this button.

One other critical point to remember about using AE Lock: The camera establishes and locks exposure differently depending on the metering mode, the focusing mode (automatic or manual), and on an autofocusing setting called AF Point Selection mode. (Chapter 6 explains this option thoroughly.) Here's the scoop:

- **Evaluative metering and automatic AF Point Selection:** Exposure is locked on the focusing point that achieved focus.

- **Evaluative metering and manual AF Point Selection:** Exposure is locked on the selected autofocus point.

- **All other metering modes:** Exposure is based on the center autofocus point, regardless of the AF Point Selection mode.

- **Manual focusing:** Exposure is based on the center autofocus point.

Again, if all of this focusing lingo just sounded like gibberish, check out Chapter 6 to get a full explanation.

By combining autoexposure lock with Partial metering, you can ensure a good exposure for photographs in which you want your subject to be off-center, and that subject is significantly darker or lighter than the background. Imagine, for example, a dark statue set against a light blue sky. First, select Partial metering, so that the camera only considers the object located in the center of the frame. Frame the scene initially so that your statue is located in the center of the viewfinder. Press and hold the shutter button halfway to establish focus and then lock exposure by pressing the AE Lock button. Now reframe the shot to your desired composition and take the picture. (See Chapter 6 for details on selecting an autofocus point.)

Note that all of these bits of advice assume that you haven't altered the function of the AE Lock button, which you can do via a Custom Function. You can swap the tasks of the shutter button and AE Lock button, for example, so that pressing the shutter button halfway locks exposure and pressing the AE Lock button locks focus. Chapter 11 offers details on the relevant Custom Function.

Bracketing Exposures Automatically

One of my favorite exposure features on the Rebel XS/1000D is *automatic exposure bracketing,* or AEB for short. This feature makes it easy to *bracket exposures* — which simply means to take the same shot using several exposure settings to up the odds that you come away with a perfectly exposed image.

When you enable AEB, your first shot is recorded at the current exposure settings; the second, with settings that produce a darker image; and the third, with settings that produce a brighter image. You can specify how much change in exposure you want in the three images when you turn on the feature.

You can take advantage of AEB in any of the advanced exposure modes. However, the feature isn't available when you use flash. If you want to bracket exposures when using flash, you have to do it yourself, either by using exposure compensation or, in manual exposure mode, by changing the aperture and shutter speed directly.

Speaking of exposure compensation, you can combine that feature with AEB if you want. The camera simply applies the compensation amount when it calculates the exposure for the three bracketed images.

One feature you may want to disable when you use AEB, however, is the Auto Lighting Optimizer option. Because that feature is designed to automatically adjust images that are underexposed or lacking in contrast, it can render AEB ineffective. See the section "Disabling Auto Lighting Optimization," earlier in this chapter, for information on where to find and turn off the feature.

With that preamble out of the way, take these steps to turn on AEB:

1. **Display Shooting Menu 2 and highlight AEB, as shown on the left in Figure 5-20.**

Figure 5-20: Auto exposure bracketing records your image at three exposure settings.

2. **Press Set to activate the little exposure meter, as shown on the right in Figure 5-20.**

3. **Press the right cross key to establish the amount of exposure change you want between images.**

After you press the right cross key, you see three exposure indicators under the meter. These indicators show you the amount of exposure shift in the three shots the camera will record. Each whole number represents one full exposure stop.

For example, if you use the setting shown in Figure 5-20, the camera shoots one image at the actual exposure settings, and it then takes the second image using settings that allow half as much light into the camera. The third image is recorded using settings that allow twice as much light.

To reduce the amount of exposure shift, press the left cross key, which moves the exposure indicators closer together.

4. **Press Set.**

AEB is now enabled. To remind you of that fact, the exposure meter in the Shooting Settings display shows the three exposure indicators to represent the exposure shift you established in Step 3, as shown in Figure 5-21. You see the same markers in the viewfinder and in the Live View display.

Auto Exposure Bracketing indicators

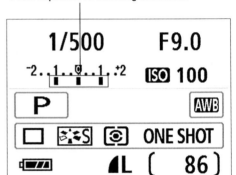

Figure 5-21: The three bars under the meter remind you that automatic exposure bracketing is enabled.

How you actually record your trio of exposures depends on whether the Drive mode is set to Single or Continuous. The Drive mode, which I introduce in Chapter 2, determines whether the camera records a single image or multiple images with each press of the shutter button. (Press the left cross key to access the screen that enables you to change this setting.)

- ✔ **AEB in Single mode:** You take each exposure separately, pressing the shutter button fully three times to record your trio of images.

  If you forget which exposure you're taking, look at the exposure meter. After you press the shutter button halfway to lock focus, the meter shows just a single indicator bar instead of three. If the bar is at 0, you're ready to take the first capture. If it's to the left of 0, you're on capture two, which creates the darker exposure. If it's to the right of 0, you're on capture three, which produces the brightest image.

- ✔ **AEB in Continuous mode:** The camera records all three exposures with one press of the shutter button. To record another series, release and then press the shutter button again. In other words, when AEB is turned on, the camera doesn't keep recording images until you release the shutter button as it normally does in Continuous mode — you can take only three images with one press of the shutter button.

> ✏ **Self-Timer/Remote modes:** All three exposures are recorded with a single press of the shutter button, as with Continuous mode.

To turn off auto exposure bracketing, just revisit Shooting Menu 2 and change the AEB setting back to 0.

AEB is also turned off when you power down the camera, enable the flash, replace the camera battery, or replace the memory card. You also can't use the feature in manual exposure mode if you set the shutter speed to the Bulb option. (At that setting, the camera keeps the shutter open as long as you press the shutter button down.)

Using Flash in Advanced Exposure Modes

Sometimes, no amount of fiddling with aperture, shutter speed, and ISO produces a bright enough exposure — in which case, you simply have to add more light. The built-in flash on your camera offers the most convenient solution.

To pop up the flash, press the Flash button on the side of the camera, highlighted in Figure 5-22. To turn off the flash, just press down on the flash assembly to close it.

As you can in the fully automatic modes, you also can set the flash to Red-Eye Reduction mode. Just display Shooting Menu 1 and turn the Red Eye option on or off. When enabled, the camera lights the Red-Eye Reduction lamp on the front of the camera for a brief time before the flash goes off in an effort to constrict the subject's pupils and thereby lessen the chances of red-eye.

The next section goes into a little background detail about how the camera calculates the flash power that's needed to expose the image. This stuff is a little technical, but it will help you better understand how to get the results you want because the flash performance varies depending on the exposure mode.

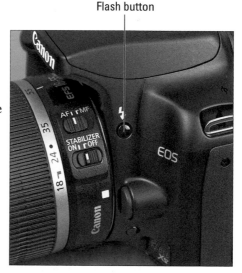

Flash button

Figure 5-22: Want flash? Just press the Flash button, and you're set to go.

Following that discussion, the rest of the chapter covers advanced flash features, including flash exposure compensation and flash exposure lock. You'll find some tips on getting better results in your flash pictures as well. For details on using Red-Eye Reduction flash, flip back to Chapter 2, which spells everything out. Be sure to also visit Chapter 7, where you can find additional flash and lighting tips related to specific types of photographs.

Understanding your camera's approach to flash

When you use flash, your camera automatically calculates the flash power needed to illuminate the subject. This process is sometimes referred to as *flash metering*. Your Rebel XS/1000D uses a flash-metering system that Canon calls E-TTL II. The *E* stands for *evaluative; TTL,* for *through the lens.* And the *II* refers to the fact that this system is an update to the first version of the system.

It isn't important that you remember what the initials stand for or even the flash system's official name. But what is helpful to keep in mind is how the system is designed to work.

First, you need to know that a flash can be used in two basic ways: as the primary light source or as a *fill flash.* When flash is the primary light source, both the subject and background are lit by the flash. In dim lighting, this typically results in a brightly lit subject and a dark background, as shown on the left in Figure 5-23.

Flash as primary light source   Fill flash

Figure 5-23: Fill flash produces brighter backgrounds.

With fill flash, the background is exposed primarily by ambient light, and the flash adds a little extra illumination to the subject. Fill flash typically produces brighter backgrounds and, often, softer lighting of the subject because not as much flash power is needed. The downside is that if the ambient light is dim, as in my nighttime photo, you need a slow shutter speed to properly expose the image, and both the camera and the subject must remain very still to avoid blurring. The shutter speed for my fill-flash image was 1/30 second, for example. Fortunately, I had a tripod, and the deer didn't seem inclined to move.

Neither choice is necessarily right or wrong, by the way: Whether you want a dark background depends on the scene and your artistic interpretation. If you want to diminish the background, you may prefer the darker background you get when you use flash as your primary light source. But if the background is important to the context of the shot, allowing the camera to absorb more ambient light and adding just a small bit of fill flash may be more to your liking.

One more note on flash: Although most people think of flash as a tool for nighttime and low-light photography, most outdoor daytime pictures, especially portraits, also benefit from a little fill flash. As a case in point, Figure 5-24 shows you the same scene, shot at a farmer's market on a sunny morning, captured with and without fill flash.

Without flash With flash

Figure 5-24: Flash often improves daytime pictures outdoors.

Using a flash in bright sunlight also produces a slight warming effect, as illustrated in Figure 5-24. This color shift occurs because when you enable the flash, the camera's white balancing mechanism warms color slightly to compensate for the bluish light of a flash. But because your scene is actually lit primarily by sunlight, which is *not* as cool as flash light, the white balance adjustment takes the image colors a step warmer than neutral. If you don't want this warming effect, see Chapter 6 to find out how to make a manual white balance adjustment.

So how does this little flash lesson relate to your camera? Well, the exposure mode you use (P, Tv, Av, M, or A-DEP) determines whether the flash operates as a fill flash or as the primary light source. The exposure mode also controls the extent to which the camera adjusts the aperture and shutter speed in response to the ambient light in the scene.

In all modes, the camera analyzes the light both in the background and on the subject. Then it calculates the exposure and flash output as follows:

✓ **P:** In this mode, the shutter speed is automatically set between 1/60 and 1/200 second. If the ambient light is sufficient, the flash output is geared to providing fill-flash lighting. Otherwise, the flash is determined to be the primary light source, and the output is adjusted accordingly. In the latter event, the image background may be dark, as in the left example in Figure 5-23.

✓ **Tv:** In this mode, the flash defaults to fill-flash behavior. After you select a shutter speed, the camera determines the proper aperture to expose the background with ambient light. Then it sets the flash power to provide fill-flash lighting to the subject.

You can select a shutter speed between 30 seconds and 1/200 second. If the aperture (f-stop) setting blinks, the camera can't expose the background properly at the shutter speed you selected. You can adjust either the shutter speed or ISO to correct the problem.

✓ **Av:** Again, the flash is designed to serve as fill-flash lighting. After you set the f-stop, the camera selects the shutter speed needed to expose the background using only ambient light. The flash power is then geared to fill in shadows on the subject.

Depending on the ambient light and your selected f-stop, the camera sets the shutter speed at anywhere from 30 seconds to 1/200 second. So be sure to note the shutter speed before you shoot — at slow shutter speeds, you may need a tripod to avoid camera shake. Your subject also must stay very still to avoid blurring.

If you want to avoid the possibility of a slow shutter altogether, you can, however. Display Setup Menu 3, select Custom Functions, and press Set. Then select Custom Function 2, as shown in Figure 5-25. At the Auto setting, the camera operates as just described. If you instead select the 1/200 second option, the shutter speed is always set to that value when you use flash. This ensures that you can handhold the camera without blur, but obviously, in dim lighting, it can result in a dark background because the camera doesn't have time to soak up much ambient light.

Figure 5-25: You can limit the camera to a fast shutter when using Av mode with flash.

✔ **M:** In this mode, the shutter speed, aperture, and ISO setting you select determine how brightly the background will be exposed. The camera takes care of illuminating the subject with fill flash. The maximum shutter speed you can select is 1/200 second.

✔ **A-DEP:** You can use flash in this mode, but doing so disables the automatic depth-of-field feature. The flash and exposure systems then operate as described for P mode. However, you can't choose from multiple combinations of aperture and shutter speed as you can in that mode; you're stuck with the combination that the camera selects.

If the flash output in any mode isn't to your liking, you can adjust it by using flash exposure compensation, explained next. Also check out the upcoming section "Locking the flash exposure" for another trick you can use to manipulate flash results.

Keep in mind, too, that in any autoexposure mode, you can use exposure compensation, discussed earlier, to tweak the ambient exposure — that is, the brightness of your background. So you have multiple points of control: exposure compensation to manipulate the background brightness, and flash compensation and flash exposure lock to adjust the flash output.

Adjusting flash power with flash exposure compensation

When you shoot with your built-in flash, the camera attempts to adjust the flash output as needed to produce a good exposure in the current lighting conditions. On some occasions, you may find that you want a little more or less light than the camera thinks is appropriate.

You can adjust the flash output by using a feature called *flash exposure compensation.* This feature works similarly to exposure compensation, discussed earlier in this chapter. But flash exposure compensation affects the output level of the flash unit, whereas exposure compensation affects the brightness of the background in your flash photos. As with exposure compensation, the flash exposure compensation settings are stated in terms of EV *(exposure value)* numbers. A setting of 0.0 indicates no flash adjustment; you can increase the flash power to +2.0 or decrease it to –2.0.

As an example of the benefit of this feature — again, available only when you shoot in the advanced exposure modes — take a look at Figure 5-26. I snapped these tomatoes during bright daylight, but they were shaded by a tent awning. The first image shows you a flash-free shot. Clearly, I needed a little more light, but at normal flash power, the flash was too strong, blowing out the highlights in some areas, as shown in the middle image. By dialing the flash power down to EV –1.3, I got a softer flash that straddled the line perfectly between no flash and too much flash.

No flash   Flash EV 0.0   Flash EV –1.3

Figure 5-26: When normal flash output is too strong, dial in a lower flash exposure compensation setting.

As for boosting the flash output, well, you may find it necessary on some occasions, but don't expect the built-in flash to work miracles even at a flash exposure compensation of +2.0. Any built-in flash has a limited range, and you simply can't expect the flash light to reach faraway objects. In other words, don't even try taking flash pictures of a darkened recital hall from your seat in the balcony — all you'll wind up doing is annoying everyone.

Whichever direction you want to go with flash power, display Shooting Menu 2 and highlight the Flash Exp Comp option, as shown on the left in Figure 5-27. Press Set to activate the little meter and then press the right or left cross key to specify the amount of flash compensation, as shown on the right in the figure. A higher value increases flash output; a lower value reduces it.

Figure 5-27: Adjust flash power via Shooting Menu 2.

TIP

By the way, if you use flash exposure compensation a lot, you can customize the camera so that pressing the Set button displays that control, saving you the trouble of using the menus. Chapter 11 shows you how.

To let you know that flash compensation is in effect, the icon labeled in Figure 5-28 appears in the Shooting Settings display. You see the same plus/minus flash symbol in the viewfinder and Live View display, although in both cases without the actual flash exposure compensation value.

Figure 5-28: This symbol tells you that flash compensation is in effect.

WARNING!

As with exposure compensation, any flash-power adjustment you make remains in force until you reset the control, even if you turn off the camera. So be sure to check the setting before you next use your flash. In addition, the Auto Lighting Optimizer feature, covered earlier in this chapter, can interfere with flash exposure compensation, so you may want to disable it.

Locking the flash exposure

You might never notice it, but when you press the shutter button to take a picture with flash enabled, the camera emits a very brief *preflash* before the actual flash. This preflash is used to determine the proper flash power needed to expose the image.

On occasion, the information that the camera collects from the preflash can be off-target because of the assumptions the system makes about what area of the frame is likely to contain your subject. To address this problem, your camera has a feature called *flash exposure lock,* or FE Lock. This tool enables you to set the flash power based only on the center of the frame.

Unfortunately, FE Lock is not available in Live View mode. So if you want to use this feature, you must abandon Live View and use the viewfinder to frame your images. Then follow these steps to FE Lock:

1. **Frame your photo so that your subject falls under the center autofocus point.**

   You want your subject smack in the middle of the frame. You can reframe the shot after locking the flash exposure if you want.

2. **Press the shutter button halfway down.**

   If you're using autofocusing, focus is set on your subject, and the green focus confirmation dot appears in the viewfinder. You can now lift your finger off the shutter button if you want.

3. **While the subject is still under the center autofocus point, press and release the AE Lock button.**

   You can see the button in the margin here. The camera emits the pre-flash, and the letters FEL display for a second in the viewfinder. (FEL stands for *flash exposure lock.*) You also see the asterisk symbol — the one that appears above the AE Lock button on the camera body — next to the flash icon in the viewfinder.

4. **If needed, re-establish focus on your subject.**

   In autofocus mode, press and hold the shutter button halfway down. (You need to take this step only if you released the shutter button after Step 2.) In manual focus mode, twist the focusing ring on the lens to establish focus.

5. **Reframe the image to your desired composition.**

   As you do, keep the shutter button pressed halfway to maintain focus if you're using autofocusing.

6. **Press the shutter button the rest of the way to take the picture.**

   The image is captured using the flash output setting you established in Step 3.

Flash exposure lock is also helpful when you're shooting portraits. The pre-flash sometimes causes people to blink, which means that with normal flash shooting, in which the actual flash and exposure occur immediately after the preflash, their eyes are closed at the exact moment of the exposure. With flash exposure lock, you can fire the preflash and then wait a second or two for the subject's eyes to recover before you take the actual picture.

Better yet, the flash exposure setting remains in force for about 16 seconds, meaning that you can shoot a series of images using the same flash setting without firing another preflash at all.

Exploring more flash options

Setup Menu 2, shown on the left in Figure 5-29, offers an option called Flash Control. Through this menu item, you can customize a few additional aspects of your camera's built-in flash as well as an external flash head.

Figure 5-29: You can customize additional flash options via Setup Menu 2.

To explore your options, highlight Flash Control, as shown on the left in Figure 5-29, and press Set. You then see the screen shown on the right in the figure. Here's the rundown of the available options:

- **Flash Firing:** Normally, this option is set to Enable. If you want to disable the flash, you can choose Disable instead. However, you don't have to take this step in most cases — just close the pop-up flash head on top of the camera if you don't want to use flash.

  What's the point of this option, then? Well, if you use autofocusing in dim lighting, the camera may need some help finding its target. To that end, it sometimes emits an *AF-assist beam* from the flash head — the beam is actually a series of rapid pulses of light. If you want the benefit of the AF-assist beam but you don't want the flash to actually fire, you can disable flash firing. Remember that you do have to pop up the flash unit to expose the lamp that emits the beam. You also can take advantage of this option when you attach an external flash head.

- **Built-In Flash Function Setting:** If you highlight this option, as shown on the right in Figure 5-29, and press Set, you display options related to the built-in flash, as shown in Figure 5-30. The first option is unavailable for the built-in flash. The other three affect the flash as follows.

- *Shutter Sync:* By default, the flash fires at the beginning of the exposure. This flash timing, known as *first-curtain sync,* is the best choice for most subjects. However, if you use a very slow shutter speed and you're photographing a moving object, first-curtain sync causes the blur that results from the motion to appear in front of the object, which doesn't make much visual sense.

Figure 5-30: These advanced flash options affect only the built-in flash.

  To solve this problem, you can change the Shutter Sync option to *second-curtain sync,* also known as *rear-curtain sync.* In that flash mode, the motion trails will appear behind the moving object. The flash actually fires twice in this mode: once when you press the shutter button and again at the end of the exposure.

- *Flash Exposure Compensation:* This setting adjusts the power of the built-in flash, just like the option with the same name that lives on Shooting Menu 2. For details, see the earlier section "Adjusting flash power with flash exposure compensation." You can set this option on either menu.

- *E-TTL II:* This option enables you to switch from the default flash metering approach, called Evaluative. In this mode, the camera operates as described in the earlier section, "Understanding your camera's approach to flash." That is, it exposes the background using ambient light when possible and then sets the flash power to serve as fill light on the subject.

  If you instead select the Average option, the flash is used as the primary light source, meaning that the flash power is set to expose the entire scene without relying on ambient light. Typically, this results in a more powerful (and possibly harsh) flash lighting and dark backgrounds.

- **External Flash controls:** The final three options on the Flash Control list (refer to the right screen in Figure 5-29) relate to external flash heads; they don't affect the performance of the built-in flash. However, they apply only to Canon EX-series Speedlites that enable you to control the flash through the camera. If you own such a flash, refer to the flash manual for details.

As you can probably discern from these descriptions, most of these features are designed for photographers who are schooled in flash photography and want to mess around with advanced flash options. If that doesn't describe you, don't worry about it. The default settings selected by Canon will serve you well in most every situation — the exception being flash exposure compensation, which you can just as easily adjust via Shooting Menu 2.

Using an external flash unit

In addition to its built-in flash, your camera has a *hot shoe,* which is photo-geek terminology for a connection that enables you to add an external flash head like the one shown in Figure 5-31. The figure features the Canon Speedlite 580EX II, which currently retails for right around $350.

Although certainly not the cheapest of camera accessories, an external flash may be a worthwhile investment if you do a lot of flash photography, especially portraits. For one thing, an external flash offers greater power, enabling you to illuminate a larger area than you can with a built-in flash. And with flash units like the one in Figure 5-31, you can rotate the flash head so that the flash light bounces off a wall or ceiling instead of hitting your subject directly. This results in softer lighting and can eliminate the harsh shadows often caused by the strong, narrowly focused light of a built-in flash. (Chapter 7 offers an example of the difference this lighting technique can make in portraits.)

Figure 5-31: An external flash with a rotating head offers greater lighting flexibility.

Whether the investment in an external flash will be worthwhile depends on the kind of photography you want to do. However, if you simply want a softer, more diffused light than your built-in flash produces, you have another option: You can buy a flash diffuser attachment like the one shown in Figure 5-32. This diffuser, made by LumiQuest (www.lumiquest.com), sells for just $13 and is a heck of a lot lighter and smaller to tuck into your camera bag than a flash head. This is just one of many diffuser designs, so visit your camera store to compare all of your options.

If you decide to purchase an external flash, I strongly recommend that you shop at a reputable camera store where the personnel can help you match the flash unit to your shooting needs. You don't have to buy a Canon flash, but be aware that non-Canon flash units do not operate in Live View mode.

You may also want to dig into some of the many books that concentrate solely on flash photography. There's a lot more to that game than you may imagine, and you'll no doubt discover some great ideas about lighting your pictures with flash. You can start with Chapter 7, which provides some specific examples of how to get better flash results when you shoot portraits, whether you go with the built-in flash, an external flash, or, my favorite, no flash.

Figure 5-32: If you don't own an external flash head, try using a diffuser to soften the light from your built-in flash.

6

Manipulating Focus and Color

*T*o many people, the word *focus* has just one interpretation when applied to a photograph: Either the subject is in focus or it's blurry. And it's true, this characteristic of your photographs is an important one. There's not much to appreciate about an image that's so blurry that you can't make out whether you're looking at Peru or Peoria.

But an artful photographer knows that there's more to focus than simply getting a sharp image of a subject. You also need to consider *depth of field,* or the distance over which objects remain sharply focused. This chapter explains all the ways to control depth of field and also discusses how to use your Canon's advanced autofocus options.

In addition, this chapter dives into the topic of color, explaining such concepts as *white balancing,* which compensates for the varying color casts created by different light sources, and *color space,* which determines the spectrum of colors your camera can capture. Finally, a section near the end of the chapter introduces you to Picture Styles, which enable you to take even greater control over image sharpness and color.

Reviewing Focus Basics

I touch on various focus issues in Chapters 1, 2, and 5. But just in case you're not reading this book from front to back, the following steps provide a recap of the basic process of focusing with your Rebel XS/1000D.

These steps assume that Live View shooting, introduced in Chapter 4, is not enabled. Focusing works a little differently in Live View mode; see the upcoming section "Autofocusing in Live View Mode" for details.

1. **If you haven't already done so, adjust the viewfinder to your eyesight.**

   Look through the view-finder and pay attention only to the autofocus points, labeled in Figure 6-1. Then nudge the diop-tric adjustment knob, to the right of the viewfinder, until the autofocus points appear sharp — don't worry about the scene in front of the lens.

Figure 6-1: The viewfinder offers these focusing aids.

2. **Set the focusing switch on the lens to manual or automatic focusing.**

   To focus manually, set the switch to the MF position. For autofocusing, set the switch to the AF position, as in Figure 6-2. (These directions are specific to the kit lens sold with the Rebel XS/1000D, shown in the figure. If you use another lens, the switch may look or operate differently, so check the product manual.)

3. **For handheld shooting, turn on Image Stabilization.**

   For sharper handheld shots, set the Stabilizer switch on the kit lens to On, as shown in Figure 6-2. If you use another lens that offers image sta-bilization (it may go by another name, depending on the manufacturer), check the lens manual to find out how to turn the feature on.

   For tripod-mounted shooting with a non-Canon lens, the manufacturer may suggest turning stabilization off, so check the lens manual. You don't need to turn the feature off for most Canon IS lenses, but you can save battery power by doing so.

TIP

Shutter speed and blurry photos

A poorly focused photo isn't always related to the issues discussed in this chapter. Any movement of the camera or subject can also cause blur. Both of these problems are actually related to shutter speed, an exposure control that I cover in Chapter 5. Be sure to also visit Chapter 7, which provides some additional tips for capturing moving objects without blur.

4. **To set focus in autofocus mode, press and hold the shutter button halfway down.**

   When focus is established, the focus lamp in the viewfinder lights, and one or more of the autofocus points turns red, as shown in Figure 6-1. A red dot indicates an *active autofocus point* and tells you that the area under the dot is in focus. You can tell the camera to base focus on a specific autofocus point by following the steps in the next section.

REMEMBER

   Focus is maintained as long as you continue to hold the shutter button down halfway. (Press the button the rest of the way when you're ready to snap the picture.)

5. **To set focus manually, twist the focusing ring on the lens.**

   Don't forget to first set the switch on the lens to the MF position to avoid possibly damaging the lens.

Auto/Manual focus switch

Image Stabilizer switch

Figure 6-2: Select AF for autofocus or MF for manual focus.

Note that even in manual mode, you can confirm focus by pressing the shutter button halfway. The autofocus point or points that achieved focus flash for a second or two, and the viewfinder's focus lamp lights up.

Adjusting Autofocus Performance

You can adjust two aspects of your Rebel XS/1000D's autofocusing system: which autofocus points are used to establish focus and the AF (autofocus) mode. The next two sections explain these features.

Selecting an autofocus point

When you shoot in any of the fully automatic exposure modes (Full Auto, Portrait, Landscape, and so on) as well as in A-DEP mode, all seven of your camera's autofocus points are active. That means that the camera's autofocusing system looks at all the points when trying to establish focus. Typically, the camera sets focus on the point that falls over the object closest to the lens. If that focusing decision doesn't suit your needs, you have two options:

- Focus manually.
- Set the camera to P, Tv, Av, or M exposure mode. In those modes, you can tell the camera to base focus on a specific autofocus point.

Chapter 1 explains how to adjust focus manually. If you want to use autofocusing and specify an autofocus point, the following steps spell out the process.

These steps assume that you are not shooting in Live View mode. I explain the intricacies of Live View autofocusing a little later in this chapter, in the section cleverly named "Autofocusing in Live View Mode." However, some of the autofocusing concepts involved in normal shooting also come into play for Live View autofocusing, so familiarize yourself with these steps before you jump to that discussion.

1. Set the Mode dial to P, Tv, Av, or M.

Again, you can specify an autofocus point only in these exposure modes.

2. Press and release the AF Point Selection button, highlighted in Figure 6-3.

When you do, you see the AF Point Selection screen on the monitor. In Automatic AF Point Selection mode, all the autofocus points appear in color, as in Figure 6-4. In Manual AF Point Selection mode, only one point is selected and appears in color, as shown in Figure 6-5. In the figure, the center AF point is selected.

AF Point Selection button

You can check the current mode by looking through the viewfinder, too. When you press and release the AF Point Selection button, all seven autofocus points turn red if you're in Automatic AF Point Selection mode. A single point turns red if you're in Manual AF Point Selection mode.

Figure 6-3: Press and release the AF Point Selection button to select an autofocus point.

3. **To choose a single autofocus point, set the camera to Manual AF Point Selection mode.**

   You can do this in two ways:

   - *Rotate the Main dial.* This option is easiest when your eye is up to the viewfinder.

   - *Press the Set button.* Pressing the button toggles you between Automatic AF Point Selection and Manual AF Point Selection with the center point activated.

4. **Specify which AF Point you want to use.**

   You can either rotate the Main dial or press the cross keys to select a point. When all autofocus points again turn red, you've cycled back to automatic AF Point Selection mode. Rotate the dial or press a cross key to switch back to single-point selection.

That's all there is to it — after you select the autofocus point, just frame your shot so that your subject falls under that point and then press the shutter button halfway to focus.

Figure 6-4: In Automatic mode, all seven autofocus points are active.

Figure 6-5: You also can base autofocus on a single point; here, the center point is selected.

If you want the benefits of autofocus but find it bothersome to have to worry about selecting an autofocus point, try this approach: Set the camera to Manual AF Point Selection and select the center point as the active point. Now the camera will always set focus based on whatever is at the center of the frame. If you want your subject to appear off-center, you still can: Just frame the picture initially so that the subject is centered, depress the shutter button halfway to establish focus, and then reframe the image before pressing the shutter button the rest of the way.

Do be careful about exposure if you use this technique, however. If the exposure metering mode is set to either Partial or Center-Weighted Average metering and you reframe the image so that your subject isn't at the center of the frame, exposure may be off. To compensate, you may need to lock exposure (using the AE Lock button) before you reframe. In Evaluative metering mode, this issue shouldn't be a big problem because exposure is based on the entire frame. Chapter 5 provides details about metering modes, autoexposure lock, and other exposure issues.

Changing the AF (autofocus) mode

Your camera offers three different autofocusing schemes, which you select through a control called AF mode. The three choices work like so:

- ✔ **One-Shot:** In this mode, which is geared to shooting stationary subjects, the camera locks focus when you depress the shutter button halfway. Focus remains locked as long as you hold the shutter button at that halfway position.

- ✔ **AI Servo:** In this mode, the camera adjusts focus continually as needed from the time you press the shutter button halfway to the time you take the picture. This mode is designed to make it easier to focus on moving objects.

For AI Servo to work properly, you must reframe as needed to keep your subject under the active autofocus point if you're working in Manual AF Point Selection mode. If the camera is set to Automatic AF Point Selection, keep the subject within the area covered by the seven autofocus points. (The preceding section explains these two modes.)

In either case, the green focus dot in the viewfinder blinks rapidly if the camera isn't tracking focus successfully. If all is going well, the focus dot does not light up at all, nor do you hear the beep that normally sounds when focus is achieved.

- ✔ **AI Focus:** This mode automatically switches the camera from One-Shot to AI Servo as needed. When you first press the shutter button halfway, focus is locked on the active autofocus point (or points), as usual in One-Shot mode. But if the subject moves, the camera shifts into AI Servo mode and adjusts focus as it thinks is warranted.

Which of these three autofocus modes are available to you, however, depends on the exposure mode, as follows:

- ✔ In P, Tv, Av, and M modes, you can select any of the three AF mode options.

- ✔ In A-DEP mode as well as in Portrait, Landscape, Night Portrait, and Close-Up modes, the camera restricts you to One-Shot mode.

- ✔ Sports mode always uses AI Servo autofocus.

- ✔ Full Auto and No Flash modes always use AI Focus.

    The AI stands for *artificial intelligence,* if that helps.

So, assuming that you can choose from all three, which mode is best? Well, here's my take: One-Shot mode works best for shooting still subjects, and AI Servo is the right choice for moving subjects. But frankly, AI Focus does a good job in most cases of making that shift for you and saves you the trouble of having to change the mode each time you go from shooting still to moving subjects. So, in my mind, there's no real reason to fiddle with the setting unless you're shooting moving objects and want to be able to lock focus at a specific position — in which case, my recommendation would be to simply switch to manual focusing anyway.

Whatever you decide, you can set the AF mode as follows:

1. **Press the right cross key (the one labeled AF).**

   The monitor displays the screen you see in Figure 6-6.

2. **Press the left or right cross keys to highlight your choice.**

3. **Press the Set button.**

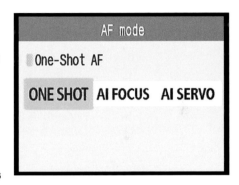

Figure 6-6: Press the right cross key to display the AF mode options.

Autofocusing in Live View Mode

Chapter 4 covers the basics of shooting in Live View mode, which enables you to compose your shots by using the camera monitor instead of the viewfinder. As I mention in that discussion, using this photography mode on a digital SLR isn't as simple as it is on a compact point-and-shoot model because of the complexities of SLR design. On the Rebel XS/1000D, shooting in Live View mode requires some tradeoffs, such as not being able to use certain exposure features or any of the fully automatic exposure modes (Full Auto, Portrait, and so on).

As for focusing, the simplest and usually most reliable choice is to focus manually, and the Chapter 4 guide to Live View shooting explains the steps involved in doing just that. (The process is a little different in Live View mode than when you use the viewfinder to preview your shots.)

You can use autofocusing in Live View mode, however. In fact, you have your choice of two autofocusing methods: Quick mode and Live mode. (Hint: Quick mode is usually the best option.)

The next three sections explain the art of autofocusing in Live View mode. Before you move on to those sections, though, note the following limitations:

✔ **Continuous autofocusing isn't possible.** You can set the AF mode to AI Servo, but even if you do, the camera behaves as if you instead selected the One-Shot option. In other words, the camera won't track focus on a moving subject during Live View shooting.

✔ **Autoexposure and autofocus are set and locked together.** When you autofocus in Live View mode, you don't press the shutter button halfway to lock focus as you normally do. Instead, you focus by pressing the AE Lock button — which also locks autoexposure, as explained in Chapter 5. If you want to lock exposure and focus separately in Live View mode, you have to reset the function of the AE Lock button.

You do this through Custom Function 9, which you can explore fully in Chapter 11. For the purpose of Live View autofocusing, select option 1, AE Lock/AF. After you do, you lock autoexposure by using the shutter button and lock autofocus by pressing the AE Lock button. (Trust me, however, that simply focusing manually is much simpler than this convoluted process. And don't make this change to the button functions while using this book, or things won't work as described.)

✔ **Autofocusing isn't possible with remote-control shooting.** If you want to control the camera with a remote unit, either switch to manual focusing or don't enable Live View.

Don't forget that the Live View function is turned off by default. You enable the feature via the Live View Function Settings option on Setup Menu 2. (Chapter 4 explains this step.)

Enabling Live View autofocusing

By default, autofocusing is disabled for Live View shooting. If you want to autofocus, take these steps:

1. **Set the camera to P, Tv, Av, M, or A-DEP mode.**

   You can't use Live View in any other mode.

2. **Display Setup Menu 3 and highlight Custom Functions, as shown on the left in Figure 6-7.**

3. **Press Set and then press the right or left cross key to navigate to Custom Function 7.**

   The Custom Function number appears in the upper-right corner of the screen. You should see options shown on the right in Figure 6-7.

4. **Press Set again to activate the options list.**

Figure 6-7: Enable Live View autofocusing through Custom Function 7.

5. Highlight your choice of autofocusing modes and then press Set.

The next two sections explain the difference between Quick mode and Live mode autofocusing. After you press Set, your selected option appears in blue text in the menu, as shown on the right in Figure 6-7. (The blue always indicates the selected option for Custom Functions.)

Live View autofocus option 1: Quick mode

As its name implies, Quick mode offers the fastest autofocusing during Live View shooting. Here's how it works:

1. Set the camera Mode dial to one of the advanced exposure modes (P, Tv, Av, M, or A-DEP).

But remember that in Live View mode, the automatic depth-of-field feature supplied by the A-DEP mode is disabled, and the camera operates as it does when set to P (programmed autoexposure). See Chapter 5 if you can't remember the difference between these two autoexposure settings.

2. Select Quick mode for Custom Function 7, as explained in the preceding section.

3. Set the AF mode to One-Shot.

To do so, press the right cross key to access the AF mode settings. Highlight One-Shot and press Set.

You can use the other two AF mode settings, but the camera can't adjust focus to track moving subjects in those modes as it normally can. In addition, the other two settings can slow the autofocusing process.

4. Set the desired autofocus point.

You do this by pressing the AF Point Selection button and then using the techniques spelled out earlier in this chapter, in the section "Selecting an autofocus point."

5. Press the shutter button halfway to return to shooting mode.

You can then release the shutter button.

6. Press Set to engage the Live View preview.

Now you see your subject on the monitor, along with either two or eight rectangles, as shown in Figure 6-8. Here's the scoop:

Focusing frame

- The large rectangle is the focusing frame that appears anytime you use Live View. It becomes involved in autofocusing if you choose to magnify the image display to check focus, as spelled out in Step 10.

- The small rectangles represent the autofocus points. If you're using Automatic AF Point

Figure 6-8: The small rectangles represent autofocus points; the large rectangle, the Live View focusing frame.

Selection, all seven points appear, as in Figure 6-8. If you're using Manual AF Point Selection, you see only a single small rectangle that represents your chosen autofocus point.

7. Frame your shot so that an autofocus point falls over your subject.

Again, the small rectangle (or rectangles) represent the autofocus point(s).

8. Press and hold the AE Lock button until you hear a beep.

As soon as you press the button, the monitor turns black, and the auto-focusing mechanism kicks into gear. Keep pressing the button until the camera beeps at you. The beep signals you that focus is set.

In P, Tv, Av, or A-DEP modes, the autoexposure system fires up and locks exposure settings along with focus.

9. When focus is set, release the AE Lock button.

The live image reappears on the monitor.

10. **Verify focus (optional).**

You can magnify the Live View display to double-check focus if you want. First press the cross keys to move the large focusing frame (refer to Figure 6-8) over the area of interest. Then press the AF Point Selection button to magnify the area inside the frame. Your first press displays a five-times magnified view; press again for a 10-times magnification.

If focus is off, you can try reframing the scene and repeating Step 8 — that is, press and hold the AE Lock button until you hear the beep that indicates that focus has been reestablished. You can't, however, select a different AF point without exiting from Live View mode. To do so, press the Set button. You then can repeat Steps 4 through 6 to change the AF point and return to Live View mode.

When you're satisfied with focus, press the AF Point Selection button again to return to the normal display magnification.

11. **Depress the shutter button fully to take the picture.**

Because the shutter button doesn't affect autofocus, as it does when you're not using Live View mode, you don't have to use the normal two-stage button press. You can press that baby all in a single motion. (But press, don't jab, or you may shake the camera and cause image blur.)

Live View autofocus option 2: Live mode

Live mode autofocusing enables you to select an autofocus point without exiting Live View shooting mode, an option you don't get with Quick mode autofocusing.

On the very significant downside, however, Live mode autofocusing is noticeably slower than Quick mode, and the camera may have more trouble finding the focus point than in Quick mode. (The difference is due to the autofocusing system that the camera employs.)

To compare the two modes, first visit Custom Function 7, on Setup Menu 3, and select Live mode from the list of options, as explained in the earlier section, "Enabling Live View autofocusing." Then set focus as follows:

1. **Press Set to switch to Live View mode.**

Remember, in order to use Live View, you must use one of the advanced exposure modes: P, Tv, Av, M, or A-DEP.

After you press Set, your subject appears on the monitor. This time, you see just the large rectangular focusing frame, labeled in Figure 6-8, without the smaller autofocus point or points.

2. **Position the focusing frame over the area on which you want to focus.**

   You can move the focusing frame by pressing the cross keys.

3. **Press and hold the AE Lock button.**

   The camera attempts to establish focus and also sets exposure, if you're using any exposure mode but M (manual).

4. **When the focusing frame turns green and you hear a beep, release the AE Lock button.**

   These signals tell you focus has been established and, in the autoexposure modes, that exposure has been set as well.

   If the focusing frame instead turns orange, the camera can't establish focus. The best option here is to switch to manual focusing. (See the instructions in Chapter 4 for help with manual focusing in Live View mode.)

5. **Verify focus (optional).**

   To zoom in on the area inside the focusing frame and check focus, press the AF Selection Point button. Press once to zoom to a five-times magnification; press again to display the scene at 10-times magnification. You can press the cross keys to shift the position of the focusing frame to inspect another area of the image.

   If focus appears off, you can press the AE Lock button again to restart autofocusing. Again, wait for the beep and green focusing frame indicator to release the button.

   When you're happy with focus, press the AF Point Selection button once more to return to normal, non-magnified view.

6. **Press the shutter button to take the picture.**

Although this option may seem like the easiest way to shoot in Live View mode, I suspect that you'll find that it's actually the least successful because of the length of time the camera needs to establish focus — assuming that it can do so at all. Once again, if you enjoy Live View shooting, I strongly encourage you to opt out of autofocusing and instead use the manual focusing technique explored in Chapter 4.

Manipulating Depth of Field

Getting familiar with the concept of *depth of field* is one of the biggest steps you can take to becoming a more artful photographer. I introduce you to depth of field in Chapters 2 and 5, but here's a quick recap just to hammer home the lesson:

✔ *Depth of field* refers to the distance over which objects in a photograph appear sharply focused.

Shallow depth of field

✔ With a shallow, or small, depth of field, only your subject and objects very close to it appear sharp. Objects at a distance from the subject appear blurry.

✔ With a large depth of field, the zone of sharp focus extends to include distant objects.

Which arrangement works best depends entirely on your creative vision and your subject. In portraits, for example, a classic technique is to use a shallow depth of field, as in Figure 6-9. This approach increases emphasis on the subject while diminishing the impact of the background. But for the photo shown in Figure 6-10, I wanted the historical marker, the lighthouse, and the cottage behind to have equal weight in the scene, so I used settings that produced a large depth of field, keeping them all in sharp focus.

Figure 6-9: A shallow depth of field blurs the background and draws added attention to the subject.

Note, though, that with a shallow depth of field, you can just as easily throw foreground objects into soft focus as background objects. In the lighthouse scene, for example, if I had used settings that produced a short depth of field and I set focus on the lighthouse, the historical marker and the cottage both might be outside the zone of sharp focus.

Large depth of field

So how do you adjust depth of field? You have three points of control, as follows:

✔ **Aperture setting (f-stop):** The aperture is one of three exposure settings, all explained fully in Chapter 5. Depth of field increases as you stop down the aperture (by choosing a higher f-stop number). For shallow depth of field, open the aperture (by choosing a lower f-stop number).

Figure 6-10: A large depth of field keeps both near and far subjects in sharp focus.

Figure 6-11 offers an example. Notice that the trees in the background are much more softly focused in the f/5.6 example than in the f/11 version. Of course, changing the aperture requires adjusting the shutter speed or ISO to maintain the equivalent exposure; for these images, I adjusted shutter speed.

f/5.6, 1/1000 second   f/11, 1/200 second

Figure 6-11: Raising the f-stop value increases depth of field.

✓ **Lens focal length:** In lay terms, *focal length* determines what the lens "sees." As you increase focal length, measured in millimeters, the angle of view narrows, objects appear larger in the frame, and — the important point for this discussion — depth of field decreases. Additionally, the spatial relationship of objects changes as you adjust focal length.

As an example, Figure 6-12 compares the same scene shot at focal lengths of 138mm and 255mm. I used the same aperture, f/22, for both examples.

Whether you have any focal-length flexibility depends on your lens: If you have a zoom lens, you can adjust the focal length — just zoom in or out. (The Rebel XS/1000D kit lens, for example, offers a focal range of 18–55mm.) If you don't have a zoom lens and can't switch to a lens offering a different focal length than your current lens, scratch this means of manipulating depth of field.

138mm, f/22 | 255mm, f/22

Figure 6-12: Zooming to a longer focal length also reduces depth of field.

For more technical details about focal length and your camera, see the sidebar "Fun facts about focal length."

✓ **Camera-to-subject distance:** As you move the lens closer to your subject, depth of field decreases. This assumes that you don't zoom in or out to reframe the picture, thereby changing the focal length. If you do, depth of field is affected by both the camera position and focal length.

Together, these three factors determine the maximum and minimum depth of field that you can achieve, as illustrated by my clever artwork in Figure 6-13 and summed up in the following list:

✓ **To produce the shallowest depth of field:** Open the aperture as wide as possible (select the lowest f-stop number), zoom in to the maximum focal length of your lens, and get as close as possible to your subject.

✓ **To produce maximum depth of field:** Stop down the aperture to the highest possible f-stop setting, zoom out to the shortest focal length your lens offers, and move farther from your subject.

Greater depth of field:
Select higher f-stop
Decrease focal length (zoom out)
Move farther from subject

Shorter depth of field:
Select lower f-stop
Increase focal length (zoom in)
Move closer to subject

Figure 6-13: Aperture, focal length, and your shooting distance determine depth of field.

Here are a few additional tips and tricks related to depth of field:

- When depth of field is a primary concern, try using aperture-priority autoexposure (Av). In this mode, detailed fully in Chapter 5, you set the f-stop, and the camera selects the appropriate shutter speed to produce a good exposure. The range of aperture settings you can access depends on your lens.

- Some of the fully automatic scene modes are also designed with depth of field in mind. Portrait and Close-Up modes produce shortened depth of field; Landscape mode produces a greater depth of field. You can't adjust aperture in these modes, however, so you're limited to the setting the camera chooses. And in certain lighting conditions, the camera may not be able to choose an aperture that produces the depth of field you expect from the selected mode.

- The Rebel XS/1000D also offers a special autoexposure mode called A-DEP, which stands for *automatic depth of field*. In this mode, the camera selects the aperture setting that it thinks will keep all objects in the frame within the zone of sharp focus. You can read more about this mode in the next section.

- Not sure which aperture setting you need to produce the depth of field you want? Good news: Your camera offers *depth-of-field preview*, which enables you to see in advance how the aperture affects the focus zone. See the section labeled "Checking depth of field" for details on how to use this feature.

Fun facts about focal length

Every lens can be characterized by its *focal length*, or in the case of a zoom lens, the range of focal lengths it offers. Measured in millimeters, focal length determines the camera's angle of view, the apparent size and distance of objects in the scene, and depth of field. According to photography tradition, a focal length of about 50mm is a "normal" lens. Most point-and-shoot cameras feature this focal length, which is a medium-range lens that works well for the type of snapshots that users of those kinds of cameras are likely to shoot.

A lens with a focal length under 35mm is typically known as a *wide-angle* lens because at that focal length, the camera has a wide angle of view and produces a long depth of field, making it good for landscape photography. A short focal length also has the effect of making objects seem smaller and farther away. At the other end of the spectrum, a lens with a focal length longer than about 80mm is considered a *telephoto* lens and often referred to as a *long lens*. With a long lens, angle of view narrows, depth of field decreases, and faraway subjects appear closer and larger, which is ideal for wildlife and sports photographers.

Note, however, that the focal lengths stated here and elsewhere in the book are so-called *35mm equivalent* focal lengths. Here's the deal: For reasons that aren't really important, when you put a standard lens on most digital cameras, including your Rebel XS/1000D, the available frame area is reduced, as if you took a picture on a camera that uses 35mm film negatives (the kind you've probably been using for years) and then cropped it.

This so-called *crop factor*, sometimes also called the *magnification factor*, varies depending on the digital camera, which is why the photo industry adopted the 35mm-equivalent measuring stick as a standard. With your camera, the cropping factor is roughly 1.6. So the 18–55mm kit lens sold with the Rebel XS/1000D, for example, actually captures the approximate area you would get from a 27–82mm lens on a 35mm film camera. In the figure here, for example, the red outline indicates the image area that results from the 1.6 crop factor.

Note that although the area the lens can capture changes when you move a lens from a 35mm film camera to a digital body, depth of field isn't affected, nor are the spatial relationships between objects in the frame. So when lens shopping, you gauge those two characteristics of the lens by looking at the stated focal length — no digital-to-film conversion math is required.

Chuck Pace

✔ The extent to which background focus shifts as you adjust depth of field also is affected by the distance between the subject and the background. For increased background blurring, move the subject farther in front of the background.

✔ If you adjust aperture to affect depth of field, be sure to always keep an eye on shutter speed as well. To maintain the same exposure, shutter speed must change in tandem with aperture, and you may encounter a situation where the shutter speed is too slow to permit hand-holding of the camera. Lenses that offer optical image stabilization do enable most people to handhold the camera at slower shutter speeds than non-stabilized lenses, but double-check your results just to be sure. You can also consider raising the ISO setting to make the image sensor more reactive to light, but remember that higher ISO settings can produce noise. (Chapter 5 has details.)

Using A-DEP mode

In addition to the four advanced exposure modes found on most digital SLR cameras, your Rebel XS/1000D offers a fifth mode called A-DEP, as shown in Figure 6-14. The initials stand for *automatic depth of field.*

This mode is designed to assist you in producing photos that have a depth of field sufficient to keep all objects in the frame in sharp focus. The camera accomplishes this by analyzing the lens-to-subject distance for all those objects and then selecting the aperture that results in the appropriate depth of field. After choosing the aperture, the camera then selects the necessary shutter speed to properly expose the image at the selected f-stop.

A-DEP mode isn't a surefire bet, however, and it does have some restrictions that may make it unsuitable for your subject. Here's what you need to know:

Figure 6-14: A-DEP stands for automatic depth of field.

✔ In very dim lighting, the shutter speed the camera selects may be too slow to allow you to handhold the camera without risking camera shake. So check the shutter speed in the viewfinder after you press the shutter button halfway to meter and focus the image.

✔ If the aperture value blinks in the viewfinder, the camera can't set the f-stop so that you get both a good exposure and the depth of field necessary to keep all objects in the frame in sharp focus. In this situation, the camera assumes that your primary goal is a good exposure and adjusts the aperture as needed based on the available light.

  ✔ If the shutter speed blinks in the viewfinder, the light is either too bright
    or too dim for the camera to properly expose the image at any combina-
    tion of aperture and shutter speed. In bright light, you can lower the ISO,
    if it isn't already at 100, or reposition or shade your subject. In dim light-
    ing, raise the ISO or add artificial light.

  ✔ You can use flash with A-DEP mode, but the minute you turn on the
    flash, the camera no longer does its automatic depth-of-field calculation.
    The same thing occurs if you switch to Live View shooting. In either
    case, the camera simply presents you with a fixed combination of aper-
    ture and shutter speed that will properly expose the image. The depth of
    field may or may not be what you want.

Given these limitations, my personal recommendation is that as soon as you
fully understand the impact of aperture on depth of field, you politely decline
the option of using A-DEP mode and instead work in aperture-priority autoexposure mode (Av) instead. Then you can simply match the f-stop to the
depth of field you have in mind, without giving up the option of using flash or
Live View shooting.

Checking depth of field

When you look through your viewfinder and press the shutter button halfway, you can get only a partial indication of the depth of field that your current camera settings will produce. You can see the effect of focal length and
the camera-to-subject distance, but because the aperture doesn't actually
open to your selected f-stop until you take the picture, the viewfinder doesn't
show you how that setting will affect depth of field.

By using the Depth-of-Field Preview button on your camera, however, you
can do just that. Almost hidden away on the front of your camera, the button
is labeled in Figure 6-15.

To use this feature, just press and hold the shutter button halfway down and
then press and hold the Depth-of-Field Preview button with the other hand.
Depending on the selected f-stop, the scene in the viewfinder may then get
darker. Or in Live View mode, the same thing happens in the monitor preview. Either way, this effect doesn't mean that your picture will be darker;
it's just a function of how the preview works.

After the preview engages, you can release the shutter button and then rotate
the Main dial to see how changing the f-stop affects the depth of field. (The
exception is when the camera is set to A-DEP mode, in which you have no
control over aperture.)

Note that the preview doesn't engage in P, Tv, Av, or A-DEP mode if your current aperture and shutter speed aren't adequate to expose the image properly. You have to solve the exposure issue before you can use the preview.

Controlling Color

Compared with understanding some aspects of digital photography — resolution, aperture and shutter speed, depth of field, and so on — making sense of your camera's color options is easy-breezy. First, color problems aren't all that common, and when they are, they're usually simple to fix with a quick shift of your camera's white balance control. And getting a grip on color requires learning only a couple of new terms, an unusual state of affairs for an endeavor that often seems more like high-tech science than art.

Depth-of-Field Preview button

Figure 6-15: Press this button to see how the aperture setting will affect depth of field.

The rest of this chapter explains the aforementioned white balance control, plus a couple of menu options that enable you to fine-tune the way your camera renders colors. For information on how to alter colors of existing pictures by using the software that shipped with your camera, see Chapter 10.

Correcting colors with white balance

Every light source emits a particular color cast. The old-fashioned fluorescent lights found in most public restrooms, for example, put out a bluish-greenish light, which is why our reflections in the mirrors in those restrooms always look so sickly. And if you think that your beloved looks especially attractive by candlelight, you aren't imagining things: Candlelight casts a warm, yellow-red glow that is flattering to the skin.

Science-y types measure the color of light, officially known as *color temperature,* on the Kelvin scale, which is named after its creator. You can see an illustration of the Kelvin scale in Figure 6-16.

When photographers talk about "warm light" and "cool light," though, they aren't referring to the position on the Kelvin scale — or at least not in the way we usually think of temperatures, with a higher number meaning hotter. Instead, the terms describe the visual appearance of the light. Warm light, produced by candles and incandescent lights, falls in the red-yellow spectrum you see at the bottom of the Kelvin scale in Figure 6-16; cool light, in the blue-green spectrum, appears at the top of the scale.

At any rate, most of us don't notice these fluctuating colors of light because our eyes automatically compensate for them. Except in very extreme lighting conditions, a white tablecloth appears white to us no matter whether we view it by candlelight, fluorescent light, or regular houselights.

Similarly, a digital camera compensates for different colors of light through a feature known as *white balancing.* Simply put, white balancing neutralizes light so that whites are always white, which in turn ensures that other colors are rendered accurately. If the camera senses warm light, it shifts colors slightly to the cool side of the color spectrum; in cool light, the camera shifts colors the opposite direction.

Figure 6-16: Each light source emits a specific color.

The good news is that, as with your eyes, your camera's Automatic White Balance setting, which carries the label AWB, tackles this process remarkably well in most situations, which means that you can usually ignore it and concentrate on other aspects of your picture. But in some lighting conditions, the AWB adjustment doesn't quite do the trick, resulting in an unwanted color cast like the one you see in the left image in Figure 6-17.

Figure 6-17: Multiple light sources resulted in a yellow color cast in Auto White Balance mode (left); switching to the Tungsten Light setting solved the problem (right).

Serious AWB problems most often occur when your subject is lit by a variety of light sources. For example, I shot the figurine in Figure 6-17 in my home studio, where I use a couple of high-powered photo lights that use tungsten bulbs, which produce light with a color temperature similar to regular household incandescent bulbs. The problem is that the windows in that room also permit some pretty strong daylight to filter through. In Automatic White Balance mode, the camera reacted to that daylight — which has a cool color cast — and applied too much warming, giving my original image a yellow tint. No problem: I just switched the white balance mode from AWB to the Tungsten Light setting. The right image in Figure 6-17 shows the corrected colors.

 Unfortunately, you can't make this kind of manual white balance selection if you shoot in the fully automatic exposure modes. So if you spy color problems in your camera monitor, you need to switch to either P, Tv, Av, M, or A-DEP mode. (Chapter 5 details all five exposure modes.)

The next section explains precisely how to make a simple white balance correction; following that, you can explore some advanced white balance features.

Changing the white balance setting

To switch from automatic to manual white balancing, follow these steps:

1. **Set the camera Mode dial to P, Tv, Av, M, or A-DEP.**

   You can tweak white balance only in these advanced exposure modes.

2. **Press the WB button.**

   You see the White Balance screen, shown on the left in Figure 6-18.

White Balance symbol

Figure 6-18: Press the WB button to access white balance options.

3. **Press the right or left cross key to highlight the setting you want to use.**

   As you scroll through the list of options, the name of the selected setting appears on the screen. For some settings, the camera also displays the approximate Kelvin temperature of the selected light source, as shown in the figure. (Refer to Figure 6-16 for a look at the Kelvin scale.)

   If the scene is lit by several sources, choose the setting that corresponds to the strongest one. The Tungsten Light setting is usually best for regular incandescent household bulbs, by the way. And with the Custom option, you can define your own white balance setting; see the next section for details.

4. **Press Set to lock in your choice.**

You can confirm the current White Balance setting by displaying the Shooting Settings screen. The symbol representing the setting appears in the position labeled in the right image in Figure 6-18. (You also can display the symbol during Live View shooting; see Chapter 4 to find out how.) Table 6-1 offers a reminder of what setting each symbol represents.

Your selected white balance setting remains in force for the P, Tv, Av, M, and A-DEP exposure modes until you change it again. So you may want to get in the habit of resetting the option to AWB (automatic white balance) after you finish shooting whatever subject it was that caused you to switch to manual white balance mode.

Table 6-1	White Balance Settings
Symbol	*Setting*
AWB	Auto
☀	Daylight
⌂	Shade
☁	Cloudy
💡	Tungsten
▭	White Fluorescent
⚡	Flash
◢📷◣	Custom

Creating a custom white balance setting

If none of the preset white balance options produces the right amount of color correction, you can create your own custom setting. To use this technique, you need a piece of card stock that's either neutral gray or absolute white — not eggshell white, sand white, or any other close-but-not perfect white. (You can buy reference cards made just for this purpose in many camera stores for under $20.)

Position the reference card so that it receives the same lighting you'll use for your photo. Then take these steps:

1. **Set the camera to the P, Tv, Av, M, or A-DEP exposure mode.**

   You can't create a custom setting in any of the fully automatic modes.

2. **Set the camera to manual focusing and then focus on your reference card.**

Chapter 1 has details on manual focusing if you need help.

3. **Frame the shot so that your reference card fills the center area of the viewfinder.**

   In other words, make sure that at least the center autofocus point and the six surrounding points fall over the reference card.

4. **Make sure that the exposure settings are correct.**

   Just press the shutter button halfway to check exposure. In M mode, make sure that the exposure indicator is at the midway point of the exposure meter. In other modes, a blinking aperture or shutter speed value indicates an exposure problem. If necessary, adjust ISO, aperture, or shutter speed to fix the problem; Chapter 5 explains how.

5. **Take the picture of your reference card.**

   The camera will use this picture to establish your custom white balance setting.

6. **Display Shooting Menu 2 and highlight Custom WB, as shown on the left in Figure 6-19.**

Figure 6-19: You can create a custom white balance setting through Shooting Menu 2.

7. **Press Set.**

   Now you see the screen shown on the right in Figure 6-19. The image you just captured should appear in the display. (The figure shows the picture I took of a gray reference card.) If not, press the right or left cross key to scroll to the image.

8. **Press Set.**

   You see the message shown on the left in Figure 6-20, asking you to confirm that you want the camera to use the image to create the custom White Balance setting.

Figure 6-20: This message indicates that your White Balance setting is stored.

9. Press the right or left cross key to highlight OK and then press Set.

Now you see the screen shown on the right in Figure 6-20. This message tells you that the White Balance setting is now stored. The little icon in the message area represents the Custom setting.

10. Press Set one more time to finalize the deal and return to Shooting Menu 2.

Your Custom White Balance setting remains stored until the next time you work your way through these steps. So anytime you're shooting in the same lighting conditions and want to apply the same white balance correction, just press the WB button to access the White Balance settings and then select the Custom option.

Fine-tuning White Balance settings

As yet another alternative for manipulating colors, your Rebel XS/1000D enables you to tweak white balancing in a way that shifts all colors toward a particular part of the color spectrum. The end result is similar to applying a traditional color filter to your lens.

To access this option, called White Balance Correction, take these steps:

1. Set the Mode dial to P, Tv, Av, M, or A-DEP exposure mode.

You can take advantage of White Balance Correction only in these modes.

2. Display Shooting Menu 2 and highlight WB Shift/Bkt, as shown on the left in Figure 6-21.

Figure 6-21: White Balance Correction offers one more way to control colors.

3. Press Set to display the screen you see on the right in Figure 6-21.

The screen contains a grid that is oriented around two main color pairs: green and magenta, represented by the G and M labels, and blue and amber, represented by B and A. The little white square indicates the current amount of white balance correction, or shift. When the square is dead center in the grid, as in the figure, no shift is applied.

4. Use the cross keys to move the square marker in the direction of the shift you want to achieve.

As you do, the Shift area of the display tells the amount of color bias that you've selected. For example, in Figure 6-22, I shifted three levels toward amber and one toward magenta.

If you're familiar with traditional lens filters, you may know that the density of a filter, which determines the degree of color correction it provides, is measured in *mireds* (pronounced *my-redds*). The white balance grid is designed around this system: Moving the marker one level is the equivalent of adding a filter with a density of 5 mireds.

Shift marker   Shift amount

Figure 6-22: Press the cross keys to move the marker and shift white balance.

5. Press Set to apply the change and return to the menu.

After you apply white balance correction, a little plus or minus sign appears next to the White Balance symbol in the Shooting Settings display, as shown on the left in Figure 6-23. That's your reminder that white balance shift is being applied. The same symbol appears in the viewfinder, right next to the ISO value.

You can see the exact shift values in Shooting Menu 2, as shown on the right in Figure 6-23, and also in the Camera Function Settings display. (Remember, to activate that display, first display any menu and then press the DISP button. Chapter 1 provides more details.)

White Balance Shift icon

Figure 6-23: The +/– symbol lets you know that white balance shift is being applied.

Your adjustment remains in force for all the advanced exposure modes until you change it. And the correction is applied no matter what White Balance setting you choose. So make it a point to check the monitor or viewfinder before your next shoot — otherwise, you may forget to adjust the white balance for the current light.

6. **To cancel White Balance Correction, repeat Steps 1–3, set the marker back to the center of the grid, and press Set.**

   Use the cross keys to move the marker back to the center of the grid. Be sure that values in the Shift area of the display are both set to 0.

   As an alternative, you can press the DISP button after you get to the grid display. However, doing so also cancels white balance bracketing, a feature explained in the next section. After you press DISP, be sure to press Set to lock in your decision.

Many film-photography enthusiasts place colored filters on their lenses to either warm or cool their images. Portrait photographers, for example, often add a warming filter to give skin tones a healthy, golden glow. You can mimic the effects of such filters by simply fine-tuning your camera's White Balance settings as just described. Experiment with shifting the white balance a tad toward amber and magenta for a warming effect or toward blue and green for a cooling effect.

Bracketing shots with white balance

Chapter 5 introduces you to your camera's automatic exposure bracketing, which enables you to easily record the same image at three different exposure settings. Similarly, you can take advantage of automatic White Balance Bracketing. With this feature, the camera records the same image three times, using a slightly different white balance adjustment for each.

This feature is especially helpful when you're shooting in varying light sources — for example, a mix of fluorescent light, daylight, and flash. Bracketing the shots ups the odds that the color renditions of at least one of the shots will be to your liking.

Note a couple of things about this feature:

- You can't use White Balance Bracketing if you set the camera's Quality setting to either Raw or Raw+Large/Fine. And frankly, there isn't any need to do so in Raw mode because you can precisely tune colors when you process the Raw files. Chapter 8 has details on Raw processing.

- White Balance Bracketing is also disabled if you turn on High ISO Speed Noise Reduction. You can read about that feature, accessed through Custom Function 4, in Chapter 5.

- Because the camera records three images, white balance bracketing reduces the maximum capture speed that is possible when you use the Continuous shooting mode. See Chapter 2 for more about Continuous mode. Of course, recording three images instead of one also eats up more space on your memory card.

- The White Balance Bracketing feature is designed around the same grid used for White Balance Correction, explained in the preceding section. As a reminder, the grid is based on two color pairs: green/magenta and blue/amber.

- When White Balance Bracketing is enabled, the camera always records the first of the three bracketed shots using a neutral white balance setting — or, at least, what it considers to be neutral, given its own measurement of the light. The second and third shots are then recorded using the specified shift along either the green/magenta or blue/amber axis of the color grid.

If all that is as clear as mud, just take a look at Figure 6-24 for an example. I captured these images using a single tungsten studio light and the candle light itself. I set up White Balance Bracketing to work along the blue/amber color axis. So the camera recorded the first image at neutral, the second with a slightly blue color bias, and the third with an amber bias.

Neutral +3 Blue bias +3 Amber bias

Figure 6-24: I captured one neutral image, one with a blue bias, and one with an amber bias.

To enable White Balance Bracketing, take these steps:

1. **Set the Mode dial to an advanced exposure mode (P, Tv, Av, M, or A-DEP).**

2. **Make sure the Quality option is not set to record Raw images.**

   You find this setting on Shooting Menu 1. If you select Raw (or Raw+Large/Fine), the camera simply records each image the same way. You then can adjust colors in your Raw processor.

3. **Display Shooting Menu 2 and highlight WB/Shift Bkt.**

4. **Press Set to display the grid shown in Figure 6-25.**

   The screen is the same one you see when you use the White Balance Correction feature, explained in the preceding section.

5. **Rotate the Main dial to set the amount and direction of the bracketing shift.**

   Rotate the dial as follows to specify whether you want the bracketing to be applied across the horizontal axis (blue to amber) or the vertical axis (green to magenta).

Figure 6-25: I used these settings to capture the bracketed candle images.

- *Blue to amber bracketing:* Rotate the dial right.
- *Green to magenta bracketing:* Rotate the dial left.

As you rotate the dial, three markers appear on the grid, indicating the amount of shift that will be applied to your trio of bracketed images. You can apply a maximum shift of plus or minus three levels of adjustment.

The BKT area of the screen also indicates the shift; for example, in Figure 6-25, the display shows a bracketing amount of plus and minus three levels on the blue/amber axis. I used the settings shown in Figure 6-25 to record the example images in Figure 6-24. As you can see, even at the maximum shift (+/− 3), the difference to the colors is subtle.

If you want to get really fancy, you can combine White Balance Bracketing with White Balance Shift. To set the amount of White Balance Shift, press the cross keys to move the square markers around the grid. Then use the Main dial to adjust the bracketing setting.

6. **Press Set to apply your changes and return to the menu.**

The bracketing symbol shown in Figure 6-26 appears in the Shooting Settings display. The Camera Function Settings display, which you bring up by pressing DISP when any menu is visible, also reports the current bracketing setting.

Your bracketing setting remains in effect until you turn the camera off. You can also cancel bracketing by revisiting the grid screen shown in Figure 6-25 and either rotating the Main dial until you see only a single grid marker or pressing the DISP button. Either way, press Set to officially turn off bracketing.

White Balance Bracketing icon

Figure 6-26: This symbol indicates that White Balance Bracketing is turned on.

Choosing a Color Space: sRGB vs. Adobe RGB

Normally, your camera captures images using the *sRGB color mode,* which simply refers to an industry-standard spectrum of colors. (The *s* is for *standard,* and the *RGB* is for *red-green-blue,* which are the primary colors in the digital imaging color world.) This color mode was created to help ensure color consistency as an image moves from camera (or scanner) to monitor and printer; the idea was to create a spectrum of colors that all of these devices can reproduce.

However, the sRGB color spectrum leaves out some colors that *can* be reproduced in print and onscreen, at least by some devices. So as an alternative, your camera also enables you to shoot in the Adobe RGB color mode, which includes a larger spectrum (or *gamut*) of colors. Figure 6-27 offers an illustration of the two spectrums.

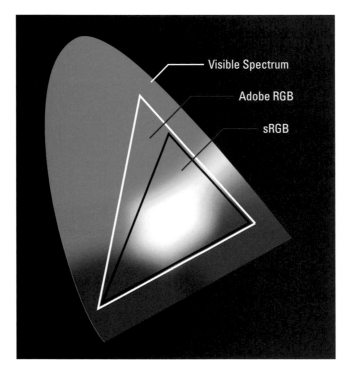

Figure 6-27: Adobe RGB includes some colors not found in the sRGB spectrum.

Which option is right for you depends on what you plan to do with your photos. If you're going to print your pictures without doing any editing to them, sRGB is probably the best choice because it typically results in the "punchy" colors that most people like. Some Internet printing services also request sRGB images.

On the other hand, if you're a color purist, will be editing your photos, making your own prints, or all of the above, experiment with Adobe RGB. For the record, this is the route that I go because I see no reason to limit myself to a smaller spectrum from the get-go. However, do note that some colors in Adobe RGB can't be reproduced in print; the printer substitutes the closest available color when necessary. Additionally, you'll need photo software that offers support for Adobe RGB as well as some basic *color management controls,* which ensure that your image colors are properly handled when you open, print, edit, and save your files. You should plan to spend a little time educating yourself about color management, too, because you can muck up the works if you don't set all the color-management options correctly. Long story short: If you're brand new to digital imaging, this option may be one you explore after you get more comfortable with the whole topic.

If you do want to capture images in Adobe RGB instead of sRGB, visit Shooting Menu 2 and highlight the Color Space option, as shown on the left in Figure 6-28. Press Set to display the screen shown on the right in the figure. Press the up or down cross key to highlight Adobe RGB and press Set again.

Remember that this color mode choice applies only when you shoot in the advanced exposure modes: P, Tv, Av, M, and A-DEP. In all other modes, the camera automatically selects sRGB as the color space.

Figure 6-28: Choose Adobe RGB for a broader color spectrum.

You can tell whether you captured an image in the Adobe RGB format by looking at its filename: Adobe RGB images start with an underscore, as in _MG_0627.jpg. Pictures captured in the sRGB color space start with the letter *I,* as in IMG_0627.jpg.

Exploring Picture Styles

In addition to all the focus and color features already covered in this chapter, your Rebel XS/1000D offers *Picture Styles.* Through Picture Styles, you can further tweak color as well as saturation, contrast, and image sharpening.

Sharpening is a software process that adjusts contrast in a way that creates the illusion of slightly sharper focus. I explain sharpening fully in Chapter 10, but the important thing to note for now is that sharpening cannot remedy poor focus, but instead produces a subtle *tweak* to this aspect of your pictures.

In fact, many of the adjustments that Picture Styles apply are pretty subtle, at least to my eye. The impact of any of these settings varies depending on your subject, but on the whole, if you want to make large-scale changes to color, contrast, or sharpening, you're probably going to need to use your computer and photo editing software. Again, though, your mileage may vary, as they say, as may your opinion of what constitutes the optimum color and sharpening characteristics.

The next section introduces you to your Picture Style options. Later sections explain how to change the Picture Style setting, customize the six prefab styles, and define your very own, custom styles.

Assessing the Picture Styles

When you set the Mode dial to Full Auto or any of the other fully automatic exposure modes, the camera selects a Picture Style for you. In P, Tv, Av, M, and A-DEP modes, however, you can specify which of the Picture Styles you want to use. Here's a quick description of the six styles:

- **Standard:** The default setting, this option captures the image using the characteristics that Canon offers as suitable for the majority of subjects.

- **Portrait:** This mode reduces sharpening slightly from the amount that's applied in Standard mode, with the goal of keeping skin texture soft. Color saturation, on the other hand, is slightly increased. If you shoot in the Portrait autoexposure mode, the camera automatically applies this Picture Style for you.

- **Landscape:** In a nod to traditions of landscape photography, this Picture Style emphasizes greens and blues and amps up color saturation and sharpness, resulting in bolder images. The camera automatically applies this Picture Style if you set the Mode dial to the Landscape autoexposure mode.

- **Neutral:** This setting reduces saturation and contrast slightly compared to how the camera renders images when the Standard option is selected.

- **Faithful:** The Faithful style is designed to render colors as closely as possible to how your eye perceives them.

- **Monochrome:** This setting produces black-and-white photos, or, to be more precise, *grayscale images* (technically speaking, a true black-and-white image contains only black and white, with no shades of gray).

If you set the Quality option on Shooting Menu 1 to Raw (or Raw + Large/Fine), the camera displays your image on the monitor in black and white during playback. But during the Raw converter process, you can either choose to go with your grayscale version or view and save a full-color version. Or, even better, you can process and save the image once as a grayscale photo and again as a color image.

If you *don't* capture the image in the Raw format, you can't access the original image colors later.

✔ **User Defined 1, 2, and 3:** These options enable you to create and save three of your own Picture Styles. I cover this feature in the last section of the chapter.

Figure 6-29 shows you how the camera rendered the same scene in each of the six preset Picture Styles. As you can see, Landscape has the most noticeable impact. To my taste, in fact, Landscape colors are a little over the top, but that's strictly a personal preference.

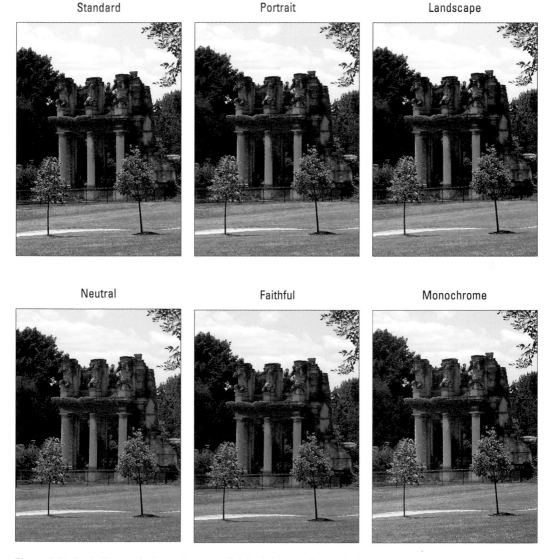

Figure 6-29: Each Picture Style produces a slightly different take on the image.

If you don't like any of the Picture Styles, you can use the options discussed in later sections to tweak them.

Setting the Picture Style

To select a Picture Style quickly, press the down cross key, highlighted in Figure 6-30. Pressing the button displays the screen you see on the monitor in the figure.

Styles

Adjustment settings   Picture Styles button

Figure 6-30: Press the down cross key to quickly change the Picture Style.

Here's what you need to know about this cryptic-looking screen:

- **Picture Style icons:** The two columns of symbols on the right represent the Picture Styles, as labeled in Figure 6-30. (Notice that the icons bear the same symbol as the down cross key.) The six prefab styles are marked with an initial (S for Standard, P for Portrait, and so on). The 1, 2, and 3 icons represent the three User Defined custom styles that you can create.

- **Adjustment setting icons:** On the left side of the screen, you see the name of the currently selected style plus four more symbols, each accompanied by a number. I labeled these four symbols "Adjustment settings" in Figure 6-30; you can get a close-up view in Figure 6-31. The icons represent the four characteristics that the styles affect: sharpness, contrast, saturation, and color tone.

If you select the Monochrome Picture Style, the saturation and color tone options are replaced by two other options, filter effect and toning effect.

✓ **Adjustment values:** As for the numbers next to the symbols, they work a little differently than you may expect. Sharpness values range from 0 to 7; the higher the value, the more sharpening is applied. At 0, no sharpening is applied.

The other values, however, all initially appear as 0, which in this case represents a middle-of-the-road setting. If you customize the style, the number indicates the level of adjustment. For example, if you customize the style so that it applies three levels more saturation than normal, you see a 3 next to the saturation icon. If you go the other direction, tweaking the style so that it applies three levels less saturation than normal, you see a –3 instead.

See the upcoming section, "Customizing Picture Styles," for a little more detail about the four picture characteristics.

Figure 6-31: For color images, Picture Styles affect these four characteristics.

To select a style, press the up or down cross key to highlight that style's icon. Press Set to lock in your style choice. As soon as you do, the Shooting Settings display appears automatically, and you can see the icon for your selected Picture Style in the position labeled in Figure 6-32.

You can also change the Picture Style through Shooting Menu 2, shown on the left in Figure 6-33. Highlight the Picture Styles option and press Set to display the screenful of options you see on the right in the figure. (You can see only the six prefab Picture Style settings on the first screen; scroll down using the cross keys to view the User Defined styles.)

Figure 6-32: The icons in the Shooting Settings display match those on the Picture Styles screen (shown in Figure 6-30).

Picture Style	$\bullet$, $\bullet$, $\&$, $\bullet$
S Standard	3, 0, 0, 0
P Portrait	2, 0, 0, 0
L Landscape	4, 0, 0, 0
N Neutral	0, 0, 0, 0
F Faithful	0, 0, 0, 0
M Monochrome	3, 0, N, N
DISP. Detail set.	SET OK

Shooting Menu 2 (left panel):

AEB	-2..1..0..1.:2
Flash exp comp	-2..1..0..1.:2
Custom WB	
WB SHIFT/BKT	0, 0/±0
Color space	Adobe RGB
Picture Style	Standard
Dust Delete Data	

Figure 6-33: You also can access Picture Style options via Shooting Menu 2.

The symbols at the top of the Picture Style screen (right image in Figure 6-33) are the same ones shown in Figure 6-30. And the numbers next to each style show you the amount of adjustment for each of the four picture characteristics.

However you set the Picture Style, remember that you must do so *before* you switch to Live View shooting, if you choose to turn on that feature. See Chapter 4 for an introduction to Live View shooting.

Customizing Picture Styles

You can customize the results that you get from the prefab Picture Styles. For the Standard, Landscape, Portrait, Neutral, and Faithful styles, you can adjust sharpness, contrast, saturation, and color tone. (The Color Tone option enables you to make your colors either a little more red or a little more yellow and is designed to help you tweak skin tones in portraits.)

For the Monochrome Picture Style, saturation and color tone are irrelevant, so they are replaced by two other options, Filter Effect and Toning Effect. The Filter Effect options mimic color filters sometimes used by photographers shooting black-and-white film. The color of the filter determines which colors in the original scene become prominent in the black-and-white image. The Toning Effect options enable you to apply a sepia, blue, purple, or green tint to your monochrome image.

To dig into Picture Style customizing, take these steps:

1. **Display Shooting Menu 2 and highlight Picture Style, as shown on the left in Figure 6-33.**

   Remember, you can access this menu and the Picture Style options only in the advanced exposure modes (P, Tv, Av, M, and A-DEP).

2. **Press Set.**

   Now you see the screen shown on the right in Figure 6-33.

3. **Press the up or down cross key to highlight the Picture Style you want to adjust.**

4. **Press the DISP button.**

   The screen shown in Figure 6-34 appears, listing the four characteristics that you can adjust for your selected Picture Style.

5. **Highlight the characteristic that you want to tweak and press Set.**

   The little scale next to the selection option becomes active.

6. **Press the right or left cross key to adjust the setting.**

   As soon as you adjust the setting, you see two markers: The gray one shows you the default setting; the white one, your customized setting, as labeled in Figure 6-34.

   For Contrast, Saturation, and Sharpness, move the little marker on the scale to the right to increase the effect. For Color Tone, move the slider toward the minus sign to make colors less yellow and more red; move the slider toward the plus sign to make colors less red and more yellow.

   Figure 6-34: To adjust the setting, highlight it and press Set.

   When you adjust the Filter Effect and Toning Effect options for the Monochrome style, the adjustment scale and slider are replaced by a simple list of options; just highlight the one you want to use.

7. **Press Set to lock in your adjustment.**

8. **Repeat Steps 5 through 7 to adjust the other settings as desired.**

9. **Press the Menu button to return to the main Picture Styles screen.**

10. **Press Set to return to Shooting Menu 2.**

    Note that any user-adjusted setting appears highlighted in blue on the Picture Style submenu.

If you later want to return to the default settings for the Picture Style, just repeat Steps 1 through 4 and then highlight Default Set (at the bottom of the screen shown in Figure 6-34) and press Set.

Unfortunately, you can't preview how your adjustments will affect your image because the Picture Style attributes are applied to the photo *after* you shoot it, during the time the image is recorded to your memory card. So I'd like to offer an alternative: If you shoot in the Raw format, you don't have to worry about in-camera adjustments to Picture Styles — or even selecting a Picture Style, for that matter — because you can apply the style when you process your Raw images. Just follow the directions laid out in Chapter 8 to use the Raw converter provided in ZoomBrowser EX (Windows) or ImageBrowser (Mac). On the Image Quality Adjustment panel, you can select a Picture Style and then make the same adjustments to the style as you can in the camera.

At the very least, experimenting with Picture Styles in the Raw converter should help you know what adjustments you may want to make to the actual camera settings. And for creating monochrome images, using the Raw converter tools enables you to try out the different Filter Effect and Toning Effect options to find the one you like best.

Creating your own Picture Style

The User Defined options on the Picture Style menu enable you to create and store up to three of your very own Picture Styles. So if you hit upon a combination of customized settings that you really like for a particular type of subject — snow scenes, for example, or pictures of your pooch — you can easily reuse those settings.

Follow these steps to create your custom Picture Style:

1. **Display Shooting Menu 2, highlight Picture Style, and press Set.**

   You see the normal list of Picture Styles.

2. **Press the down cross key to scroll the display until the User Defined options come into view.**

3. **Highlight one of the User Defined options, as shown on the left in Figure 6-35.**

4. **Press the DISP button.**

   Now you see the screen shown on the right in Figure 6-35.

5. **Highlight the Picture Style option, as shown on the right in Figure 6-35, and press Set.**

6. **Press the up or down arrow key to select the style on which you want to base your custom style and press Set.**

   If you want to create your own style for portraits, for example, select the Portrait option. Or, if you want to create a special black-and-white style, choose Monochrome. Your new style will be based on the one you select.

Figure 6-35: You can create up to three of your own Picture Styles.

7. **Set the rest of the style attributes.**

   The options available are the same as when you customize a style. Highlight the option, press Set to activate the little slider, and then use the cross keys to adjust the setting. See the preceding section for details about the options. Press Set again to lock in the adjustment.

8. **Press Menu to return to the main Picture Style screen. (See the left image in Figure 6-35.)**

9. **Press Set to store your custom style.**

To use your style, just select it from the Picture Style screen or menu as usual.

7
Putting It All Together

*E*arlier chapters of this book break down each and every picture-taking feature on your Rebel XS/1000D, describing in detail how the various controls affect exposure, picture quality, focus, color, and the like. This chapter pulls all that information together to help you set up your camera for specific types of photography.

The first few pages offer a quick summary of critical picture-taking settings that should serve you well no matter what your subject. Following that, I offer my advice on which settings to use for portraits, action shots, landscapes, and close-ups. To wrap things up, the end of the chapter includes some miscellaneous tips for dealing with special shooting situations and subjects.

Keep in mind that although I present specific recommendations here, there are no hard and fast rules as to the "right way" to shoot a portrait, a landscape, or whatever. So don't be afraid to wander off on your own, tweaking this exposure setting or adjusting that focus control, to discover your own creative vision. Experimentation is part of the fun of photography, after all — and thanks to your camera monitor and the Erase button, it's an easy, completely free proposition.

Recapping Basic Picture Settings

Your subject, creative goals, and lighting conditions determine which settings you should use for some picture-taking options, such as aperture and shutter speed. I offer my take on those options throughout this chapter. But for a few basic options, I recommend the same settings for almost every shooting scenario. Table 7-1 lists these options as well as how you access them. Figure 7-1 offers a reminder of where to find the buttons that are referenced in the table. (The ISO button isn't fully visible in this shot; the button's on top of the camera, right behind the Main dial.)

Figure 7-1: You can access several critical settings with a press of a single button.

Other chapters detail all these settings, but here's a quick reminder of how each one affects your image:

✔ **Quality:** This setting, introduced in Chapter 3, determines the file format and resolution of picture files the camera creates. For best quality and the largest possible print size, choose Large/Fine or Raw (CR2). Keep in mind that you must process Raw files in a raw converter; Chapter 8 explains that issue. For everyday images that you don't plan to print large or crop, Medium/Fine is also a good choice and creates smaller files than the other two settings.

✔ **White Balance:** White balance compensates for the color casts produced by different light sources. Auto White Balance (AWB) mode usually does the trick unless you're dealing with multiple light sources; in that case, you may need to switch to manual White Balance control. Chapter 6 tells you how. You can control this setting only in the advanced exposure modes.

 ✔ **ISO:** This setting determines the light sensitivity of the camera's image sensor. Increasing the ISO value can create noise defects, so stick with the lowest setting possible given the available light. You can't select ISO in the fully automatic exposure modes; the camera sets the value between 100 and 800 for you. Chapter 5 details ISO.

✔ **AF (autofocus) mode:** Chapter 6 details this option, which affects the autofocus system. In the AI Focus mode, the camera chooses the best autofocus mode based on whether it thinks you're shooting a still or moving subject. (The AI stands for artificial intelligence.) In most cases, this setting works well. You can control this option only in P, Tv, Av, and M exposure modes.

✔ **Drive mode:** This setting enables you to shift from Single mode, in which you record one image each time you press the shutter button, to Continuous mode, in which the camera continues to capture images as long as you hold down the shutter button.

Table 7-1	All-Purpose Picture-Taking Settings	
Option	_Recommended Setting_	_Access via Menu/ Button_
Image Quality	Large/Fine (JPEG), Medium/ Fine (JPEG), or Raw (CR2)	Shooting Menu 1
White Balance[1]	Auto	WB button
ISO[1]	100 or 200	ISO button
AF mode[2]	AI Focus	Right cross key
Drive mode	Action photos: Continuous; all others: Single	Left cross key
AF Point Selection[2]	Auto	AF Point Selection button
Metering[1]	Evaluative	Top cross key
Picture Style[1]	Standard	Bottom cross key or Shooting Menu 2
Live View[1]	Disabled	Setup Menu 2

[1]_Adjustable only in P, Tv, Av, M, and A-DEP exposure modes._

[2] _Adjustable only in P, Tv, Av, and M exposure modes._

Single mode is the best choice in most cases, but Continuous can come in handy for action shots, as covered later in this chapter. But you can select Continuous or Single only in the advanced exposure modes. In the fully automatic modes, the camera chooses for you. Note that your camera also offers three other settings that permit self-timer and remote-control shooting; see Chapter 2 for details on all the Drive modes.

 ✓ **AF Point Selection:** This control enables you to choose from two autofocusing setups when you shoot in the P, Tv, Av, or M exposure mode. In Automatic AF Point Selection mode, all seven of the camera's autofocus points are active, and the camera typically locks focus on the point that covers the nearest object or person. In Manual AF Point Selection mode, you can specify which of the autofocus points you want the camera to use when establishing focus. The camera always uses the automatic option when you shoot in the fully automatic exposure modes or A-DEP mode.

✓ **Metering mode:** This option determines what part of the frame the camera analyzes when calculating exposure. Evaluative metering takes the whole frame into account, which produces good results for most scenes. See Chapter 5 for the scoop on the other options, Partial and Center-Weighted Average metering, which are selectable only when you shoot in the advanced exposure modes. All fully automatic modes use Evaluative metering.

✓ **Picture Style:** When you shoot in the advanced exposure modes, you can manipulate color, saturation, sharpness, and contrast by selecting from one of six preset Picture Style settings or by defining your own custom style. In the fully automatic modes, the camera selects the Picture Style for you based on which mode you're using. For example, in Portrait exposure mode, the camera selects the Portrait Picture Style setting. See Chapter 6 for a review of all the Picture Style controls.

✓ **Live View:** Enabling Live View shooting, in which you use the monitor as a viewfinder, results in the loss of control over some important photography options, including Metering mode, Drive mode, AF mode, and Flash Exposure Lock (FE Lock). For this reason, along with some other caveats that you can explore at the end of Chapter 4, I suggest that you disable Live View for most shots. The exception is the scenario for which Live View is really intended: still-life photography in which you can use a tripod or otherwise stabilize the camera. In any case, you can use Live View only in the advanced exposure modes.

Setting Up for Specific Scenes

For the most part, the settings detailed in the preceding section fall into the "set 'em and forget 'em" category. That leaves you free to concentrate on a handful of other camera options, such as aperture and shutter speed, that you can manipulate to achieve a specific photographic goal.

The next four sections explain which of these additional options typically produce the best results when you're shooting portraits, action shots, landscapes, and close-ups. I offer a few compositional and creative tips along the way — but again, remember that beauty is in the eye of the beholder, and for every so-called rule, there are plenty of great images that prove the exception.

Shooting still portraits

By "still portrait," I mean that your subject isn't moving. For subjects who aren't keen on sitting still long enough to have their picture taken — children, pets, and even some teenagers I know — skip ahead to the next section and use the techniques given for action photography instead.

Assuming that you do have a subject willing to pose, the classic portraiture approach is to keep the subject sharply focused while throwing the background into soft focus, as shown in the examples in this section. This artistic choice emphasizes the subject and helps diminish the impact of any distracting background objects in cases where you can't control the setting. The following steps show you how to achieve this look:

1. **Set the Mode dial to Av (aperture-priority auto exposure) and then select the lowest f-stop value possible.**

   As Chapter 5 explains, a low f-stop number opens the aperture, which shortens depth of field, or the range of sharp focus. So dialing in a low f-stop value is the first step in softening your portrait background. (The f-stop range available to you depends on your lens.) Also keep in mind that the farther your subject is from the background, the more background blurring you can achieve.

   I recommend aperture-priority autoexposure when depth of field is a primary concern because you can control the f-stop while relying on the camera to select the shutter speed that will properly expose the image. Just rotate the Main dial to select your desired f-stop. But if you aren't comfortable with this advanced exposure mode, Portrait mode also results in a more open aperture, although the exact f-stop setting is out of your control. Chapter 2 details Portrait mode.

Whichever mode you choose, you can monitor the current aperture and shutter speed both in the Shooting Settings display, as shown on the left in Figure 7-2, and in the viewfinder display, as shown on the right.

Figure 7-2: You can view exposure settings in the Shooting Settings display or viewfinder.

2. To further soften the background, zoom in, get closer, or both.

As covered in Chapter 6, zooming in to a longer focal length also reduces depth of field, as does moving physically closer to your subject.

Avoid using a lens with a short focal length (a wide-angle lens) for portraits. They can cause features to appear distorted — sort of like how people look when you view them through a security peephole in a door.

3. For indoor portraits, shoot flash-free if possible.

Shooting by available light rather than flash produces softer illumination and avoids the problem of red-eye. To get enough light to go flash-free, turn on room lights or, during daylight, pose your subject next to a sunny window.

In the Av exposure mode, simply keeping the built-in flash unit closed disables the flash. In Portrait mode, unfortunately, you can't disable the flash if the camera thinks more light is needed. Your only option is to change the exposure mode to No Flash, in which case the camera may or may not choose an aperture setting that throws the background into soft focus.

If flash is unavoidable, see my list of flash tips at the end of the steps to get better results.

4. For outdoor portraits, use a flash.

Even in bright daylight, a flash adds a beneficial pop of light to subjects' faces, as discussed in Chapter 5 and illustrated here in Figure 7-3.

No flash

With flash

Figure 7-3: To properly illuminate the face in outdoor portraits, use fill flash.

Unfortunately, the camera doesn't let you use flash in Portrait mode if the light is very bright. In the Av exposure mode, just press the Flash button on the side of the camera to enable the flash.

 Remember that in dim lighting, the camera may select a shutter speed as slow as 1/30 second when you enable flash in Av mode, so keep an eye on that value and use a tripod if necessary to avoid blurring from camera shake. On the flip side of the coin, the fastest shutter speed you can use with the built-in flash is 1/200 second, and in extremely bright conditions, that may be too slow to avoid overexposing the image. If necessary, move your subject into the shade.

5. **Press and hold the shutter button halfway to engage exposure metering and, in autofocus mode, to lock in focus.**

   Make sure that an active autofocus point falls over your subject. (In the viewfinder, active autofocus points turn red.) For best results, try to set focus on your subject's eyes.

   Chapter 6 explains more about using autofocus, but if you have trouble, simply set your lens to manual focus mode and then twist the focusing ring to set focus.

6. **Press the shutter button the rest of the way to capture the image.**

Again, these steps just give you a starting point for taking better portraits. A few other tips can also improve your people pics:

✓ **Before pressing the shutter button, do a quick background check.** Scan the entire frame looking for intrusive objects that may distract the eye from the subject. If necessary, reposition the subject against a more flattering backdrop if possible. Inside, a softly textured wall works well; outdoors, trees and shrubs can provide nice backdrops as long as they aren't so ornate or colorful that they diminish the subject (for example, a magnolia tree laden with blooms).

✓ **Frame the subject loosely to allow for later cropping to a variety of frame sizes.** Your camera produces images that have an aspect ratio of 3:2. That means that your portrait perfectly fits a 4-x-6-inch print size but will require cropping to print at any other proportions, such as 5 x 7 or 8 x 10. Chapter 9 talks more about this issue.

✓ **Pay attention to white balance if your subject is lit by both flash and ambient light.** If you set the White Balance control to automatic (AWB), as I recommend in Table 7-1, enabling flash tells the camera to warm colors to compensate for the cool light of a flash. If your subject is also lit by room lights or daylight, the result may be colors that are slightly warmer than neutral. This warming effect typically looks nice in portraits, giving the skin a subtle glow. But if you aren't happy with the result or want even more warming, see Chapter 6 to find out how to fine-tune white balance. Again, you can make this adjustment only in P, Tv, Av, M, or A-DEP exposure mode.

✓ **When flash is unavoidable, try these tricks to produce better results.** The following techniques can help solve flash-related issues:

   • *Indoors, turn on as many room lights as possible.* With more ambient light, you reduce the flash power that's needed to expose the picture. This step also causes the pupils to constrict, further reducing the chances of red-eye. (Pay heed to my white balance warning, however.)

   • *Try setting the flash to Red-Eye Reduction mode for nighttime and indoor portraits.* Warn your subject to expect both a light coming from the Red-Eye Reduction lamp, which constricts pupils, and the actual flash. See Chapter 2 for details about using this flash mode, which you enable through Shooting Menu 1.

   • *For nighttime pictures, try Night Portrait mode.* In this autoexposure mode, the camera automatically selects a slower shutter speed than normal. This enables the camera to soak up more ambient light, producing a brighter background and reducing the flash power that's needed to light the subject. A slow shutter, however, means that you need to use a tripod to avoid camera shake, which can blur the photo. You also need to warn your subjects to remain very still during the exposure.

- *Soften the flash light by attaching a diffuser to the flash head.* This inexpensive tool both softens and spreads the light. You can see a picture of one type of diffuser in Chapter 5. You may need to bump up exposure slightly to compensate for the light filtering that occurs; the camera doesn't know that you attached the diffuser and so doesn't adjust the exposure on its own. In the P, Tv, Av, or A-DEP autoexposure modes, you can use exposure compensation to adjust the image brightness or, as an alternative, you can increase the flash power slightly. Again, Chapter 5 has details on these exposure features.

- *For professional results, use an external flash with a rotating flash head.* Then aim the flash head upward so that the flash light bounces off the ceiling and falls softly down onto the subject. An external flash isn't cheap, but the results make the purchase worthwhile if you shoot lots of portraits. Compare the two portraits in Figure 7-4 for an illustration. In the first example, the built-in flash resulted in strong shadowing behind the subject and harsh, concentrated light. To produce the better result on the right, I used the Canon Speedlite 580EX II and bounced the light off the ceiling.

Direct flash

Bounce flash

Figure 7-4: To eliminate harsh lighting and strong shadows (left), I used bounce flash and moved the subject farther from the background (right).

• *To reduce shadowing from the flash, move your subject farther from the background.* I took this extra step for the right image in Figure 7-4. The increased distance not only reduced shadowing but also softened the focus of the wall a bit (because of the short depth of field resulting from my f-stop and focal length).

A good general rule is to position your subjects far enough from the background that they can't touch it. If that isn't possible, though, try going the other direction: If the person's head is smack up against the background, any shadow will be smaller and less noticeable. For example, you get less shadowing when a subject's head is resting against a sofa cushion than if that person is sitting upright, with the head a foot or so away from the cushion.

• *Study the flash information in Chapter 5 and practice before you need to take important portraits.* How the camera calculates the aperture, shutter speed, and flash power needed to expose your subject and background varies depending on the exposure mode you use. So to fully understand how to get the flash results you want, it pays to experiment with each of the advanced exposure modes, all covered in Chapter 5.

For the maximum control over aperture, shutter speed, and flash power, try working in manual exposure mode and make friends with the Flash Exposure Compensation and FE Lock (flash exposure lock) features.

Capturing action

A fast shutter speed is the key to capturing a blur-free shot of any moving subject, whether it's a spinning Ferris wheel, a butterfly flitting from flower to flower, or in the case of Figures 7-5 and 7-6, a hockey-playing teen. In the first image, a shutter speed of 1/125 second was too slow to catch the subject without blur. For this subject, who was moving at a fairly rapid speed, I needed to bump the shutter speed all the way up to 1/1000 second to freeze the action cleanly, as shown in Figure 7-6.

Along with the basic capture settings outlined in Table 7-1, I use the techniques in the following steps to photograph a subject in motion:

1. **Set the Mode dial to Tv (shutter-priority autoexposure).**

   In this mode, you control the shutter speed, and the camera takes care of choosing an aperture setting that will produce a good exposure.

   If you aren't ready to step up to this advanced autoexposure mode, explained in Chapter 5, try using Sports mode, detailed in Chapter 2. But be aware that you have no control over any other aspects of your picture (such as white balance, flash, and so on) in that mode.

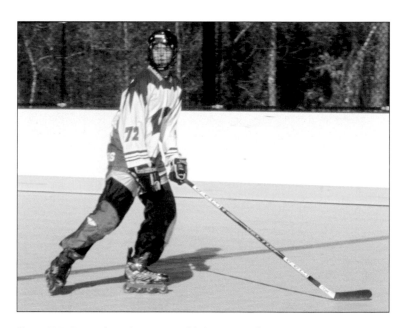

Figure 7-5: A too-slow shutter speed (1/125 second) causes the skater to appear blurry.

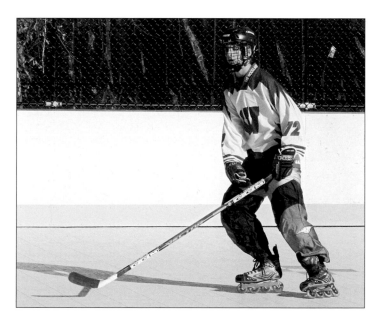

Figure 7-6: Raising the shutter speed to 1/1000 second "froze" the action.

2. **Rotate the Main dial to select the shutter speed.**

Drive mode   Shutter speed   AF mode

   In the Shooting Settings display, the option that appears in purple, with the little arrow pointers at each side, is the one that you can adjust with the Main dial. In Tv mode, the shutter speed is the active option, as shown in Figure 7-7. After you select the shutter speed, the camera selects the aperture (f-stop) necessary to produce a good exposure.

Figure 7-7: Changing the Drive mode to Continuous allows rapid-fire shooting.

   What shutter speed you need depends on how fast your subject is moving, so some experimentation is needed. But generally speaking, 1/500 second should be plenty for all but the fastest subjects — speeding hockey players like my subject, race cars, boats, and so on. For slower subjects, you can even go as low as 1/250 or 1/125 second.

   If the aperture value blinks after you set the shutter speed, the camera can't select an f-stop that will properly expose the photo at that shutter speed. See Chapter 5 for more details about how the camera notifies you of potential exposure problems.

3. **Raise the ISO setting or add flash to produce a brighter exposure if needed.**

   In dim lighting, you may not be able to get a good exposure at your chosen shutter speed without taking this step. Raising the ISO does increase the possibility of noise, but a noisy shot is better than a blurry shot. The current ISO setting appears just below the f-stop value in the Shooting Settings display, as shown in Figure 7-7.

   Note that in Sports mode, the camera automatically overrides your ISO setting if it deems necessary, but it can go only as high as ISO 800. For more on all of these ISO issues, see Chapter 5.

   Adding flash is a bit tricky for action shots, unfortunately. First, the flash needs time to recycle between shots, so try to go without if you want to capture images at a fast pace. Second, the built-in flash has limited range — so don't waste your time if your subject isn't close by. And third, remember that the fastest possible shutter speed when you enable the built-in flash is 1/200 second, which may not be fast enough to capture a quickly moving subject without blur. For more on this issue, check out Chapter 5.

   If you do decide to use flash, you must bail out of Sports mode, though; it doesn't permit you to use flash.

4. For rapid-fire shooting, set the Drive mode to Continuous.

In this mode, you can take as many as three pictures per second. The camera continues to record images as long as the shutter button is pressed. You can switch the Drive mode by pressing the left cross key; the icon representing the current mode appears in the Shooting Settings display, as labeled in Figure 7-7. Chapter 2 explains more about all the Drive mode options.

5. For fastest shooting, switch to manual focusing.

You then eliminate the time the camera needs to lock focus in autofocus mode. Chapter 1 shows you how to focus manually, if you need help.

If you do use autofocus, try these two autofocus settings for best performance:

- Set the AF Point Selection mode to Automatic. Press the button shown in the margin here to adjust this setting.

- Set the AF (autofocus) mode to AI Servo (continuous-servo autofocus). Press the right cross key to access this setting.

Chapter 6 details these autofocus options.

6. Turn off automatic image review to speed up the camera even more.

You do this via the Review Time option on Shooting Menu 1. Turning the option off can help speed up the time your camera needs to recover between shots.

7. Compose the subject to allow for movement across the frame.

You can always crop the photo later to a tighter composition. (I did so for my example images, which originally contained quite a bit more background than you see in the book.) Chapter 10 shows you how to crop pictures.

8. Lock in autofocus (if used) in advance.

Press the shutter button halfway to do so. Now when the action occurs, just press the shutter button the rest of the way. Your image-capture time is faster because the camera has already done the work of establishing focus. Remember that in AI Servo mode, you must keep the subject under the active autofocus point (or points) in order for the camera to maintain focus. Again, Chapter 6 details this feature.

Using these techniques should give you a better chance of capturing any fast-moving subject. But action-shooting strategies also are helpful for shooting candid portraits of kids and pets. Even if they aren't currently running, leaping, or otherwise cavorting, snapping a shot before they do move or change positions is often tough. So if an interaction or scene catches your eye, set your camera into action mode and then just fire off a series of shots as fast as you can.

Capturing scenic vistas

Providing specific capture settings for landscape photography is tricky because there's no single best approach to capturing a beautiful stretch of countryside, a city skyline, or other vast subject. Take depth of field, for example: One person's idea of a super cityscape might be to keep all buildings in the scene sharply focused. But another photographer might prefer to shoot the same scene so that a foreground building is sharply focused while the others are less so, thus drawing the eye to that first building.

That said, I can offer a few tips to help you photograph a landscape the way *you* see it:

✔ **Shoot in aperture-priority autoexposure mode (Av) so that you can control depth of field.** If you want extreme depth of field, so that both near and distant objects are sharply focused, as in Figure 7-8, select a high f-stop value. I used an aperture of f/16 for this shot.

You can also use the Landscape autoexposure mode to achieve a large depth of field. In this mode, the camera automatically selects a high f-stop number, but you have no control over the exact value (or any other picture-taking settings.) Of course, if the light is dim, the camera may be forced to open the aperture, reducing depth of field, to properly expose the image. (Don't confuse Landscape autoexposure mode with the Landscape Picture Style; the Landscape mode you want is the one you select from the Mode dial on top of the camera. See Chapter 6 for more details about Picture Styles.)

Figure 7-8: Use a high f-stop value (or Landscape mode) to keep foreground and background sharply focused.

✔ **If the exposure requires a slow shutter, use a tripod to avoid blurring.** The downside to a high f-stop is that you need a slower shutter speed to produce a good exposure. If the shutter speed drops below what you can comfortably hand-hold — for me, that's about 1/50 second — use a tripod to avoid picture-blurring camera shake. No tripod handy? Look for any solid surface on which you can steady the camera. You can always increase the ISO setting to increase light sensitivity, which in turn allows a faster shutter speed, too, but that option brings with it the chances of increased image noise. See Chapter 5 for details. Also see Chapter 1 for details about image stabilization, which can help you get sharper handheld shots at slow shutter speeds.

✔ **For dramatic waterfall and fountain shots, consider using a slow shutter to create that "misty" look.** The slow shutter blurs the water, giving it a soft, romantic appearance. Figure 7-9 shows you a close-up of this effect. Again, use a tripod to ensure that the rest of the scene doesn't also blur due to camera shake.

✔ **At sunrise or sunset, base exposure on the sky.** The foreground will be dark, but you can usually brighten it in a photo editor if needed. If you base exposure on the foreground, on the other hand, the sky will become so bright that all the color will be washed out — a problem you usually can't fix after the fact.

This tip doesn't apply, of course, if your sunrise or sunset is merely serving as a gorgeous backdrop for a portrait. In that case, you should enable your flash and expose for the subject.

Figure 7-9: For misty waterfalls, use a slow shutter speed (and tripod).

✔ **For cool nighttime city pics, experiment with slow shutter.** Assuming that cars or other vehicles are moving through the scene, the result is neon trails of light like those you see in the foreground of the image in Figure 7-10, taken by my friend Jonathan Conrad. Shutter speed for this image was 8 seconds.

Jonathan Conrad

Figure 7-10: A slow shutter also creates neon light trails in city-street scenes.

Instead of changing the shutter speed manually between each shot, try setting the speed to Bulb. Available only in M (manual) exposure mode, this option records an image for as long as you hold down the shutter button. So just take a series of images, holding the button down for different lengths of time for each shot. In Bulb mode, you also can exceed the minimum (slowest) shutter speed of 30 seconds. Note that in Bulb mode, the camera displays the elapsed capture time on the monitor.

Because long exposures can produce image noise, you also may want to enable the Long Exposure Noise Reduction feature. You access this option via the Custom Function option on Setup Menu 3; select Custom Function 3 and change the setting from Off to Auto or On. Chapter 5 discusses this option in more detail.

✔ **For the best lighting, shoot during the "magic hours."** That's the term photographers use for early morning and late afternoon, when the light cast by the sun is soft and warm, giving everything that beautiful, gently warmed look.

Can't wait for the perfect light? Tweak your camera's White Balance setting, using the instructions laid out in Chapter 6, to simulate magic-hour light.

✔ **In tricky light, bracket shots.** *Bracketing* simply means to take the same picture at several different exposures to increase the odds that at least one of them will capture the scene the way you envision. Bracketing is especially a good idea in difficult lighting situations such as sunrise and sunset.

Your camera offers automatic exposure bracketing when you shoot in the advanced exposure modes. See Chapter 5 to find out how to take advantage of this feature.

Capturing dynamic close-ups

For great close-up shots, start with the basic capture settings outlined in Table 7-1. Then try the following additional settings and techniques:

✔ **Check your owner's manual to find out the minimum close-focusing distance of your lens.** How "up close and personal" you can get to your subject depends on your lens, not the camera body itself.

✔ **Take control over depth of field by setting the camera mode to Av (aperture-priority autoexposure) mode.** Whether you want a shallow, medium, or extreme depth of field depends on the point of your photo. For the romantic scene shown in Figure 7-11, for example, I wanted to blur the background to help the subjects stand out more, so I set the aperture to f/5.6. But if you want the viewer to be able to clearly see all details throughout the frame — for example, if you're shooting a product shot for your company's sales catalog — you need to go the other direction, stopping down the aperture as far as possible.

Not ready for the advanced exposure modes yet? Try the Close-Up scene mode instead. (It's the one marked with the little flower on your Mode dial.) In this mode, the camera automatically opens the aperture to achieve a short depth of field and bases focus on the center of the frame.

- **Remember that zooming in and getting close to your subject both decrease depth of field.** So back to that product shot: If you need depth of field beyond what you can achieve with the aperture setting, you may need to back away, zoom out, or both. (You can always crop your image to show just the parts of the subject that you want to feature.)

Figure 7-11: Shallow depth of field helps set the subject apart from the similarly colored background.

- **When shooting flowers and other nature scenes outdoors, pay attention to shutter speed, too.** Even a slight breeze may cause your subject to move, causing blurring at slow shutter speeds. (Chapter 5 offers some examples that illustrate this issue.)

- **Use fill flash for better outdoor lighting.** Just as with portraits, a tiny bit of flash typically improves close-ups when the sun is your primary light source. You may need to reduce the flash output slightly, via the camera's Flash Exposure Compensation control. Chapter 5 offers details about using flash.

  Also keep in mind that the maximum shutter speed possible when you use flash is 1/200 second. So in very bright light, you may need to use a high f-stop setting to avoid overexposing the picture. You also can lower the ISO speed setting, if it's not already all the way down to ISO 100.

- **When shooting indoors, try not to use flash as your primary light source.** Because you'll be shooting at close range, the light from your flash may be too harsh even at a low Flash Exposure Compensation setting. If flash is inevitable, turn on as many room lights as possible to reduce the flash power that's needed — even a hardware-store shop light can do in a pinch as a lighting source. (Remember that if you have multiple light sources, though, you may need to tweak the white balance setting.)

- **To really get close to your subject, invest in a macro lens or a set of diopters.** A true macro lens, which enables you to get really, really close to your subjects, is an expensive proposition; expect to pay around $200 or more. But if you enjoy capturing the tiny details in life, it's worth the investment.

For a less expensive way to go, you can spend about $40 for a set of *diopters,* which are sort of like reading glasses that you screw onto your existing lens. Diopters come in several strengths — +1, +2, +4, and so on — with a higher number indicating a greater magnifying power. I took this approach to capture the rose in Figure 7-12. The left image shows you the closest I could get to the subject with my regular lens; to produce the right image, I attached a +6 diopter. The downfall of diopters, sadly, is that they typically produce images that are very soft around the edges, as in Figure 7-12 — a problem that doesn't occur with a good macro lens.

No diopter   +6 diopter

Figure 7-12: To extend your lens' close-focus ability, you can add magnifying diopters.

Coping with Special Situations

A few subjects and shooting situations pose some additional challenges not already covered in earlier sections. So to wrap up this chapter, here's a quick list of ideas for tackling a variety of common "tough-shot" photos:

- **Shooting through glass:** To capture subjects that are behind glass, try putting your lens flat against the glass. Then switch to manual focusing; the glass barrier can give the autofocus mechanism fits. Disable your flash to avoid creating any unwanted reflections, too. I used this technique to capture the image of the turtle sticking his neck out in Figure 7-13.

- **Shooting out a car window:** Set the camera to shutter-priority autoexposure or manual mode and dial in a fast shutter speed to compensate for the movement of the car. Oh, and keep a tight grip on your camera.

✔ **Shooting in strong backlighting:** When the light behind your subject is very strong and illuminating the subject with flash isn't an option, you can expose the image with the subject in mind, in which case the background may be overexposed.

As an alternative, you can expose for the background and purposely underexpose the subject to create a silhouette effect. I opted for this technique when capturing the image in Figure 7-14, which shows a young friend standing mesmerized in front of an aquarium. Be sure to disable your flash when trying to shoot silhouettes.

Figure 7-13: To shoot through glass, place your lens flat against the glass.

Figure 7-14: Experiment with shooting backlit subjects in silhouette.

✔ **Shooting fireworks:** First off, use a tripod; fireworks require a long exposure, and trying to handhold your camera simply isn't going to work. If using a zoom lens, zoom out to the shortest focal length. Switch to manual focusing and set focus at infinity (the farthest focus point possible on your lens). Set the exposure mode to manual, choose a relatively high f-stop setting — say, f/16 or so — and start a shutter speed of 1 to 3 seconds. From there, it's simply a matter of experimenting with different shutter speeds.

TIP

Be especially gentle when you press the shutter button — with a very slow shutter, you can easily create enough camera movement to blur the image. If you purchased the accessory remote control for your camera, this is a good situation in which to use it.

You also may want to enable your camera's Long Exposure Noise Reduction feature because a long exposure also increases the chances of noise defects. See Chapter 5 for details. (Keep the ISO setting low to further dampen noise.)

✔ **Shooting reflective surfaces:** In outdoor shots taken in bright sun, you can reduce glare from reflective surfaces such as glass and metal by using a *circular polarizing filter,* which you can buy for about $60. A polarizing filter can also help out when you're shooting through glass.

But know that in order for the filter to work, the sun, your subject, and your camera lens must be precisely positioned. Your lens must be at a certain angle from the sun, for example, and the light source must also reflect off the surface at a certain angle and direction. In addition, a polarizing filter also intensifies blue skies in some scenarios, which may or may not be to your liking. In other words, a polarizing filter isn't a surefire cure-all.

A more reliable option for shooting small reflective objects is to invest in a light cube or light tent such as the ones shown in Figure 7-15, from Cloud Dome (www.clouddome.com) and Lastolite (www.lastolite.com), respectively. You place the reflective object inside the tent or cube and then position your lights around the outside. The cube or tent acts as a light diffuser, reducing reflections. Prices range from about $50 to $200, depending on size and features.

Cloud Dome, Inc.   Lastolite Limited

Figure 7-15: Investing in a light cube or tent makes photographing reflective objects much easier.

Part III
Working with Picture Files

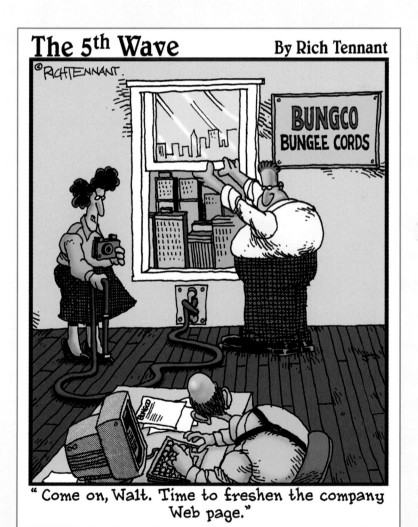

The 5th Wave   By Rich Tennant

BUNGCO
BUNGEE CORDS

" Come on, Walt. Time to freshen the company Web page."

In this part . . .

You've got a memory card full of pictures. Now what? Now you turn to the first chapter in this part, which explains how to get those pictures out of your camera and onto your computer and, just as important, how to safeguard them from future digital destruction. After downloading your files, head for Chapter 9, which offers step-by-step guidance on printing your pictures, sharing them online, and even viewing them on your television.

8

Downloading, Organizing, and Archiving Your Photos

*F*or many novice digital photographers (and even some experienced ones), the task of moving pictures to the computer and then keeping track of all of those image files is one of the more confusing aspects of the art form. In fact, students in my classes have more questions about this subject than just about anything else.

Frankly, writing about the download and organizing process isn't all that easy, either. (I know, poor me!) The problem is that providing you with detailed instructions is pretty much impossible because the steps you need to take vary widely depending on what software you have installed on your computer and whether you use the Windows or Macintosh operating system.

To give you as much help as possible, however, this chapter shows you how to transfer and organize pictures using the free software that came in your camera box. After exploring these discussions, you should be able to adapt the steps to any other photo program you may prefer.

This chapter also covers a few other aspects of handling your picture files, including converting pictures taken in the Raw format to a standard image format. Finally — and perhaps most important — this chapter explains how to ensure that your digital images stay safe after they leave the camera.

Sending Pictures to the Computer

You can take two approaches to moving pictures from your camera memory card to your computer:

- **Connect the camera directly to the computer.** For this option, you need to dig out the USB cable that came in your camera box. (The camera manual refers to the cable as the *interface cable.*) Your computer must also have a free USB slot, or *port,* in techie talk. If you aren't sure what these gadgets look like, Figure 8-1 gives you a look.

USB symbol

Figure 8-1: You can connect the camera to the computer using the supplied USB cable.

The little three-pronged icon you see on the plug and to the left of the two ports in Figure 8-1 is the universal symbol for USB. Be sure to check for this symbol because a different type of slot, called a FireWire slot, looks very similar to a USB slot, and your USB cable can even seem to fit (sort of) into a FireWire slot.

- **Transfer images using a memory card reader.** Many computers now also have built-in memory card readers. If yours has one that accepts a Secure Digital (SD) card, you can simply pop the card out of your camera and into the card reader instead of hooking the camera up to the computer. Note that if you're using the new SDHC (high capacity) cards, the reader must specifically support that type.

As another option, you can buy stand-alone card readers such as the SanDisk model shown in Figure 8-2. This particular model accepts a variety of memory cards. Check your photo printer, too; many printers now have card readers that accept the most popular types of cards.

I prefer to use a card reader, for three reasons: First, when you transfer via the camera, the camera must be turned on during the process, wasting battery power. Second, with a card reader, I don't have to keep track of that elusive camera cable. And third, when I copy photos to my desktop system, transferring via the camera requires that I get down on all fours to plug the cable into the computer's USB slot, which is of course located in the least convenient spot possible. The card reader, by contrast, stays perched on my desk, connected to my computer at all times, so there's very little physical activity involved in transferring pictures, which is how I prefer to live my life.

If you want to transfer directly from the camera, however, the next section explains some important steps you need to take to make that option work. If you choose to use a card reader, skip ahead to the section "Starting the transfer process" to get an overview of what happens after you insert the card into the reader.

Courtesy SanDisk Corporation

Figure 8-2: A card reader offers a more convenient method of image transfer.

Connecting camera and computer

You need to follow a specific set of steps when connecting the camera to your computer. Otherwise, you can damage the camera or the memory card.

Also note that in order for the process to work smoothly, Canon suggests that your computer be running one of the following operating systems:

- Windows Vista
- Windows XP with Service Pack 2
- Windows 2000 with Service Pack 4 or later
- Mac OS X 10.3 and higher

If you use another OS (operating system, in case you're a non-geek), check the support pages on the Canon Web site (www.canon.com) for the latest news about any updates to system compatibility. You can always simply transfer images with a card reader, too.

With that preamble out of the way, the next steps show you how to get your camera to talk to your computer:

1. **Assess the level of the camera battery.**

   Just look at the little battery-status indicator at the bottom of the Shooting Settings display. If the battery is low, charge it before continuing. Running out of battery power during the transfer process can cause problems, including lost picture data. Alternatively, if you purchased the optional AC adapter, use that to power the camera during picture transfers.

2. **Turn on the computer and give it time to finish its normal startup routine.**

3. **Turn off the camera.**

4. **Insert the smaller of the two plugs on the USB cable into the USB port on the side of the camera.**

   The slot is hidden under a little rubber door just around the corner from the buttons that flank the left side of the monitor, as shown in Figure 8-3. Gently pry open the little door and insert the cable end into the slot.

5. **Plug the other end of the cable into the computer's USB port.**

   Be sure to plug the cable into a port that's actually built into the computer, as opposed to one that's on your keyboard or part of an external USB hub. Those accessory-type connections can sometimes foul up the transfer process.

USB port

Figure 8-3: The USB port is hidden under the little rubber door on the left rear side of the camera.

6. **Turn on the camera.**

   The Shooting Settings screen appears briefly on the camera monitor, displaying a "Busy" message. Then the monitor goes black, and the card access lamp (just to the right of the Erase button) begins flickering, letting you know that the camera is communicating with the computer. After a few moments (or minutes, depending on the speed of your computer), the Direct Transfer screen appears on the camera monitor, as shown in Figure 8-4, and the Print/Share light, in the center of the WB button, glows blue.

   For details about the next step in the downloading routine, move on to the next section.

The options you see on the Direct Transfer screen relate to a method of image downloading that requires you to handle everything through the camera menus. I don't cover this download technique because I think that most people will find the alternative methods I discuss here easier and more user-friendly. Nor do I cover the Transfer Order item on the Playback menu, which is related to the process. However, if you're curious about the Wallpaper option on the Direct Transfer screen, turn to Chapter 11, which explains it. Your camera manual also includes specifics about the other download technique.

Figure 8-4: When the camera is ready to download images, the Direct Transfer screen appears.

Starting the transfer process

After you connect the camera to the computer (be sure to carefully follow the steps in the preceding section) or insert a memory card into your card reader, your next step depends, again, on the software installed on your computer and the computer operating system.

Here are the most common possibilities and how to move forward:

- ✓ **On a Windows-based computer, a Windows message box like the one in Figure 8-5 appears.** The box suggests different programs that you can use to download your picture files. Which programs appear depend on what you have installed on your system; if you installed the Canon software, for example, one or more of those programs should appear in the list. To proceed, just click the transfer program that you want to use and then click OK. (The figure features the Windows XP Home Edition version of the dialog box.)

Figure 8-5: Windows may display this initial boxful of transfer options.

If you want to use the same program for all of your transfers, select the Always Use This Program for This Action check box, as I did in Figure 8-5. The next time you connect your camera or insert a memory card, Windows will automatically launch your program of choice instead of displaying the message box.

✔ **An installed photo program automatically displays a photo-download wizard.** For example, if you installed the Canon software, the EOS Utility window or MemoryCard Utility window may leap to the forefront. Or, if you installed some other program, such as Photoshop Elements, its downloader may pop up instead. On the Mac, the built-in iPhoto software may display its auto downloader. (Apple's Web site, www.apple. com, offers excellent video tutorials on using iPhoto, by the way.)

Usually, the downloader that appears is associated with the software that you most recently installed. Each new program that you add to your system tries to wrestle control over your image downloads away from the previous program.

If you don't want a program's auto downloader to launch whenever you insert a memory card or connect your camera, you should be able to turn off that feature. Check the software manual to find out how to disable the auto launch.

✔ **Nothing happens.** Don't panic; assuming that your card reader or camera is properly connected, all is probably well. Someone — maybe even you — simply may have disabled all the automatic downloaders on your system. Just launch your photo software and then transfer your pictures using whatever command starts that process. (I show you how to do it with the Canon software tools later in the chapter; for other programs, consult the software manual.)

As another option, you can use Windows Explorer or the Mac Finder to simply drag and drop files from your memory card to your computer's hard drive. The process is exactly the same as when you move any other file from a CD, DVD, or other storage device onto your hard drive.

As I say in the introduction to this chapter, it's impossible to give step-by-step instructions for using all the various photo downloaders that may be sprinkled over your hard drive. So in the next sections, I provide details on using Canon software to download and organize your files.

If you use some other software, the concepts are the same, but check your program manual to get the small details. In most programs, you also can find lots of information by simply opening the Help menu.

Safeguarding your digital photo files

To make sure that your digital photos enjoy a long, healthy life, follow these storage guidelines:

- Don't rely on your computer's hard drive for long-term, archival storage. Hard drives occasionally fail, wiping out all files in the process. This warning applies to both internal and external hard drives.

- Camera memory cards, flash memory keys, and other portable storage devices are similarly risky. All are easily damaged if dropped or otherwise mishandled. And being of diminutive stature, these portable storage options also are easily lost.

- The best way to store important files is to copy them to nonrewritable CDs. (The label should say CD-R, not CD-RW.) Look for brand-name CDs that have a gold coating and are advertised as archival quality,

which offer a higher level of security than other coatings.

- Recordable DVDs offer the advantage of holding lots more data than a CD. However, as of today, the industry still hasn't settled on a single, standard DVD format, and the archival-level gold coating isn't available for all of those formats. For those reasons, I'm not quite as comfortable with DVDs as I am with CDs. So I use DVDs only for noncritical images; precious family photos go on CDs.

- Online photo-sharing sites such as Shutterfly, Kodak Gallery, and the like aren't designed to be long-term storage tanks for your images. Consider them only a backup to your backup, and read the site terms carefully so that you understand how long the site will hold onto your files if you stop buying prints and other products.

Downloading images with Canon tools

The software CD that shipped with your Rebel XS/1000D includes several programs for transferring, organizing, and editing your photos. For downloading images, I suggest that you use the tools discussed in the next two sections.

Before you try the download steps, however, you may want to visit the Canon Web site and download the latest versions of the software in the suite. Even if you recently bought your camera, the shipping CD may be a little out of date. Just go to www.canon.com and follow the links to locate the software for your camera. (You can also download updated manuals.)

In this book, the steps relate to version 2.4 of the EOS Utility and version 6.1.1 for ZoomBrowser EX (Windows) and ImageBrowser (Mac). As I write this, those versions are the most recent available.

After taking care of the software download and installation chores, see the next two sections for details on how to transfer your images.

Using EOS Utility to transfer images from your camera

Follow these steps to transfer images directly from your camera to the computer using the Canon EOS Utility software:

1. **Connect your camera to the computer.**

   See the first part of this chapter for specifics.

2. **Turn on the camera.**

   After a few moments, the EOS Utility window should appear automatically. If it doesn't, just launch the program as you would any other on your system. Figure 8-6 shows the Windows version of the screen; the Mac version looks the same.

Figure 8-6: EOS Utility is designed for sending pictures from the camera to the computer.

3. **Click the option named Lets You Select and Download Images.**

   With this option, you can specify which pictures you want to download from the camera. After you click the option, you see a browser window that looks similar to the one in Figure 8-7. The figure shows the Windows version, but the Mac version contains the same components.

   Along the right third of the window, you see thumbnails of the images currently on your camera or card. (Click the magnifying glass icons in the lower-right corner of the window to enlarge or reduce the thumbnail size.)

Figure 8-7: Select the thumbnails of the images you want to transfer.

4. **Select the images that you want to copy to the computer.**

   Each thumbnail contains a check box in its lower-left corner. To select an image for downloading, click the box to put a check mark in it.

   For a quick way to select all images, press Ctrl+A (Windows) or ⌘+A (Mac). Or choose Edit⇨Select Image⇨Select All.

5. **Click the Download button at the bottom of the window.**

   Now you see a screen that tells you where the program wants to store your downloaded pictures. Figure 8-8 shows the Windows version of this notice; the Mac version contains the same options.

   By default, pictures are stored in the My Pictures or Pictures folder in Windows (depending on the version of Windows you use) and in the Pictures folder on a Mac. You can put your images anywhere you like; however, most photo editing programs look first for photos in those folders, so sticking with this universally accepted setup makes some sense.

6. **Verify or change the storage location for your pictures.**

   If you want to put the pictures in a location different from what the program suggests, click the Destination Folder button and specify the storage location and folder name you prefer. You also can choose to have the picture files renamed when they're copied; click the File Name button to access the renaming options.

Figure 8-8: You can specify where you want to store the photos.

7. Click OK to begin the download.

A progress window appears, showing you the status of the download. As the images are downloaded, each one appears for a brief moment in a preview window.

8. When the download is complete, turn off the camera.

You can then safely remove the cables connecting it to the computer.

That's the basic process, but I need to share a couple of fine points:

✔ **Setting download preferences:** While the camera is still connected and turned on, you can click the Preferences button at the bottom of the EOS Utility browser (refer to Figure 8-7) to open a dialog box where you can specify many aspects of how the transfer program works. Figure 8-9 shows the Windows version; Figure 8-10, the Mac version.

In Windows, click the tabs at the top of the Preferences dialog box to reveal all your options. (You may need to use the scroll arrows at the right side of the tabs to access hidden tabs.) On a Mac, display the various panels by choosing them from the drop-down list at the top of the dialog box.

✔ **Auto-launching the other Canon programs:** After the download is complete, the EOS Utility may automatically launch Canon Digital Photo Professional or ZoomBrowser EX (Windows) or ImageBrowser (Mac) so that you can immediately start working with your pictures. (You must have installed the programs for this to occur.)

Figure 8-9: In Windows, click the tabs at the top of the window to access download options.

Figure 8-10: On a Mac, select a panel of options from the drop-down list at the top of the dialog box.

If you want to change the program that's launched, visit the Linked Software panel of the EOS Utility's Preferences dialog box. You then can select the program that you want to use or choose None to disable auto-launch altogether.

✔ **Closing the EOS Utility:** The utility browser window doesn't close automatically after the download is complete. So you must return to it and click the Quit button to shut it down. (Refer to Figure 8-7.)

Using MemoryCard Utility for card-to-computer transfers

Transferring images from a memory card reader involves a different Canon tool, MemoryCard Utility. This tool is actually a component of ZoomBrowser EX (Windows) and ImageBrowser (Mac). To try it out, take these steps:

1. **Put your card in your card reader.**

   If all the planets are aligned — meaning that the Canon software was the last photo software you installed, and some other program doesn't try to handle the job for you — the MemoryCard Utility window shown in Figure 8-11 appears automatically when you put your memory card into the card reader. The figure shows the Windows version of the window; the Mac version is identical except that the top of the window refers to ImageBrowser, which is the Mac version of ZoomBrowser EX.

Figure 8-11: The MemoryCard Utility enables you to transfer pictures using a card reader.

If the window doesn't appear, you can access it as follows:

- *Windows:* Open the program called ZoomBrowser EX MemoryCard Utility, using the steps you usually take to start a program.

- *Mac:* Start the program called Canon Camera Window. The program should detect your memory card and display the MemoryCard Utility window.

2. **Click Lets You Select and Download Images.**

   You then see the browser window shown in Figure 8-12. The figure shows the Windows version; the Mac version contains the same basic components but follows conventional Mac design rules. Either way, thumbnails of the images on your memory card are displayed in the window.

Figure 8-12: Select the images that you want to download.

3. **Select the images that you want to download.**

   Use these techniques:

   - To select the first photo, click its thumbnail.

   - To select additional pictures, Ctrl+click (Windows) or ⌘+click (Mac) their thumbnails.

   - To quickly select all images in Windows, choose Select All from the Select drop-down list, located on the toolbar near the top of the window. On a Mac, the list is called Select Image and is located at the bottom of the window. (You also can just press Ctrl+A in Windows or ⌘+A on a Mac.)

4. **Click the Image Download button.**

   In Windows, the button is near the top-left corner of the browser window; on a Mac, it's in the bottom-left corner.

   Either way, a new window appears to show you where the downloader wants to put your files and the name it plans to assign the storage folder, as shown in Figure 8-13.

   If you're not happy with the program's choices, click the Change Settings button to open a dialog box where you can select a different storage location. In the same dialog box, you can also choose to have the picture files renamed when they're copied. Click OK to close the Change Settings dialog box when you finish.

Figure 8-13: Click the Change Settings button to specify a different download folder.

Most programs look first for photos stored in the location suggested initially by the downloader. In Windows, that folder is named either My Pictures or Pictures, depending on what version of Windows you use. On a Mac, the folder is named Pictures. Sticking with these default storage locations can simplify your life down the road, but of course, you're free to set up whatever image-organization system works best for you.

5. **Click the Starts Download button.**

   Your files start making their way to your computer. When the download is finished, the MemoryCard Utility window closes, and either ZoomBrowser EX (Windows) or ImageBrowser (Mac) appears, displaying your downloaded files. See the next section for details on using that program.

Using ZoomBrowser EX/ImageBrowser

In addition to the aforementioned software tools, your Canon CD contains two additional programs: ZoomBrowser EX (Windows) or ImageBrowser (Mac), plus Digital Photo Professional. In this section, you can find out how to organize your photos using the ZoomBrowser EX/ImageBrowser tool. Although you can view thumbnails of your images in Digital Photo Professional, that tool is designed for advanced users, so I don't cover it in this book.

The next sections give you the most basic of introductions to ZoomBrowser EX/ImageBrowser, which, in the interest of saving type, I may refer to from here on in as just "the browser." If you want more details, the CD that ships with the program offers a very good online manual.

Before you move on, though, I want to clear up one common point of confusion: You can use Canon's software to download and organize your photos and still use any photo editing software you prefer. And to do your editing, you don't need to re-download photos — after you transfer photos to your computer, you can access them from any program, just as you can any file that you put on your system.

Getting acquainted with the program

Figure 8-14 offers a look at the ZoomBrowser EX window; Figure 8-15, the ImageBrowser window. As you can see, the windows contain most of the same basic components, although the Mac version of the browser is lacking the row of task buttons found in the upper-left corner of the Windows version. The two versions also offer a different set of image-viewing modes — Preview Mode and List mode on the Mac, and Zoom, Scroll, and Preview modes in Windows.

Figure 8-14: Click a folder in the Explore panel to display its images.

Figure 8-15: Click a thumbnail to view that image in the main preview area.

Whichever version you use, you can customize the window layout via the View menu. The arrangement you see in the figures is the Preview mode setup. I prefer this mode because it provides easy access not just to your images, but also to details about the camera settings you used to shoot the picture. Note that in Windows, you can display and hide the Explore and Information panels by clicking the little vertical buttons that border the preview area (the "Information panel" label in Figure 8-14 points to one of the little guys.) On a Mac, choose View⇨View Settings to display a submenu where you can toggle the panels on and off.

Here's a quick guide to viewing your photos in Preview mode:

✔ **Select the folder you want to view.** Click the folder's icon in the Explore panel, found on the left side of the window and labeled in Figures 8-14 and 8-15. If you click the Favorite Folders tab, you see only the My Pictures or Pictures (Windows) or Pictures folder (Mac) along with any custom Favorites folders that you create, a topic that you can visit in the upcoming section "Organizing your photos." By default, picture files that you transfer from your camera or memory card using the Canon software go into these folders. To view all folders on your computer, click the All Folders button.

✔ **Preview the images in the selected folder.** In Preview mode, the current image appears at a large size in the middle of the window, as shown in the figures, and a "filmstrip" of smaller thumbnails appears beneath.

To view the next image in the filmstrip, click its thumbnail. On a Mac, you then can press the right and left arrow keys on your keyboard to view your photos one by one. In Windows, the same technique works on some keyboards; if not, click the Next and Previous buttons (under the large preview) instead. Drag the scroll bar under the thumbnails to scroll the thumbnail display as needed.

✔ **View an image in full-screen mode.** For a larger view of a photo, double-click its thumbnail. (You must double-click the thumbnail, not the larger preview image.) Doing so opens the image in its own browser window, displaying the image as large as possible to fit the available screen space. This full-screen window is the Viewer window. The next section explains more about the controls therein. To exit the Viewer window and return to the main browser, just click the window's close button.

✔ **View shooting information.** Check out the Information panel, located on the right side of the window. If you click the Shooting Information button, you display all the settings that you used to capture the selected image, as shown in Figures 8-14 and 8-15. Reviewing this data — known as *metadata* — is a great way to better understand what settings work best for different types of pictures, especially when you're just getting up to speed with aperture, shutter speed, white balance, and all the other digital photography basics. (Note that you may need to scroll the Information panel display to access the Shooting Information button, depending on the size of the program window.

Those are the basics of navigating through your images. In the next section, you can find some hints about viewing your photos in full-screen mode, inside the Viewer window. After that, the section "Organizing your photos" explains how to customize the folder setup that the Canon software creates for you.

Viewing photos in full-screen mode

Double-clicking a thumbnail in the main browser window displays the image inside the Viewer window. Figure 8-16 shows the Windows version of the Viewer; Figure 8-17 shows the Mac alternative.

After opening an image in the Viewer window, use these tricks to inspect it more closely:

✔ **Magnify the image.** You can zoom in on your image for a closer look by using these techniques:

    • *In ZoomBrowser EX (Windows):* Drag the Zoom slider or click the preview with the Zoom In tool, both labeled in Figure 8-16.

Zoom in

Next Zoom out

Previous Hand tool

Fit to window Zoom slider

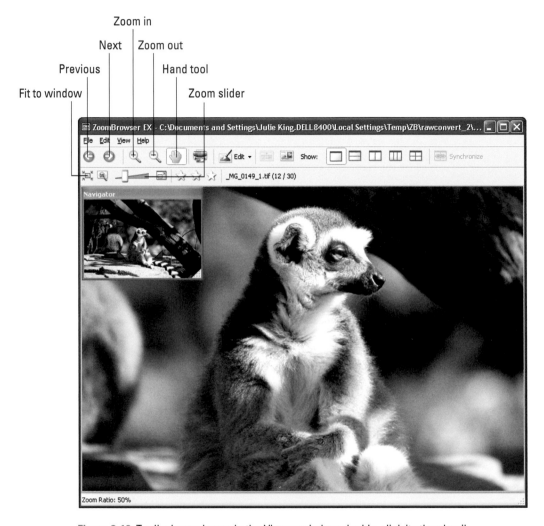

Figure 8-16: To display an image in the Viewer window, double-click its thumbnail.

- *In ImageBrowser (Mac):* Choose a specific magnification level from the Display Size drop-down list, labeled in Figure 8-17.

✔ **Scroll a magnified image.** After you magnify the photo, a tiny Navigator window appears in the top-left corner of the screen, as shown in the figures. The little red triangles in the Navigator window indicate the area that you're viewing in the main preview. To scroll the display to see another portion of the image, put your cursor in the Navigator window, within the area bounded by those little red triangles, and drag.

Navigator window

Edit list   Display Size list

Figure 8-17: The Mac version of the Viewer window looks like this.

In Windows, you also can click the Hand tool, labeled in Figure 8-16, and drag in the preview itself. On a Mac, just drag in the preview; your cursor automatically sets itself to Hand-tool mode as soon as you enlarge the image display.

✓ **Reduce the view size.** In Windows, click the preview with the Zoom Out tool or use the Zoom slider. (Refer to Figure 8-16.) On a Mac, choose a smaller zoom size from the Display Size drop-down list.

To zoom out so that you can see the entire image, click the Fit to Window button in Windows. (Refer to Figure 8-16.) On a Mac, choose Fit to Window from the Display Size list instead.

✓ **View the next image in the folder.** If you want to inspect more images in the Viewer, just click the Previous and Next buttons, labeled in Figure 8-16, if you use Windows. On a Mac, click the Back or Next button located under the preview.

> ✔ **Edit the photo.** To use the editing tools provided with the program, open the Edit drop-down list, found above the preview in Windows and beneath it on a Mac. Then select the editing task you want to perform. Chapter 10 provides more details about shifting into Editing mode and using the available tools.

Keep in mind that the preceding tidbits just give you the basics of using the Viewer window; for additional tips, check out the program manual.

Organizing your photos

By default, the Canon download software puts your picture files into either the My Pictures or Pictures folder in Windows and the Pictures folder on a Mac. Within that folder, the downloading tools organize the images by their shooting dates, creating a new folder for each date found on the memory card, as shown in Figure 8-18. Each folder contains only the images shot on that particular day.

If you don't like this organizational structure, you can change it. For example, you may want to organize images by category — family, travel, work, and so on. I took this approach to customize my folder collection in Figure 8-18.

Figure 8-18: You can create custom folders to organize images by category.

To keep things simple, I suggest that you add these custom folders within the My Pictures or Pictures folder (Windows) or Pictures folder (Mac). That way, you'll always know where to look for images on your computer's hard drive. And programs that default to looking to those folders for photos will be able to find them as well. The next mini-sections show you the basics you need to create custom folders and then organize images in them.

Creating custom folders

Take these steps to add a folder to the My Pictures or Pictures list. (Again, which folder is the default image-storage tank depends on your computer's operating system.)

1. **Click the Favorite Folders tab of the Explore panel, if it isn't already visible.**

2. **Click My Pictures or Pictures.**

   The folder should appear highlighted.

3. **Choose File⇨New Folder.**

   The New Folder dialog box appears.

4. **Type the name of the folder in the text box and click OK.**

   Your folder appears as a subfolder under the My Pictures or Pictures folder.

To create a subfolder within your new folder, follow the same process, but click the new folder in Step 2. For example, I created two subfolders within my Travel folder in Figure 8-18.

Managing your image collection

After you create your folders, you can place images into them in two ways:

- **Move an image from one folder to another.** Display the image thumbnail and then drag it to the desired folder. The program moves the image file to the new folder and removes it from the old one.

- **Download new images directly to your desired folder.** You can specify a custom folder as the download destination when you use the EOS Utility and MemoryCard Utility software to transfer images. See the earlier sections of this chapter for details.

Use these techniques to maintain and further organize your image collection:

- **Delete a folder.** First, click the folder name to select it. Then, in Windows, choose File⇨Delete. On a Mac, choose File⇨Send to Trash. In both cases, the program displays a message asking you to confirm that you want to get rid of the folder; click Yes (Windows) or OK (Mac) to proceed.

   Be careful: This step deletes both the folder and all images inside it!

- **Rename a folder.** Click the folder and choose File⇨Rename. In the dialog box that appears, type the new folder name and then click OK.

- **Rename a picture file.** Click the image thumbnail and choose File⇨ Rename. Type the new name in the dialog box that appears and then click OK. *Note:* Do not type the three-letter file extension (.jpg or .CR2) at the end of the new filename. The program adds that data automatically to the filename for you.

- **Delete a picture.** Click the image thumbnail to select it. Then, in Windows, choose File⇨Delete; on a Mac, choose File⇨Send to Trash. As with deleting a folder, you're presented with a dialog box asking you whether you really, really want to dump that image. Respond in the affirmative to do so.

Exploring Other Software Options

The Canon browser software is a nifty tool for viewing and organizing your photos. And it enables you to perform basic retouching: You can crop your image and make some adjustments to color, exposure, and sharpness. Chapter 10 shows you how.

But the program isn't designed for serious photo editing. For one thing, you can't perform *selective editing* — changing only the part of your image that needs help. And you don't get any tools for removing flaws such as blemishes in portraits and the like.

So my recommendation is that you consider the browser as a good, free tool for organizing your photos and doing simple picture fixes. But if you find yourself doing a lot of photo editing, invest in something more capable. Here are just some of the products to consider:

- **Beginning/consumer programs:** Unless you're retouching photos for professional purposes or want to get into photo editing at a serious level for other reasons, a program such as Adobe Photoshop Elements ($100, www.adobe.com) is a good fit. Elements has been the best-selling consumer photo editor for some time, and for good reason. With a full complement of retouching tools, onscreen guidance for novices, a built-in photo organizer, and an assortment of tools and templates for creating artistic photo projects, Elements offers all the features that most consumers need.

  Figure 8-19 offers a look at Elements 6 for Windows; the program is also available in a Mac version. (By the time this book is published, Elements 7 for Windows will also be available.)

  For other candidates in this category and price range, visit the Web sites of Corel (www.corel.com) and ArcSoft (www.arcsoft.com). Both companies offer multiple programs aimed at the beginner-to-intermediate user.

- **Advanced/professional tools:** The best-known option in this category is Adobe Photoshop, shown in Figure 8-20. Photoshop offers professional-grade photo editing tools, a built-in photo organizer, and features needed by people preparing images for commercial printing, Web design, and other high-end uses.

  Of course, all that power comes at a price: $650. And expect to spend lots of time getting up to speed with the program, too, because you don't get the friendly interfaces and guidance offered by the beginner-level programs. Nor does Photoshop offer the automated photo-creation features, such as greeting card templates and clip art, that you find in consumer programs.

  Other programs aimed at the professional market include Apple Aperture ($200, www.apple.com) and Adobe Lightroom ($300). These two programs are geared toward users who routinely need to process lots of images but who typically do only light retouching work.

Figure 8-19: Adobe Photoshop Elements offers a good balance of power and ease-of-use.

A few important tips before you buy:

- ✔ Check the software's system requirements to make sure that your computer can run the program. Some of the products I mention here aren't available for Macintosh computers; Apple Aperture, on the other hand, isn't available for Windows-based systems. Also make sure that your computer offers the system memory (RAM), processor speed, and other components that the software requires.

- ✔ You also can buy stand-alone photo organizing programs if you aren't interested in serious photo editing but want a more powerful image-management tool than you get with the Canon software. Check out the offerings in this category from ACDSee (www.acdsee.com), ThumbsPlus (www.thumbsplus.com), and Extensis (www.extensis.com).

You may be amused, as I am, to know that the photo industry uses the term *DAM* software — for digital asset management — to refer to the function provided by image-organizing programs. (I dare you to walk into your local computer store and ask where you can find the DAM software. Wait; I double-dare you.)

- ✔ Many software companies enable you to download free trials from their Web sites so that you can actually use the software for a short period to make sure that it fits your needs.

Using your mouse as a shutter button

Along with providing a convenient way for you to download images, the EOS Utility software enables you to use your computer to actually shoot pictures.

While your camera is connected to your computer, clicking the Camera Settings/Remote Shooting button in the main EOS Utility window displays a panel containing clickable controls for adjusting the major camera settings, such as aperture, white balance, ISO, and metering mode. After you establish those settings, you click another button to record whatever scene is in front of your camera lens.

What's the point? Well, this feature is great in scenarios that make having a live photographer close to the subject either difficult or dangerous — for example, trying to get a shot of a chemical reaction in a science lab or capture an image of an animal that's shy around humans. Additionally, the software enables easy time-lapse photography, enabling you to set the camera to take pictures automatically at specified intervals over a period of minutes, hours, or even days.

Figure 8-20: Adobe Photoshop is designed for advanced users and imaging professionals.

Processing Raw (CR2) Files

Chapter 3 introduces you to the Camera Raw file format, which enables you to capture images as raw data. The advantage of capturing Raw files, which are called CR2 files on your Rebel XS/1000D, is that you make the decisions about how to translate the raw data into an actual photograph. You can specify attributes such as color intensity, image sharpening, contrast, and so on — all of which are handled automatically by the camera if you use its other file format, JPEG.

The bad news: You have to specify attributes such as color intensity, image sharpening, contrast, and so on before you can do anything with your pictures. Although you can print them immediately if you use the Canon software, you can't take them to a photo lab for printing, share them online, or edit them in your photo software until you process them using a tool known as a *raw converter*. At the end of the conversion process, you save the finished file in a standard file format, such as JPEG or TIFF.

If you decide to shoot in the Raw format, you can process your images with ZoomBrowser EX (Windows) or ImageBrowser (Mac). Follow these steps:

1. **Click the image thumbnail in the browser window.**

2. **In Windows, choose Tools⇨Processing Raw Images; on a Mac, choose File⇨Processing Raw Image.**

   A message window may appear in order to provide you with general instructions about the conversion. Just click OK to close the window and move on. (If you don't want to be bothered with it each time you want to process a Raw image, select the Don't Show This Message Again check box before you close the window.)

   Now your photo appears inside the Raw Image Task window, shown in Figure 8-21. (The window may appear slightly different, depending on the options you choose from the View menu.)

3. **Use the controls on the Image Quality adjustment panel to adjust the image as needed.**

   Figure 8-22 gives you a look at the Windows version of the panel; the Mac version contains the same components but is arranged a little differently. Drag the scroll bar on the right side of the panel if necessary to scroll the display as needed to access all the controls.

   The panel offers the following controls:

   - *Digital Exposure Compensation:* Drag this slider to adjust image brightness.

Figure 8-21: You can convert Raw images using the browser's Raw Image Task tool.

- *White Balance:* These controls, based on the white balance options discussed in Chapter 6, adjust color. You can click one of the white balance icons in the large panel, or you can drag the A/B (amber/blue) and M/G (magenta/green) sliders to tweak the colors. Or click the little white balance eyedropper, labeled in Figure 8-22, and then click an area of the image that should be white, black, or gray to remove any color cast.

- *Picture Style:* Here, you can actually apply one of the camera's Picture Style options to the photo. Or you can customize the style by dragging the Sharpness, Contrast, Color Saturation, and Color Tone sliders. (If you select Monochrome as the Picture Style, the Color Saturation and Color Tone sliders are replaced by the Filter Effect and Toning Effect sliders.) Chapter 6 talks about Picture Styles.

- *Color Space:* You can select either sRGB or Adobe RGB as the image color space. As discussed in Chapter 6, the latter offers a broader range of colors, although some of them may be beyond the printable range.

- *Noise Reduction:* If you select On for this option, the converter applies a filter designed to soften noise, a defect that gives the image a grainy look. The filter works by applying a slight blur to the photo, so use with caution.

At any time, you can revert the image to the original settings by clicking the Shot Settings button underneath the Image Adjustment panel. (See Figure 8-21; the button is just above the Preview check box.)

4. **Choose File⇨Save Image.**

   You see the Save dialog box shown in Figure 8-23.

5. **Set the Save options.**

   Here's the rundown on the options that may be foreign to you:

   - *Conversion Target (Windows) or Images to Save (Mac):* These options matter only if you are processing multiple images at a time. If you want to do this, the Help system available in the Raw Image Task window provides how-to's.

   - *Image Type:* This one is the critical setting. Choose EXIF-Tiff (8 bits/channel). This saves your image in the TIFF file format, which preserves all image data. Don't choose the JPEG format; doing so is destructive to the photo because of the lossy compression that is applied. Chapter 3 has details.

White balance eyedropper

Figure 8-22: Set the characteristics of your photo here.

- *Resolution:* This option *does not* adjust the pixel count of your image, as you might imagine. It only sets the default output resolution that will be used if you send the photo to a printer. Most photo editing programs enable you to adjust this value before printing. The Canon software does not, however, so if you plan to print through the browser, I suggest you set this value to 300. Chapter 9 talks more about printing.

- *Save Folder and Rename File:* Use these options to specify a storage folder and filename for your converted image.

6. **Click Save.**

   A progress box appears in order to let you know that the conversion and file-saving is going forward.

7. **Close the Raw Image Task window to return to the browser.**

Figure 8-23: Always save your processed files in the TIFF format.

As you can probably tell from looking at the Raw Image Task window in Figure 8-21, these steps give you only a basic overview of the process. If you regularly shoot in the Raw format, take the time to explore the Raw Image Task window Help system so that you can take advantage of its other features.

Also know that this raw processor isn't your only option. Digital Photo Professional, provided in the Canon software suite, offers its own raw conversion tools. Because that program is designed for the more advanced user, the conversion tools are slightly more complex, but they're also a little more powerful in some regards. Additionally, both Adobe Photoshop and Photoshop Elements offer excellent raw converters.

Whichever converter you choose, keep these final pointers in mind:

✔ Always save your processed files in a nondestructive format, such as TIFF. (If you use Adobe Photoshop Elements or Photoshop, its format, PSD, is also nondestructive.) If you need a JPEG image to share online, Chapter 9 shows you how to create a duplicate of your original, converted image in that format.

✓ Some raw converters, including the ones in the Canon programs, give you the option of creating a 16-bit image file. A *bit* is a unit of computer data; the more bits you have, the more colors your image can contain. Many photo editing programs either can't open 16-bit files or limit you to a few editing tools, so I suggest you stick with the standard, 8-bit image option unless you know your software can handle the higher bit depth. (If you do prefer 16-bit files, choose the TIFF (16bit/ch) option in Step 5 of the preceding steps.)

✓ Resist the temptation to crank up color saturation too much. Doing so can actually destroy image detail. Likewise, be careful about overdoing sharpening, or else you can create noticeable image defects. Chapter 10 offers some additional information about sharpening and saturation to help you find the right amounts of each.

9

Printing and Sharing Your Photos

*W*hen my first digital photography book was published, way back in the 1990s, consumer digital cameras didn't offer the resolution needed to produce good prints at anything more than postage-stamp size — and even then, the operative word was good, not *great*. And if you did want a print, it was a pretty much a do-it-yourself proposition unless you paid sky-high prices at a professional imaging lab. In those days, retail photo labs didn't offer digital printing, and online printing services hadn't arrived yet, either.

Well, time and technology march on, and, at least in the case of digital photo printing, to a very good outcome. Your Rebel XS/1000D can produce dynamic prints even at large sizes, and getting those prints made is easy and economical, thanks to an abundance of digital printing services now in stores and online. And for home printing, today's printers are better and cheaper than ever, too.

That said, getting the best prints from your picture files still requires a little bit of knowledge and prep work on your part. To that end, this chapter tells you exactly how to ensure that your pictures will look as good on paper as they do in your camera monitor.

In addition, this chapter explores ways to share your pictures electronically. First, I show you how to prepare your picture for e-mail — an important step if you don't want to annoy friends and family by cluttering their inboxes with ginormous, too-large-to-view photos. Following that, you can find out how to create a digital slide show, view your pictures on a television, and more.

Avoiding Printing Problems

Although digital printing has come a long way in the past couple of years, a few issues still can cause hiccups in the process. So before you print your photos, whether you want to do it on your own printer or send them to a lab, read through the next three sections, which show you how to avoid the most common trouble spots.

Check the pixel count before you print

Resolution, or the number of pixels in your digital image, plays a huge role in how large you can print your photos and still maintain good picture quality. You can get the complete story on resolution in Chapter 3, but here's a quick recap as it relates to printing:

- ✓ On your Rebel XS/1000D, you set picture resolution via the Quality option, found on Shooting Menu 1. You must select this option *before* you capture an image, which means that you need some idea of your ultimate print size before you shoot. And remember that if you crop your image, you eliminate some pixels, so take that factor into account when you do the resolution math.

- ✓ For good print quality, the *minimum* pixel count (in my experience, anyway) is 200 pixels per linear inch, or 200 *ppi*. That means that if you want a 4-x-6-inch print, you need at least 800 x 1200 pixels.

- ✓ Depending on your printer, you may get even better results at 200+ ppi. Some printers do their best work when fed 300 ppi, and a few (notably those from Epson) request 360 ppi as the optimum resolution. However, going higher than that typically doesn't produce any better prints.

Unfortunately, because most printer manuals don't bother to tell you what image resolution produces the best results, finding the right pixel level is a matter of experimentation. (Don't confuse the manual's statements related to the printer's *dpi* with *ppi*. DPI refers to how many dots of color the printer can lay down per inch; many printers use multiple dots to reproduce one image pixel.)

✔ If you're printing your photos at a retail kiosk or at an online site, the software that you use to order your prints should determine the resolution of your files and then suggest appropriate print sizes. But if you're printing on a home printer, you need to be the resolution cop.

So what do you do if you find that you don't have enough pixels for the print size you have in mind? You just have to decide what's more important — print size or print quality.

If your print size exceeds your pixel supply, you have the following two choices, neither of which provides a good outcome:

✔ Keep the existing pixel count, in which case pixels simply grow in size to fill the requested print size. And if pixels get too large, you get a defect known as *pixelation*. The picture starts to appear jagged, or stairstepped, along curved or digital lines. Or at worst, your eye can actually make out the individual pixels, and your photo begins to look more like a mosaic than, well, a photograph.

✔ Add more pixels, also known as *resampling the image*. Some photo programs enable you to do so, and some programs resample the photo automatically for you, depending on the print settings you choose. Although this option sounds good, it really doesn't solve your problem. You're asking the software to make up photo information out of thin air, and the resulting image usually looks worse than the original. You don't get pixelation, but details turn muddy, giving the image a blurry, poorly rendered appearance.

Just to hammer home the point and remind you one more time of the impact of resolution picture quality, Figures 9-1 and 9-2 show you the same image as it appears at 300 ppi (the resolution required by the publisher of this book), at 50 ppi, and resampled from 50 ppi to 300 ppi. As you can see, there's just no way around the rule: If you want the best-quality prints, you need the right pixel count from the get-go.

300 ppi　　　　　　　　　　　　　　50 ppi

Figure 9-1: A high-quality print depends on a high-resolution original.

Allow for different print proportions

Unlike many digital cameras, yours produces images that have an aspect ratio of 3:2. That is, images are 3 units wide by 2 units tall — just like a 35mm film negative — which means that they translate perfectly to the standard 4-x-6-inch print size. (Most digital cameras produce 4:3 images, which means the pictures must be cropped to fit a 4-x-6-inch piece of paper.)

If you want to print your digital original at other standard sizes — 5 x 7, 8 x 10, 11 x 14, and so on — you need to crop the photo to match those proportions. Alternatively, you can reduce the photo size slightly and leave an empty margin along the edges of the print as needed.

As a point of reference, both images in Figure 9-3 show you an original, 3:2 image. The blue outlines indicate how much of the original can fit within a 5-x-7-inch frame and an 8-x-10-inch frame.

Chapter 10 shows you how to crop your image using the free Canon software that shipped with your camera. You also can usually crop your photo using the software provided at online printing sites and at retail print kiosks. But if you plan to simply drop off your memory card for printing at a lab, be sure to find out whether the printer automatically crops the image without your input. If so, use your photo software to crop the photo, save the cropped image to your memory card, and deliver that version of the file to the printer.

50 ppi resampled to 300 ppi

Figure 9-2: Adding pixels in a photo editor doesn't rescue a low-resolution original.

To allow yourself printing flexibility, leave at least a little margin of background around your subject when you shoot, as I did for the example in Figure 9-3. Then you don't clip off the edges of the subject no matter what print size you choose. (Some people refer to this margin padding as *head room,* especially when describing portrait composition.)

Get print and monitor colors in sync

Your photo colors look perfect on your computer monitor. But when you print the picture, the image is too red, or too green, or has some other nasty color tint. This problem, which is probably the most prevalent printing issue, can occur because of any or all of the following factors:

✔ **Your monitor needs to be calibrated.** When print colors don't match what you see on your computer monitor, the most likely culprit is actually the monitor, not the printer. If the monitor isn't accurately calibrated, the colors it displays aren't a true reflection of your image colors. The same caveat applies with regard to monitor brightness: You can't accurately gauge the exposure of a photo if the brightness of the monitor is cranked way up or down.

5 x 7 frame area   8 x 10 frame area

Figure 9-3: Composing your shots with a little head room enables you to crop to different frame sizes.

To ensure that your monitor is displaying photos on a neutral canvas, you can start with a software-based calibration utility, which is just a small program that guides you through the process of adjusting your monitor. The program displays various color swatches and other graphics and then asks you to provide feedback about what you see on the screen.

If you use a Mac, the operating system offers a built-in calibration utility, the Display Calibrator Assistant; Figure 9-4 shows the welcome screen that appears when you run the program. (Access it by opening the System Preferences dialog box, clicking the Displays icon, clicking the Color button, and then clicking the Calibrate button.) You also can find free calibration software for both Mac and Windows systems online; just enter the term *free monitor calibration software* into your favorite search engine.

Figure 9-4: Mac users can take advantage of the operating system's built-in calibration tool.

Software-based tools, though, depend on your eyes to make decisions during the calibration process. For a more reliable calibration, you may want to invest in a hardware solution, such as the Pantone Huey ($90, www.pantone.com) or the ColorVision Spyder2express ($70, www. colorvision.com). These products use a device known as a *colorimeter* to accurately measure your display colors.

Whichever route you go, the calibration process produces a monitor *profile,* which is simply a data file that tells your computer how to adjust the display to compensate for any monitor color casts. Your Windows or Mac operating system loads this file automatically when you start your computer. Your only responsibility is to perform the calibration every month or so, as monitor colors drift over time.

✔ **One of your printer cartridges is empty or clogged.** If your prints look great one day but are way off the next, the number-one suspect is an empty ink cartridge or a clogged print nozzle or head. Check your manual to find out how to perform the necessary maintenance to keep the nozzles or print heads in good shape.

If black-and-white prints have a color tint, you might assume that your black ink cartridge is to blame, if your printer has one. But the problem is usually a color cartridge instead. Most printers use both color and black inks even for black-and-white prints, and if one color is missing, a tint results.

When you buy replacement ink, by the way, keep in mind that third-party brands, while they may save you money, may not deliver the performance you get from the cartridges made by your printer manufacturer. A lot of science goes into getting ink formulas to mesh with the printer's ink-delivery system, and the printer manufacturer obviously knows most about that delivery system.

✔ **You chose the wrong paper setting in your printer software.** When you set up your print job, be sure to select the right setting from the paper-type option — glossy, matte, and so on. This setting affects how the printer lays down ink on the paper.

✔ **Your photo paper is low quality.** Sad but true: The cheap, store-brand photo papers usually don't render colors as well as the higher-priced, name-brand papers. For best results, try papers from your printer manufacturer; again, those papers are engineered to provide top performance with the printer's specific inks and ink-delivery system.

✔ **Your printer and photo software are fighting over color management duties.** Some photo programs offer *color management* tools, which are features that enable the user to control how colors are handled as an image passes from camera to monitor to printer. Most printer software also offers color management features. The problem is, if you enable color management controls both in your photo software and your printer software, you can create conflicts that lead to wacky colors. So check your photo software and printer manuals to find out what color management options are available to you and how to turn them on and off.

Even if all the aforementioned issues are resolved, however, don't expect perfect color matching between printer and monitor. Printers simply can't reproduce the entire spectrum of colors that a monitor can display. In addition, monitor colors always appear brighter because they are, after all, generated with light.

Finally, be sure to evaluate your print colors and monitor colors in the same ambient light — daylight, office light, whatever — because that light source has its own influence on the colors you see. Also allow your prints to dry for 15 minutes or so before you make any final judgments.

Printing Online or In-Store

Normally, I'm a do-it-yourself type of gal. I mow my own lawn, check my own tire pressure, hang my own screen doors. I am woman; hear me roar. Unless, that is, I discover that I can have someone *else* do the job in less time and for less money than I can — which just happens to be the case for digital photo printing. Although I occasionally make my own prints for fine-art images that I plan to sell or exhibit, I have everyday snapshots made at my local retail photo lab.

Unless you're already very comfortable with computers and photo printing, I suggest that you do the same. Compare the cost of retail digital printing with the cost of using a home or office photo printer — remember to factor in the required ink, paper, and your precious time — and you'll no doubt come out ahead if you delegate the job.

You can choose from a variety of retail printing options:

- **Drop-off printing services:** Just as you used to leave a roll of film at the photo lab in your corner drugstore or camera store, you can drop off your memory card, order prints, and then pick up your prints in as little as an hour.

- **Self-serve print kiosks:** Many photo labs, big-box stores, and other retail outlets also offer self-serve print kiosks. You insert your memory card into the appropriate slot, follow the onscreen directions, and wait for your prints to slide out of the print chute.

- **Online with mail-order delivery:** You can upload your photo files to online printing sites and have prints mailed directly to your house. Photo-sharing sites such as Shutterfly, Kodak Gallery, and Snapfish are well-known players in this market. But many national retail chains, such as Ritz Camera, Wal-Mart, and others also offer this service.

- **Online with local pickup:** Here's my favorite option. Many national chains enable you to upload your picture files for easy ordering but pick up your prints at a local store.

This service is a great way to share prints with friends and family who don't live nearby. I can upload and order prints from my desk in Indianapolis, for example, and have them printed at a store located a few miles from my parents' home in Texas.

Printing from ZoomBrowser EX/ImageBrowser

If you prefer to print your own pictures on a home or office printer, the process is much the same as printing anything from your computer: You open the picture file in your photo software of choice, choose File➪Print, and specify the print size, paper size, paper type, and so on, as usual.

The following steps show you how to get the job done using Canon ZoomBrowser EX (Windows) or ImageBrowser (Mac). Chapter 8 introduces you to this free software, so you may want to pop over to that chapter to find out how to browse your images using the program, if you haven't already done so. Then walk this way:

1. **Click the thumbnail for the image that you want to print.**

2. **Choose File⇨Print⇨Photo Print.**

   Your image then appears inside the Photo Print window, shown in Figure 9-5. The figure shows the Windows XP version of the Photo Print features. If you're a Mac user, your window lacks the gray task panel that appears on the left in Windows, but don't fret: The critical printing settings remain the same, albeit with a slightly different look.

Figure 9-5: Your first step is to select a printer and paper size.

3. **Select a printer.**

   In Windows, choose the printer from the Name drop-down list. On a Mac, select your printer from the Printer drop-down list.

4. **Specify your printer settings.**

   - *Windows:* Click the Properties button.
   - *Mac:* Click the Page Setup button.

   Either way, you're taken to the standard print-setup dialog box for your printer. The options therein depend on your printer, so check your manual for guidance. But be sure to specify the following settings:

- Paper size

- Paper type (glossy, plain paper, and so on)

- Borderless printing on or off (if your printer offers this feature)

The browser software automatically chooses the print orientation (portrait or landscape) that best fits the image on the page. Even though you can select an orientation option in your printer setup dialog box, the program overrides you later if it deems necessary.

When you finish establishing the printer settings, click OK to return to the Photo Print window.

5. **Adjust the image cropping as necessary.**

By default, the browser automatically enlarges and/or crops your image to fit your chosen paper size if necessary. To see exactly what has been cropped in Windows, click the Trim Image button. On a Mac, click the button labeled Remove Unwanted Regions of Your Photo.

In both cases, your image opens in the Trim Image editing window, shown in Figure 9-6, which contains some of the controls that you see when you use the program's editing functions.

Figure 9-6: You can adjust the image cropping if needed.

Chapter 10 details the Trim Image editing controls, but here's the short story:

- The box with the little white squares around it indicates the crop box. Anything outside the box isn't printed.

- Drag any of those squares to adjust the size of the crop box. You're limited to setting the box to the same proportions as your selected paper size.

- Drag inside the box to move it over a different part of the photo.

- Click the Orientation icons (Windows) or Trimming Frame buttons (Mac) if you want to change the layout of the cropping box (horizontal or vertical).

- Click OK to apply the new cropping and return to the Photo Print window.

If you don't want your photo to be cropped or enlarged, you need to exit the printing process and adjust a program preference. See the end of these steps for details.

6. **Add the shooting date/time (optional).**

   You can print the date and time that the photo was taken by choosing an option from the Shooting Date/Time drop-down list in the Photo Print window (refer to Figure 9-5). The program determines the date and time from data in the image file.

   If you choose to print the date and time, click the Properties button that appears underneath the Shooting Date/Time drop-down list to set the font, size, and placement of the type.

7. **Add a caption to the photo (optional).**

   To add more type to your photo, click the Insert Text button (Windows) or the Add or Modify Text to Print with This Photo button (Mac). Either way, you're taken to the Insert Text window, which offers most of the same text tools as the regular Insert Text window, which I cover at the end of Chapter 10. If you add text, click OK to close the Insert Text window and return to the Photo Print window when you're finished.

8. **Click the Print button.**

   Your photo file is shipped to the printer.

As I mentioned in Step 5, you can choose to turn off the automatic cropping that occurs by default. First, close the Photo Print window if it's open. Then take these steps:

- ✔ *Windows:* Choose Tools⇨Preferences to open the Preferences dialog box. Click the Printing tab and select the Do Not Allow Trimming of the Image option. Click OK to close the dialog box.

✔ *Mac:* Choose ImageBrowser⇨Preferences. Select Photo Print from the drop-down list at the top of the dialog box that appears. Then select Do Not Trim and click OK.

If you take this step, the Trim function inside the Photo Print dialog box becomes disabled, so you must do any cropping before you print.

Although it's fine for casual printing, Photo Print lacks some features that are typically found in most photo editors and even in the software that ships with most photo printers. You can't print multiple images on the same page, for example, or even multiple copies of the same photo. So if you own other software, you may find it more convenient than using the browser's print functions.

Whatever software you use, be sure to follow the resolution guidelines set out near the beginning of this chapter. And note that the Photo Print window doesn't warn you if your image doesn't contain enough pixels to produce a good print at the size you select. So before you begin printing, check that pixel count by displaying the Shooting Information panel in the main browser window. The Image Size listing, highlighted in Figure 9-7, shows you the pixel count.

Photo resolution

Figure 9-7: Make sure that the pixel count is adequate for the print size.

DPOF, PictBridge, and computerless printing

Your Rebel XS/1000D offers two features that enable you to print directly from your camera or memory card — without using the computer as middle-machine — assuming that your printer offers the required options.

The first of these features, *DPOF*, stands for Digital Print Order Format. With this option, accessed via the Print Order option on your camera's Playback menu, you select the pictures on your memory card that you want to print, and you specify how many copies you want of each image. Then, if your photo printer has a Secure Digital (SD) memory card slot and supports DPOF, you just pop the memory card into that slot. The printer reads your "print order" and outputs just the requested copies of your selected images. (You use the printer's own controls to set paper size, print orientation, and other print settings.)

A second direct-printing feature, *PictBridge,* works a little differently. If you have a PictBridge-enabled photo printer, you can connect the camera to the printer using the USB cable supplied with your camera. A PictBridge interface appears on the camera monitor, and

you use the camera controls to select the pictures you want to print. With PictBridge, you specify additional print options, such as page size and whether you want to print a border around the photo, from the camera.

Both DPOF and PictBridge are especially useful in scenarios where you need fast printing. For example, if you shoot pictures at a party and want to deliver prints to guests before they go home, DPOF offers a quicker option than firing up your computer, downloading pictures, and so on. And if you invest in one of the tiny portable photo printers on the market today, you can easily make prints away from your home or office — you can take both your portable printer and camera along to your regional sales meeting, for example.

For the record, I prefer DPOF to PictBridge because with PictBridge, you have to deal with cabling the printer and camera together. Also, the camera must be turned on for the whole printing process, wasting battery power. But if you're interested in exploring either printing feature, your camera manual provides complete details.

Preparing Pictures for E-Mail

How many times have you received an e-mail message that looks like the one in Figure 9-8? Some well-meaning friend or relative has sent you a digital photo that is so large that it's impossible to view the whole thing on your monitor.

The problem is that computer monitors can display only a limited number of pixels. The exact number depends on the monitor's resolution setting and the capabilities of the computer's video card, but suffice it to say that the average photo from one of today's digital cameras has a pixel count in excess of what the monitor can handle.

In general, a good rule is to limit a photo to no more than 450 pixels at its longest dimension. That ensures that people can view your entire picture without scrolling, as in Figure 9-9. This image measures 450 x 300 pixels.

This recommendation means that even if you shoot at your camera's lowest-resolution setting (1936 x 1288 pixels), you need to dump pixels from your images before sending them to the cyber post office. You can take care of that task and then send the resized image right from ZoomBrowser EX (Windows) or ImageBrowser (Mac).

As a first step, however, you need to check the file format of the photos you want to share; they must be in the JPEG format. If they are Raw (CR2) or TIFF images, the next section shows you how to create JPEG copies for online sharing. If the pictures are already JPEGs, skip ahead to the section "E-mailing photos from the browser."

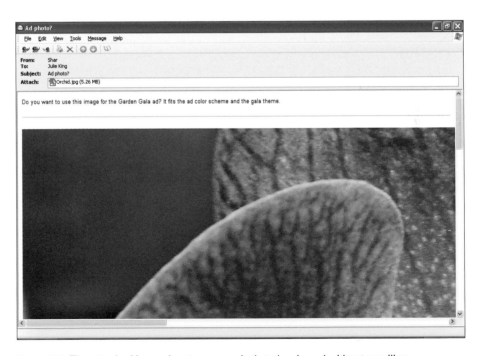

Figure 9-8: The attached image has too many pixels to be viewed without scrolling.

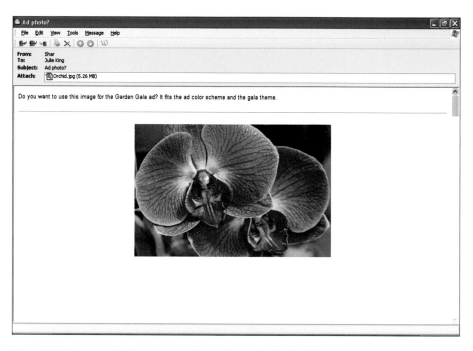

Figure 9-9: Keep e-mail pictures to no larger than 450 pixels wide or tall.

Creating Web-friendly copies of Raw and TIFF photos

In Chapter 8, I advise you to save Raw files in the TIFF format after you process them in a raw converter. TIFF is ideal because it is a *nondestructive format* — that is, it retains all your picture data, resulting in the highest image quality. But there's one problem with TIFF files: E-mail programs and Web browsers can't display them. If you want to share your converted raw files online, you need to create a copy of the file in the standard online format, JPEG.

Why not just save your converted raw files as JPEG images at the processing stage? Because JPEG *is* a destructive format, eliminating some image data as a tradeoff for producing smaller file sizes. So the best practice is to save your original raw conversions as TIFF files and then create JPEG copies for online use.

In ZoomBrowser EX (Windows) or ImageBrowser (Mac), you can use the Export command to create a JPEG copy and reduce the pixel count to a resolution suitable for onscreen display at the same time. Follow these steps:

1. **Select the image by clicking its thumbnail in the browser.**

2. **Choose File➪Export➪Export Still Images (Windows) or File➪Export Image (Mac).**

   Export is the geekspeak way of saying "save this file in a different format."

   In Windows, you next see a window that contains the file-saving options, as shown in Figure 9-10. On a Mac, you see the Write a Still Image box instead; click Edit and Save Image and then click the Next button to get to the file-saving options. They're arranged a little differently on the Mac than in Figure 9-10, but the basic controls are the same.

Figure 9-10: Use the Export command to create a JPEG copy of a TIFF photo.

3. **Set the image size.**

   To keep the original pixel count, deselect the Resize Images During Export check box (Windows) or Resize the Image box (Mac). If you want to resample the image (trim the pixel count), select the box, as shown in the figure. Then click the Long Side option (Windows) or Specify the

Length Dimension (Mac) and type a value in the neighboring box. The value you enter determines the number of pixels the image contains along its longest side. The program automatically sets the pixel count of the shortest side to retain the original image proportions.

For e-mail images, I suggest setting the long side of the image to 450 pixels or less. This ensures that the recipient can view the entire image without scrolling the e-mail window.

4. **Select the Change Image Type check box.**

5. **Select the JPEG format from the drop-down list under the check box.**

6. **Use the Quality slider to set the desired image quality.**

At the highest Quality setting, the program applies the least amount of *JPEG compression,* which is the process that reduces file sizes by dumping image data. For the best image quality, set the slider to either Highest or High. (Your file size is already pretty small because of the reduced pixel count.)

7. **Specify a filename.**

You have two options: If you deselect the Add a Prefix check box (Windows) or the Rename the File box (Mac), the program gives your JPEG copy the same name as the original — for example, IMG_7813.TIF becomes IMG_7813.JPG.

You also can assign a new filename. First, select the Add a Prefix check box (Windows) or the Rename the File box (Mac). Then type the text in the adjacent text box. Note that the program automatically adds the numbers 0001 to the end of whatever text you enter. For example, if you type **Web** in the box, the filename of your JPEG copy will be Web0001. jpg. If you stick with the text that the program enters in the box for you automatically — IMG_ — the filename will be IMG_0001.jpg.

8. **Choose the folder where you want to store the JPEG file.**

In Windows, you do this by using the Save to Folder option. Click Current Folder to put the copy in the same folder as the original. Click My Pictures (or Pictures, depending on the version of Windows you use) to put the copy in that folder instead, or click Browse to select another folder.

In Windows, you may need to scroll the window display to access the Save to Folder option, as shown in Figure 9-11.

On a Mac, the current folder destination appears at the bottom of the dialog box; click the Browse button to select a different storage bin.

9. **Click Finish to save the copy.**

After creating your Web-ready image, you can attach it to an e-mail message just as you do any file.

Figure 9-11: Scroll the window display to reveal the Save to Folder option.

E-mailing photos from the browser

You can resize and e-mail JPEG photos directly from ZoomBrowser EX (Windows) or ImageBrowser (Mac). Follow these steps:

1. **In the browser, select the images that you want to share.**

   Click the first image and then either Ctrl+click (Windows) or ⌘+click (Mac) additional images.

2. **Start the e-mail tool.**

   How you do it depends on your operating system:

   - *Windows:* Choose Internet⇨Send Images by Email.
   - *Mac:* Choose Internet⇨Create Image for Email.

   In Windows, you see the dialog box shown in Figure 9-12. The Mac version looks a little different, but it contains the same critical controls.

3. **Click the Using Custom Settings button.**

   Why not use the program's recommended settings? Because if you do, your e-mail image is sized to 640 x 480 pixels. On some computer screens, even that size is too large to be viewed without scrolling.

Figure 9-12: Select Using Custom Settings and click Custom Settings to specify the pixel count.

4. Click the Custom Settings button.

In Windows, you see the dialog box shown in Figure 9-13. The Mac version contains the same basic options, plus a couple additional options related to digital movies, which you can ignore. In both versions, the dialog box enables you to specify the width or height of your picture and then preview the resulting file size and onscreen display size.

5. Open the Image Size (Windows) or Still Image Size (Mac) dropdown list and click Custom Size.

Now a second dialog box opens, offering the options shown in Figure 9-14. Here, you can specify the exact pixel count you want the photo to have.

Figure 9-13: You can create a custom setting to apply to all your e-mail photos.

6. **Click the Long Side button and enter a size value in the adjacent box.**

   This value determines the maximum height of a vertically oriented picture or the maximum width of a horizontally oriented picture. Again, I recommend a value of 450 pixels, but you make the call.

   Whatever value you enter, the program will handle setting the value for the shortest side when it resizes the image.

Figure 9-14: Set the pixel count for the picture's longest side.

7. **Click OK to close the dialog box.**

   The image size you specified now appears as an option in the drop-down list. So the next time you send an image, you can skip Steps 5 and 6 and simply select that size from the list.

8. **Specify the picture quality by dragging the Quality slider.**

   This setting determines how much JPEG compression is applied. As Chapter 3 explains, *JPEG compression* reduces the size of a picture file by getting rid of some image data. The more compression you apply, the smaller the file and the lower the picture quality.

   After you drag the slider, click the Calculate button. The program does a quick calculation, and the Modified File Size value then shows you the file size that will result from the chosen Quality setting. And if you click the Preview button, you can view a preview of how the image will look at the selected setting.

   Because the new pixel count of your photo already results in a very small file, you can use a high Quality setting without worrying too much about download times. The exception is if you are sending a picture to someone who uses a dial-up connection, in which case I would bump the Quality slider down a notch. You also may want to reduce the Quality slightly if you are attaching multiple pictures to the same e-mail message so that the combined download time isn't excessive.

9. **Tell the program to automatically fire up your e-mail program after it resizes the photo.**

   - *Windows:* Select the Attach to Email option.
   - *Mac:* Select the Start Email Application After Closing option.

10. **Click OK to close the Custom Settings dialog box.**

    You return to the main e-mail utility window.

11. **Click the arrow labeled Confirm Current to review the image size settings.**

    If anything is amiss, click the Custom Settings button to adjust the settings.

12. **Click Attach to Email (Windows) or Finish (Mac).**

    The program creates your e-mail copy, fires up your e-mail program, and creates a new message window. The images are automatically attached to the message, so all you have to do is enter the recipient's e-mail address and any message you want to include. Then just send the message as you normally do.

The software does not save a copy of the resized e-mail image on your computer's hard drive. If you do want to create and save a small copy of the photo, follow Steps 1 through 8 and then proceed like so:

- *Windows:* Select the Save to Folder button and then click the Browse button to select the folder where you want to store the resized copy of the photo. In Step 12, click the Save to Folder button.

- *Mac:* Deselect the Attach to Email button in Step 9. Click OK to close the Custom Settings box and then click the Finish button. You can't specify a different folder location; the copy is automatically placed in the same folder as the original.

Windows or Mac, the program gives the resized image the same name as the original but tags the characters "_1" onto the end of the name so that you don't overwrite the original. Your e-mail program isn't started automatically, but you can take care of that step yourself, creating your message and attaching the picture files just as you do any file that you want to share by e-mail.

Online photo sharing: Read the fine print

If you want to share more than a couple of photos, consider posting your images at an online photo-album site instead of attaching them to e-mail messages. Photo-sharing sites such as Shutterfly, Kodak Gallery, and Picasa all enable you to create digital photo albums and then invite friends and family to view your pictures and order prints of their favorites.

At most sites, picture-sharing is free, but your albums and images are deleted if you don't order prints or make some other purchase from the site within a specified amount of time. Additionally, many free sites enable you to upload high-resolution files for printing but then don't let you retrieve those files from the site. (In other words, don't think of album sites as archival storage solutions.) And here's another little bit of fine print to investigate: The membership agreement at some sites states that you agree to let the site use your photos, for free, for any purpose that it sees fit.

Creating an In-Camera Slide Show

Many photo-editing and cataloging programs offer a tool for creating digital slide shows that can be viewed on a computer or, if copied to a DVD, on a DVD player. You can even add music, special transition effects, and the like to jazz up your presentations.

But if you just want a simple slide show — that is, one that just displays all the photos on the camera memory card one by one — you don't need a computer or any photo software. You can create and run the slide show right on your camera. And by connecting your camera to a television, as outlined in the next section, you can present your show to a whole roomful of people.

Follow these steps:

1. **Display the Playback menu and highlight Auto Play, as shown in Figure 9-15.**

2. **Press Set.**

   The images are displayed sequentially on the monitor, with each image appearing for about four seconds. After the last image is displayed, the show automatically begins again.

Figure 9-15: Choose Auto Play to set up automatic playback of all pictures on your memory card.

During auto playback, you can control the display as follows:

- ✔ **Pause playback.** Press the Set button. Press the button again to restart playback.

- ✔ **Change the information display style.** Press the DISP button. (See Chapter 4 for details about the available display styles.)

- ✔ **Exit Auto playback mode.** Press the Menu button.

Viewing Your Photos on a Television

Your camera is equipped with a *video-out port,* which is tucked under the little rubber cover on the left rear side of the camera, as shown in Figure 9-16. That feature means that you can output your pictures for display on a television screen.

Video out port   Video in port

Figure 9-16: You can connect your camera to a television, VCR, or DVD player.

To take advantage of this option, dig through your camera box until you find the video cable. One end of the cable has a yellow plug; the other end has a black plug. Then, making sure that the camera is off, plug the black end into the camera's video-out port, and plug the yellow end into the video-in port on your television, as shown on the right in Figure 9-16. You can also insert the yellow plug into the video-in port on a VCR or DVD player that's connected to your TV, as shown in the figure.

When the two devices are connected, turn the camera and TV (or VCR or DVD) on. At this point, you need to consult your TV/VCR/DVD manual to find out what channel to select for playback of signals from auxiliary input devices. After you sort out that issue, you can control playback using the same camera controls as you normally do to view pictures on your camera monitor. (See Chapter 4 for help.) You can also run a slide show by following the steps outlined in the preceding section.

Note that you may need to adjust one camera setting, Video System, which is found on Setup Menu 2. You get just two options here: NTSC and PAL. Select the video mode that's used by your part of the world. (In the United States, Canada, and Mexico, NTSC is the standard).

Part IV
The Part of Tens

In this part . . .

*I*n time-honored *For Dummies* tradition, this part of the book contains additional tidbits of information presented in the always popular "Top Ten" list format.

Chapter 10 shows you how to do some minor picture touchups, such as cropping and adjusting exposure, by using the free software that shipped with your camera. Following that, Chapter 11 introduces you to ten camera functions that I consider specialty tools — bonus options that, while not at the top of the list of the features I suggest you study, are nonetheless interesting to explore when you have a free moment or two.

Ten Fast Photo-Editing Tricks

*E*very photographer produces a clunker image now and then. When it happens to you, don't be too quick to reach for the Erase button on your camera. Many common problems are surprisingly easy to fix using the tools found in most photo editing programs.

In fact, you can perform many common retouching tasks using one of the free programs provided with your camera. Called ZoomBrowser EX in Windows and ImageBrowser on the Mac, this software offers tools for removing red-eye, adjusting exposure, tweaking colors, sharpening focus, and more.

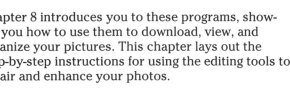

Chapter 8 introduces you to these programs, showing you how to use them to download, view, and organize your pictures. This chapter lays out the step-by-step instructions for using the editing tools to repair and enhance your photos.

A few other notes before you start:

   ✔ If you shot your pictures using the Raw file format, you must process them using the raw-conversion instructions laid out in Chapter 8 before you can edit them.

   ✔ Although the tools provided in the free software are pretty good, they don't allow selective editing. That is, you can't apply them just to the part of your photo that needs help. For that kind of retouching work, you need a more sophisticated photo editor. Chapter 8 offers some recommendations.

✓ Most figures in this chapter feature the Windows versions of the Canon software. Although the Mac version looks different, the retouching steps are the same unless I state otherwise.

✓ For simplicity's sake, I refer to ZoomBrowser EX and ImageBrowser generically in the instructions here as just "the browser."

✓ Finally, Canon occasionally posts updates to its software on its Web site (www.canon.com). So if you've owned your camera for a while, check the Web site to make sure that you're using the most current versions of the available programs. This book features version 6.1.1 of ZoomBrowser EX and ImageBrowser.

Removing Red-Eye

From my experience, red-eye is not a major problem with the Rebel XS/1000D. But if you spot red-eye in your flash pictures, take these steps to fix the problem:

1. **In the main browser window, double-click the image thumbnail.**

   Again, Chapter 8 shows you how to get your images into the browser and keep track of your picture files.

   After you double-click a thumbnail, the picture opens in its own Viewer window. Figure 10-1 offers a look at how the window appears in Windows; Figure 10-2 shows the Mac version.

2. **Open the Edit drop-down list, as shown in Figures 10-1 and 10-2.**

3. **Choose Red Eye Correction from the Edit list.**

   Your photo appears in the Red Eye Correction retouching window. Figure 10-3 shows the Windows version; Figure 10-4, the Mac version.

4. **Zoom in on your photo so that you can get a good view of the eyes.**

   • *Windows:* Zoom and scroll the display using the controls labeled in Figure 10-3, which work the same way as they do when you view your photo in the initial Viewer window. Chapter 8 details all the controls, but here's a quick reminder: The fastest way to zoom in and out is to drag the Zoom slider; to scroll the display, just drag in the Navigator window, which appears whenever the entire image isn't visible at the current preview size. Or click the Hand tool, labeled in Figure 10-3, and drag in the preview itself.

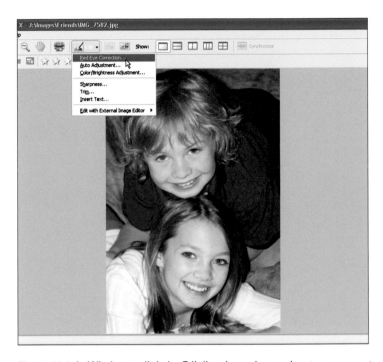

Figure 10-1: In Windows, click the Edit list above the preview to access retouching tools.

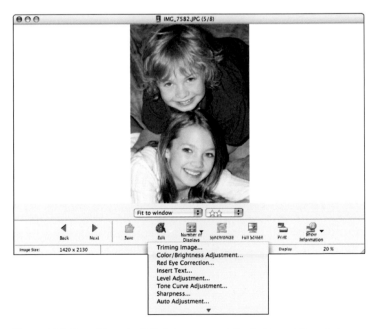

Figure 10-2: On a Mac, the Edit list appears at the bottom of the window.

   ● *Mac:* Zoom by choosing a magnification level from the Display Size drop-down list, labeled in Figure 10-4, or by clicking the Zoom In and Zoom Out buttons. The Mac version of the retouching window does not sport a Navigator window — instead, you use the scroll bars to scroll the display.

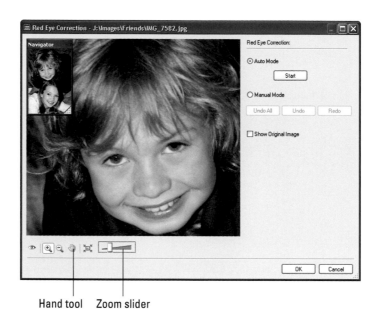

Hand tool   Zoom slider

Figure 10-3: Zoom in for a close look at the eyes.

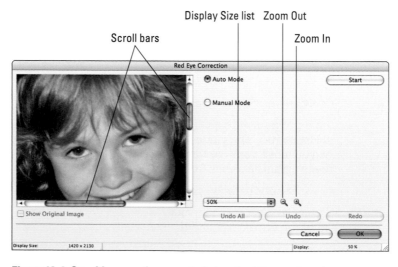

Figure 10-4: On a Mac, use these controls to adjust the preview size.

5. Click the Manual Mode option.

In Auto mode, the red-eye correction tool can sometimes trip up, "correcting" red pixels that aren't actually in the eye, so stick with Manual mode, which enables you to specify exactly where you want the program to do its retouching work.

6. In Windows, select the Red Eye tool, labeled in Figure 10-5.

The tool is ready to go if it appears highlighted, as in the figure. If not, click the tool icon. Mac users can ignore this step.

Red Eye tool

Figure 10-5: The little green circle indicates the eye area that will be replaced.

7. Position your mouse cursor over one of the red eyes.

If the program detects fixable red pixels, a green circle appears, as shown in Figure 10-5. The circle indicates the area that the tool will try to correct. As you move your cursor around the eye, the circle may change size as the program searches for pixels that meet its red-eye criteria.

8. Click to initiate the repair.

If you like what you see, move on to the next eye. Or click Undo to get rid of the correction and then try again.

9. **After you finish all eye repairs, click OK.**

The Red Eye Correction window closes, and your repaired photo appears in the Viewer window.

10. **Save your picture in the TIFF file format.**

The last section of this chapter provides details.

Like most red-eye removal tools, the Canon version can do a good job in the right circumstances. But if the eyes are very bright, the tool may not be able to make the repair. In addition, no red-eye remover works on animal eyes; red-eye tools detect and replace only red-eye pixels, and animal eyes typically turn yellow, white, or green in response to a flash. The best solution is to simply paint in the correct eye colors. For that type of retouching, you need a more capable photo-editing program; see Chapter 8 for a look at some options.

Cropping Your Photo

To *crop* a photo simply means to trim away some of its perimeter. Removing excess background can often improve an image, as illustrated by my original frog scene, shown on the left in Figure 10-6, and its cropped cousin, shown on the right. In the original image, there's just too much going on — the eye has a hard time figuring out what's important. Eliminating all but a little of the surrounding foliage returned emphasis to the subject and created a stronger composition.

You may also want to crop an image so that it fits a specific frame size. As Chapter 8 explains, the original images from your camera fit perfectly in 4-x-6-inch frames, but if you want a 5 x 7, 8 x 10, or other standard print size, you need to crop your image to those new proportions. (If you don't, the photo printer software or retail print lab will crop for you, and the result may not be the composition that you'd choose.)

Follow these steps to get the job done:

1. **In the main browser window, double-click the image thumbnail.**

Your photo appears all by its lonesome in a new Viewer window.

2. **Choose Trim (Windows) or Trimming Image (Mac) from the Edit drop-down list.**

Refer to Figures 10-1 and 10-2, in the preceding section, if you need help finding the list.

Your image appears in the Trim Image retouching window, and a dotted outline, called a *crop box,* appears around your photo, as shown in Figure 10-7.

Figure 10-6: Cropping creates a better composition, eliminating background clutter.

3. **Click the Advanced Options button to display all the crop-size controls.**

   Figure 10-7 labels the button and shows the controls that appear when you click it. (On a Mac, the control panel pops out of the side of the dialog box instead of appearing within it.)

4. **Choose an option from the Aspect Ratio drop-down list.**

   Your selection determines the proportions of the cropped image. You can go in three directions:

   - *Manual:* This option enables you to crop the image to any proportions. I chose this setting for my frog photo.

   - *Maintain Original:* The program restricts you to cropping to the same proportions as your original, which is 3:2.

   - *Specific Aspect Ratios:* You also can select from six specific aspect ratios: 2:3, 3:2, 3:4, 4:3, 9:16, and 16:9. The first number in the pair indicates the width, and the second indicates the height.

5. **In Windows, make sure that the Trim button is selected (refer to Figure 10-7).**

   It should already be selected unless you used the adjacent controls to zoom or scroll the preview. Just click the button to select it if needed. Mac users can skip this step.

Handle

Click to display advanced options

Trim button

Figure 10-7: You can specify a crop size via the Advanced Options controls.

6. Adjust the size and position of the crop box as needed.

Use these techniques:

- *Move the crop box.* Drag inside the box.

- *Resize the crop box.* Drag any of the *handles* — those little squares around the perimeter of the crop box. I labeled one of the handles in Figure 10-7.

As you drag the handles, the W and H boxes in the Size of Trimming Area portion of the dialog box reflect the new dimensions of the crop box, with the measurement shown in pixels. Keep in mind that pixel count is critical to print quality. Chapters 3 and 9 provide details, but the short story is that you need roughly 200 to 300 pixels per linear inch of your print. So if you have a finished print size in mind, monitor the W and H values as you adjust the crop box size to make sure that you aren't clipping away too many pixels.

● *Set a specific crop size.* You also can enter specific pixel dimensions in the W and H boxes. The crop box automatically adjusts to the dimensions you enter.

Using the third option is the easiest way to crop your photo to a size that doesn't mesh with any of the specific aspect ratio choices. Say that you want to produce a 5-x-7-inch print from your cropped photo, and you want an image resolution of 300 pixels per inch. Just multiply the print dimensions by the desired resolution and then enter those values into the W and H boxes. For the 5 x 7 at 300 ppi example, the W and H values are 1500 and 2100, respectively. If the resulting crop boundary encompasses too much or too little of your photo, just keep adjusting the W and H values, making sure to always keep the two at the same proportions you originally entered.

7. **Turn on the Use the Rule of Thirds gridlines (optional).**

   A classic composition rule is to imagine that your image is divided into thirds vertically and horizontally and then position the subject at a spot where two dividing lines intersect. To help you visualize that concept, the Trim box can display those horizontal and vertical grid lines as shown in Figure 10-8. Just click the Use the Rule of Thirds check box to toggle the grid on and off.

Display grid

Figure 10-8: The Rule of Thirds gridlines offer a compositional guide.

8. **When you're happy with the crop box, click the Trim Image button.**

   The cropped photo appears in the preview. If you don't like the results, click the Undo button and try again.

9. **Click OK to close the retouching window.**

10. **Choose File⇨Save As to save your cropped image.**

   The last section of this chapter has details.

Adjusting Color Saturation

Saturation refers to the intensity and purity of color. A fully saturated color contains no black, white, or gray. In other words, saturated colors are deep, rich, and bold.

On occasion, an image can benefit from a little saturation bump. Figure 10-9 offers an example. I was drawn to this scene by the mix of colors, and the original photo, shown on the left, seemed a little lackluster in that regard. So I increased the saturation ever so slightly to produce the image shown on the right.

Original Increased saturation

Figure 10-9: I slightly increased saturation to make the colors pop a little more.

Be careful about increasing saturation too much, however. Doing so actually can destroy picture detail as areas that previously contained a range of saturation levels all shift to the fully saturated state.

Whichever direction you want to go, take these steps to adjust saturation:

1. **In the main browser window, double-click the image thumbnail.**

   Your photo opens inside its own Viewer window.

2. **Click the Edit drop-down list.**

   The list appears above the image preview in Windows; it appears below the preview on a Mac.

3. **Choose Color/Brightness Adjustment from the list.**

Your image appears in the Color/Brightness Adjustment retouching window. The window contents vary depending whether you're using the Windows or Mac version of the program; Figures 10-10 and 10-11 show you both versions.

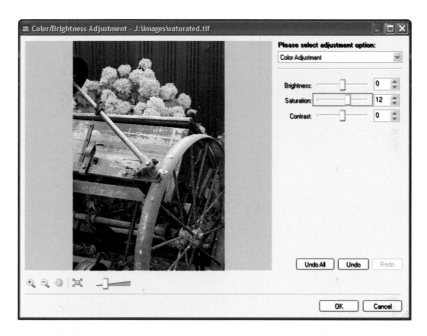

Figure 10-10: Desaturating colors slightly can sometimes reveal hidden details

Figure 10-11: In Windows, select Color Adjustment from the top drop-down list.

4. **Set the Retouching mode to Color Adjustment.**

   • *Windows:* Select Color Adjustment from the drop-down list at the top of the window (refer to Figure 10-10). After you do so, the window offers three sliders: Brightness, Saturation, and Contrast.

   • *Mac:* Click the Color Adjustment button. The Mac version of the tool offers just a Saturation and Brightness slider.

One note about the Brightness and Contrast controls: These tools aren't the best options for adjusting exposure and contrast. You can get much better results by using the Level Adjustment and Tone Curve Adjustment tools, both explained later in this chapter.

5. **Drag the Saturation slider to adjust the image as desired.**

6. **Click OK to apply the change and close the retouching window.**

7. **Save the edited image, following the steps provided at the end of this chapter.**

Tweaking Color Balance

Chapter 6 explains how to use your camera's white balance and Picture Style controls to manipulate the colors in your pictures. If you can't get the results you want by using those features, you may be able to do the job using the RGB Adjustment filter offered by the Canon browser. In Figure 10-12, for example, I used the filter to tone down the amount of blue in the image and bring out the warm yellow tones of the building instead.

Follow these steps to use the filter:

1. **Open the image in its own Viewer window.**

   You do this by double-clicking the image thumbnail in the main browser window.

2. **Choose Color/Brightness Adjustment from the Edit drop-down list.**

   Look for the list above the image preview if you're a Windows user; on a Mac, the list is below the preview. After you choose the command, your photo appears in a retouching window. Figure 10-13 shows you both the Windows and Mac versions of the window.

3. **Select RGB Adjustment as the edit mode.**

   In Windows, select that option from the drop-down list at the top of the window, as shown in the top image in Figure 10-13. On a Mac, just click the RGB Adjustment button, as shown in the lower image. Either way, you gain access to three sliders: Red, Green, and Blue.

4. **Drag the sliders to adjust image colors.**

Original   Colors Adjusted

Figure 10-12: I warmed colors to emphasize the buildings rather than the sky.

Figure 10-13: Select RGB Adjustment to tweak color balance.

The filter is based on three color pairs: red-cyan; green-magenta; and blue-yellow. (Those six colors happen to be the primary and secondary colors of the RGB color world, which is the one in which all digital images reside.) As you move the sliders, you affect both the primary color and its secondary opposite, as follows:

- *Red slider:* As you drag the slider to the right, you increase red and decrease cyan. Drag the slider to the left to diminish reds and embolden cyans.

- *Green slider:* Drag this slider to the right to add green and reduce magenta. Drag to the left to produce the opposite result.

- *Blue slider:* Dragging this slider to the right increases the amount of blue and reduces the amount of yellow. Go the other direction to increase yellow and tone down blues.

In imaging lingo, tools of this type are known as *color balancing* filters because they shift the balance between the two opposite colors.

I used the slider settings shown in the figure for my photo.

5. **Click OK to apply the change and close the retouching window.**

6. **Save your work in the TIFF format as explained in the last section of this chapter.**

Adjusting Exposure

Getting exposure just right is one of the trickiest aspects of photography. Fortunately, the Canon software gives you several tools for tweaking exposure. The next sections introduce the two most capable: the Level Adjustment filter and the Tone Curve Adjustment filter.

Stay away from the exposure options that appear when you open the Color Adjustment filter (shown in Figures 10-10 and 10-11, however. In Windows, the filter offers a Brightness and Contrast slider; on a Mac, you get just the Brightness slider. The problem is that both sliders affect all pixels in your image; you can't brighten just the shadows, for example, without also brightening the midtones (areas of medium brightness) and highlights. For that reason, these sliders rarely produce good results.

Three-point exposure control with the Level Adjustment filter

With this filter, you can adjust shadows, midtones, and highlights individually. Figure 10-14 shows the filter as it appears in Windows; the Mac version contains the same options in a slightly different layout.

Figure 10-14: The Level Adjustment tool isn't nearly as difficult to use as it appears.

Now, I know what you're thinking: "Wow, that looks *way* too complicated for me." Trust me, though, that this filter is actually pretty easy to use. First, ignore everything but the graph in the middle of the box, known as a *histogram,* and the three sliders underneath, labeled Shadows, Midtones, and Highlights in Figure 10-15. See? Easier already.

Shadows   Midtones   Highlights

Figure 10-15: All you need to worry about are these three sliders.

The histogram works just like the Brightness histogram that you can display while reviewing your images on your camera monitor, a topic that I discuss in Chapter 4. To recap, the horizontal axis of the graph represents the possible brightness values in an image, ranging from black on the left side to white on the right. The vertical axis shows you how many pixels fall at a particular brightness value. So if you have a tall spike, you have lots of pixels at that brightness value.

To adjust exposure, you just drag the three sliders underneath the histogram, depending on whether you want to shift shadows, midtones, or highlights. Take these steps to try it out:

1. **In the main browser window, double-click the image thumbnail to open it in a new Viewer window.**

2. **Open the Level Adjustment retouching window.**

   - *In Windows:* Choose Color/Brightness Adjustment from the Edit drop-down list, found above the image preview. Then select Level Adjustment from the drop-down list at the top of the retouching window, as shown in Figure 10-14.

   - *On a Mac:* Choose Level Adjustment from the Edit drop-down list, which appears underneath the image preview.

3. **Set the Channel option to RGB.**

   On a Mac, the option is unlabeled; it's the pop-up list above the histogram.

4. **Drag the sliders underneath the histogram to adjust exposure.**

   - *To darken shadows:* Drag the Shadows slider to the right.

   - *To adjust midtones:* Drag the middle slider to the right to darken midtones; drag it to the left to brighten them.

   - *To brighten highlights:* Drag the Highlights slider to the left.

   As you drag the Shadows or Highlights slider, the Midtones slider moves in tandem. So you may need to readjust that slider after you set the other two.

You can compare your original image with the adjusted one by toggling the dialog box preview on and off. In Windows, click the Show Original Image box to turn off the preview; click again to return to the preview. On a Mac, click the Preview box instead.

I dragged the sliders to the positions shown in Figure 10-16 to produce the results you see in the preview.

5. **Click OK to accept the changes and close the dialog box.**

6. **Save your image in the TIFF file format.**

   See the last section of this chapter to find out how.

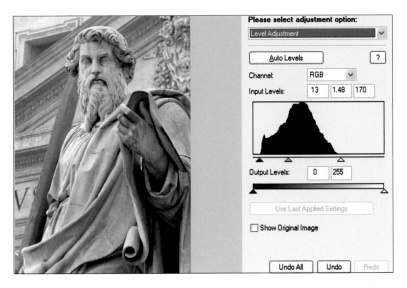

Figure 10-16: I brightened highlights and midtones but darkened shadows slightly.

Gaining more control with the Tone Curve Adjustment filter

With the Level Adjustment filter, you get three points of exposure-correction control — highlights, shadows, and midtones. The Tone Curve Adjustment filter takes things a step further, enabling you to manipulate specific values along the entire brightness spectrum.

Figure 10-17 offers a look at the Windows version of the Tone Curve Adjustment retouching window. The Mac version is slightly different in appearance, but it contains the same main components.

Again, the controls inside the window seem mighty perplexing at first. But here's all you need to know to take advantage of the filter:

- See that line that runs diagonally through the white grid? That's just another representation of the possible brightness values in a digital image. Black falls at the lower end of the line; white, at the top. (The shaded bars that run alongside the left and lower edges of the grid remind you of that orientation.) Medium brightness falls dead center on the line.

- To adjust exposure, click and drag at the spot on the line that corresponds to the brightness value you want to change. Drag up to brighten the image; drag down to darken it. For example, in Figure 10-18, I dragged the center of the line up. The resulting curve — *tone curve,* in imaging parlance — produced the exposure change shown in the preview.

Figure 10-17: With the Tone Curve Adjustment filter, you get even greater exposure control.

🖛 After a drag, a control point appears at the spot on the line you dragged to anchor that part of the tone curve, as shown in Figure 10-18.

🖛 You can bend the tone curve as much as you want, in any direction you want. Just keep clicking and dragging to add control points. But be careful — extreme curves or curves with tons of points can produce really ugly results and odd breaks in color and brightness. I usually aim for a gentle curve that has no more than six points, including the ones that are provided automatically at the black and white ends of the curve.

🖛 To increase contrast, create an s-shaped curve; to decrease contrast, create a reverse-s shape. I used the gentle s-shaped curve, shown in Figure 10-19, to produce the finished mushroom photo that you see in the preview. The curve resulted in a slight bump in exposure to medium and medium bright pixels and a slight darkening of medium dark and dark pixels. The white and black areas of the image remain unchanged.

The best way to understand this filter is to try it for yourself. So take these steps:

1. **Open the image in its own Viewer window.**

   You know the drill: Just double-click the thumbnail in the main browser window. (See Chapter 8 if you need help.)

Tone curve

Control point

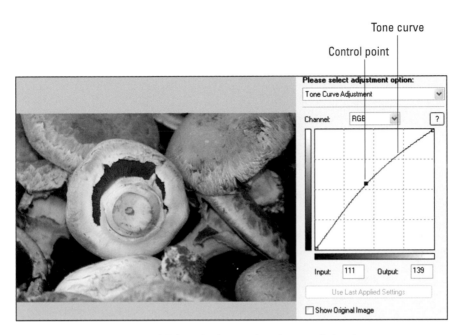

Figure 10-18: Drag upward to brighten the image; drag down to darken it.

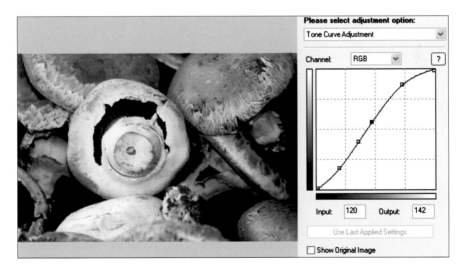

Figure 10-19: An s-shaped curve boosts contrast.

2. **Open the Tone Curve Adjustment retouching window.**

   - *Windows:* Click the Edit drop-down list at the top of the browser window and choose Adjust Color/Brightness. When the retouching window appears, select Tone Curve Adjustment from the drop-down list at the top.

   - *Mac:* Click the Edit drop-down list underneath the image preview and choose Tone Curve Adjustment.

3. **Set the Channel option to RGB.**

   On a Mac, the option is the unlabeled pop-up list just above the grid.

4. **Bend the tone curve by adding and dragging control points.**

   See the preceding list for details on this step. If you need to delete a point, click it to select it and then press Delete. (The selected control point appears black.)

   If your image doesn't appear to change in the preview, check the status of the box labeled Show Original Image. Deselect the box to turn on the dialog box preview.

5. **Click OK to apply the adjustment and close the retouching window.**

6. **Save your image in the TIFF file format, following the steps at the end of this chapter.**

Sharpening Focus (Sort Of)

Have you ever seen one of those spy-movie thrillers where the good guys capture a photo of the villain's face — only the picture is so blurry that it could just as easily be a picture of pudding? The heroes ask the photo-lab experts to "enhance" the picture, and within seconds, it's transformed into an image so clear you can make out individual hairs in the villain's mustache.

It is with heavy heart that I tell you that this kind of image rescue is pure Hollywood fantasy. You simply can't take a blurry image and turn it into a sharply focused photo, even with the most sophisticated photo software on the market. There is, however, a digital process called *sharpening* that can *slightly* enhance the apparent focus of pictures that are *slightly* blurry, as illustrated by the before and after images in Figure 10-20. Notice that I say "apparent" focus: Sharpening doesn't really adjust focus but instead creates the *illusion* of sharper focus by increasing contrast in a special way.

Original

Sharpened

Figure 10-20: A slightly blurry image (left) can benefit from a sharpening filter (right).

Here's how it works: Wherever pixels of different colors come together, the sharpening process boosts contrast along the border between them. The light side of the border gets lighter; the dark side gets darker. Photography experts refer to those light and dark strips as *sharpening halos.* You can get a close-up look at the halos in the right, sharpened example in Figure 10-21, which shows a tiny portion of the pencil image from Figure 10-20. Notice that in the sharpened example, the yellow side of the boundary between the pencils received a light halo, and the blue side received a dark halo.

A little sharpening can go a long way toward improving a slightly soft image. But too much sharpening does more damage than good. The halos become so strong that they're clearly visible, and the image takes on a sandpaper-like texture. And again, no amount of sharpening can repair a truly out-of-focus image, so all you do when you crank up sharpening is make matters worse.

Both the Windows and Mac versions of the Canon software offer a simple Sharpening tool, shown in its Mac incarnation in Figure 10-22. To use this tool, just follow the usual steps: Double-click the image thumbnail to open it in its own Viewer window and then choose Sharpness from the Edit drop-down list. (See Figures 10-1 and 10-2 if you have trouble finding the list.) Drag the slider to the right to add sharpening and then click OK to finish the job.

Original   Sharpened

Figure 10-21: Sharpening adds light and dark halos along color boundaries.

Figure 10-22: The Mac version of the browser offers only a simple sharpening slider.

Windows users, however, have the option of using a more flexible sharpening tool, called an Unsharp Mask filter. To switch to this filter, just click the Unsharp Mask tab at the top of the Sharpness retouching window, as shown in Figure 10-23

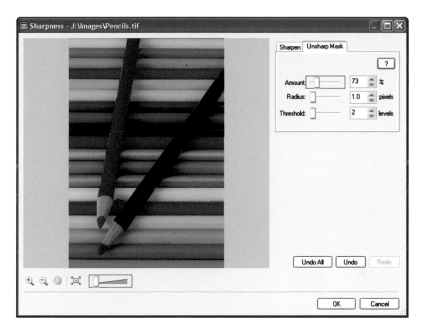

Figure 10-23: The Unsharp Mask filter provides three levels of sharpening control.

The three sliders provided for the Unsharp Mask filter enable you to control where and how the sharpening halos are applied, as follows:

- **Amount:** This slider adjusts the intensity of the sharpening halos.

- **Radius:** This slider adjusts the width of the halos. Don't go too high, or else the sharpening halos will become very noticeable.

- **Threshold:** With this slider, you can limit the sharpening effect just to high-contrast color boundaries. Try raising the value a few notches up from 0 when sharpening portraits to sharpen the image without adding unwanted texture to the skin. I also used this technique to keep the surface of the pencils smooth in my photo while sharpening the edges between them.

Whichever sharpening filter you use, don't forget to save the altered image in the TIFF file format. The last section of this chapter explains this critical part of the retouching process.

Shifting to AutoPilot

You may have noticed as you explored the Edit drop-down list an option called Auto Adjustment. If you select this option, the program opens your image in a retouching window, as usual. Figure 10-24 shows the Windows flavor of the window; the Mac version is virtually identical. After the window opens, you simply click the Auto Adjust Image button and sit back and wait. The program analyzes your image and then makes whatever changes it deems necessary. You can compare the "before" and "after" views of your photo by clicking the Show Original Image box on and off.

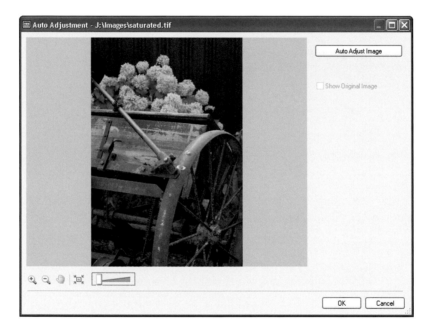

Figure 10-24: Click Auto Adjust Image to see what changes the program thinks are needed.

As a rule, I don't recommend this type of automatic image correction tool because it so often doesn't produce results as good as what you can do by using the manual filter controls. That said, if you aren't working on important images or you just don't have the time or interest in using the more sophisticated tools, go ahead and give that Auto Adjust Image button a click. If you don't like what you see, click the Cancel button and do the job yourself, using the tricks laid out elsewhere in this chapter.

Adding Text

You know that saying, "A picture is worth a thousand words." Well, you can increase that count by adding text to your photo. You can do so as follows:

1. **Open your photo in its own Viewer window by double-clicking the image thumbnail in the main browser window.**

2. **Choose Insert Text from the Edit drop-down list.**

   Look for the list at the top of the window if you use the Windows version of the program and at the bottom if you're a Mac user. Either way, you see your photo in the Insert Text retouching window. Figure 10-25 gives you a look at the Windows version of the window. (Again, the Mac version is virtually identical except for sporting different controls for zooming and scrolling the display. See the first section of this chapter for help with those controls.)

Figure 10-25: You can add captions and other text information.

3. **Click in the preview at the spot you want to add the text.**

   (In Windows, be sure that the Text tool, located under the preview, next to the Zoom tools, is selected before you click.) After you click, a text box appears, as shown in the figure. At any time, you can resize the box as needed by dragging the little boxes that appear around its perimeter. To move the box (and any text inside), just drag inside the box.

4. **Type your text.**

   The text appears both in the image preview and in the Text area on the right side of the window.

   If you want to add the date and time you shot the picture, just click the Import Shooting Date/Time button, and the program finds the data in the image file and adds it to the text box for you. Similarly, if you added comment text when organizing your pictures in the main browser, clicking the Import Comment button enters that text for you. (You can add comments via the Comment pane that appears when you browse images in Preview display mode. Chapter 8 explains the basics of browsing images.)

5. **Use the controls at the top of the dialog box to set the type characteristics.**

   You can specify a font (type design), size, and color and add bold, underline, or italic formatting.

   The Antialias option smoothes the jagged edges that can occur when letters contain diagonal or curved lines. As a rule, keeping this option enabled is a good idea.

6. **When you finish creating your text, click OK.**

   The retouching window closes.

7. **Save your edited file as outlined in the next section.**

Saving Your Edited Files

Whatever retouching task you do, the last step is to save your edited picture file. After you click OK to close the retouching window and return to the Viewer window, choose the Save As command from the File menu. You then see the standard Windows or Mac file-saving dialog box that appears when you save any type of file.

You need to take two critical steps inside the dialog box:

- ✔ **Select TIFF as the file type.** TIFF is an image file format that produces the best picture quality for saved images.

  Do *not* use JPEG as the file type. Every time you edit and save a picture in the JPEG format, you damage the picture quality slightly because of the *lossy compression* that is applied in that format. Chapter 3 has details on this issue. Should you need a JPEG version of your edited photo for online use, save it first as a TIFF file and then follow the steps provided in Chapter 9 to create a Web-sized copy of the picture in the JPEG format.

- ✔ **Type a name for the picture in the File Name box (Windows) or the Save As box (Mac).** The filename of the original image appears automatically in the box. You don't have to change the filename — you won't overwrite the original file when you save because you aren't saving it in the JPEG format (and you can't save in the Raw format). But I like to add a tag to the filename that indicates the status of the image — for example, IMG_7582 retouched, or PencilsSharpened, or the like.

After taking care of those two pieces of business, specify where you want to store the file as you usually do. Then click the Save button to save the file and close the dialog box.

Ten Special-Purpose Features to Explore on a Rainy Day

Consider this chapter the literary equivalent of the end of one of those late-night infomercial offers — the part where the host exclaims, "But wait! There's more!"

The ten features covered in these pages fit the category of "interesting bonus." They aren't the sort of features that drive people to choose one camera over another, and they may come in handy only for certain users, on certain occasions. Still, they're included at no extra charge with your camera, so check 'em out when you have a few spare moments. Who knows; you may discover that one of these bonus features is actually a hidden gem that provides just the solution you need for one of your photography problems.

Many of the features I discuss here involve Custom Functions, a group of 12 advanced options that you access via Setup Menu 3. If you're not familiar with how to navigate the Custom Functions, the next section spells things out.

Changing the Function of the Set Button

Normally, the Set button serves three functions: When a menu is displayed, you press the button to lock in menu selections. When a menu is not displayed, you can press the button to turn the monitor on and off instead of using the DISP button. And if you enable Live View shooting, a feature introduced in Chapter 4, you press Set to switch from normal shooting to Live View mode.

To make the Set button more helpful when Live View is *not* enabled, you can change the function of the button so that pressing it displays the Quality options or the Flash Exposure Compensation options. Doing so enables you to access those settings more quickly than by using the menus.

You also can assign the Set button the same function as the Menu button, in which case you can use either button to display the menus. You can also disable the button entirely so that it works only when you're choosing options from menus. I don't think either of these options is terribly useful, but you be the judge.

To customize the button, take these steps:

1. **Set your camera to one of the advanced exposure modes (P, Tv, Av, M, or A-DEP).**

   You can't adjust the performance of the Set button in the fully automatic exposure modes. Nor does the button perform whatever alternative function you may assign when the camera is set to those modes.

2. **Display Setup Menu 3 and highlight Custom Functions, as shown on the left in Figure 11-1.**

   This menu item enables you to customize 12 aspects of the camera's performance.

3. **Press Set.**

   The screen should look something like the one on the right in Figure 11-1, at least along the bottom of the screen. What appears in the rest of the screen depends on which Custom Function is selected.

   The Custom Functions are grouped into four categories. The category number and name appear in the top-left corner of the screen; the number of the selected function appears in the top-right corner and is marked with a bar at the bottom of the screen. And the blue text indicates the current setting of the selected Custom Function. You also can see the number of the option that's selected at the bottom of the screen, underneath the Custom Function number. A zero represents the default setting.

Custom Function number

Custom Function category

Figure 11-1: The Custom Function menu item provides access to 12 customization options.

4. If needed, press the right or left cross key to display Custom Function 10.

Now you should see the options shown on the right in Figure 11-1.

5. Press the Set button.

Now the list of options for Custom Function 10 becomes accessible, and a yellow high-light box appears around one of the options, as shown in Figure 11-2. Again, the option that appears in blue is the selected setting; 0 represents the default setting.

Figure 11-2: You can use the Set button to access Flash Exposure Compensation settings.

6. Press the up or down cross keys to highlight your choice.

I highlighted the Flash Exposure Compensation option in Figure 11-2.

7. Press the Set button.

Now whenever you shoot in the advanced exposure modes and press Set while no menus are displayed, the button takes on the function you just assigned to it. To go back to the default setting, repeat these steps and select option 0 in Step 6. The button then turns the monitor on and off when no menu is displayed, just like the DISP button.

Again, though, your custom Set button is available only when Live View is disabled (through Setup Menu 2) and only when you set the Mode dial to one of the advanced exposure modes (P, Tv, Av, M, or A-DEP). In Live View mode, the button always toggles the Live View preview on and off.

Customizing Exposure and Focus Lock Options

By default, pressing your shutter button halfway establishes and locks focus when you use autofocusing. When you shoot in the advanced autoexposure modes, you also can lock in the exposure settings the camera selects by pressing and holding the AE (autoexposure) Lock button, labeled in Figure 11-3.

AE Lock button

Figure 11-3: By default, pressing the AE Lock button locks the autoexposure setting.

You can customize the locking behaviors of the two buttons via Custom Function 9. Here's how:

1. **Set the Mode dial to an advanced exposure setting.**

   As with all Custom Functions, you can take advantage of this option only in the P, Tv, Av, M, or A-DEP exposure mode. Additionally, the locking setup you specify applies only to those modes.

2. **Display Setup Menu 3, highlight Custom Functions, and press Set.**

3. **Select Custom Function 9.**

   Press the right or left cross key to scroll through the Custom Functions.

4. **Press Set to activate the list of settings, as shown in Figure 11-4.**

   A highlight box appears, as shown in the figure. The option that appears in blue text is the current setting; option number 0 represents the default setting.

5. **Press the up and down cross keys to highlight the option you want to use.**

Figure 11-4: Adjust autoexposure/autofocus lock behavior via Custom Function 10.

You have the following four choices. (The first part of the setting name indicates what happens with a half-press of the shutter button; the second part indicates the function of the AE Lock button.)

- *AF/AE Lock:* This is the default setting. Pressing the shutter button halfway establishes and locks autofocus; pressing the AE Lock button locks autoexposure.

- *AE Lock/AF:* With this option, pressing the shutter button halfway locks autoexposure instead of focus. To initiate autofocusing, you instead press the AE Lock button. In other words, this mode is the exact opposite of the default setup.

- *AF/AF Lock, no AE Lock:* This mode is designed to prevent focusing mishaps when you use AI Servo autofocusing, explained in Chapter 6. Here's the deal: In the AI Servo mode, the autofocus motor continually adjusts focus from the time you press the shutter button halfway until the time you actually take the image. This feature helps you keep moving objects sharply focused. But if something moves in front of your subject, the camera may mistakenly focus on that object, which may leave your subject blurry.

  To cope with that possibility, this locking option enables you to initiate autofocusing as usual, by pressing the shutter button halfway. But at any time before you take the picture, you can press the AE Lock button to temporarily stop the autofocusing motor from adjusting focus if an intruder moves into the frame. When you release the button, the autofocusing mechanism starts up again.

  If you choose this option, autoexposure is set when you press the shutter button all the way. You can't lock autoexposure.

- *AE/AF, no AE Lock:* Similar to the preceding mode, this one also is designed to help you capture moving subjects in the AI Servo mode. Pressing the shutter button halfway initiates autoexposure metering, which is adjusted continuously as needed until the time you snap the picture. Pressing the AE Lock button starts the autofocusing servo system; releasing the button stops it. You cannot lock autoexposure in this mode.

6. **Press the Set button to finalize your choice.**

   Now when you shoot in an advanced exposure mode, the camera locks focus and exposure according to the option you selected. In the fully automatic modes, the settings have no effect; you still press the shutter button halfway to focus, and you can't lock autoexposure.

Disabling the AF-Assist Beam

In dim lighting, your camera may emit an AF (autofocus)-assist beam from the built-in flash when you press the shutter button halfway — assuming that the flash unit is open, of course. This pulse of light helps the camera "see" its target better, improving the performance of the autofocusing system.

If you're shooting in a situation where the AF-assist beam may be distracting to your subject or to others in the room, you can disable it. Take these steps to control this aspect of your camera:

1. **Set the Mode dial to P, Tv, Av, M, or A-DEP.**

   As with the other customization options discussed in preceding sections, this one is available only in these advanced exposure modes.

2. **Display Setup Menu 3, highlight Custom Functions, and press Set.**

   You're taken to the main launching pad for adjusting all the Custom Functions.

3. **Press the right or left cross key as needed to select Custom Function 6.**

4. **Press the Set button.**

   Now the options shown in Figure 11-5 become accessible.

5. **Press the up or down cross key to highlight your desired setting.**

   Setting 1 disables the AF-assist beam of both the built-in flash and compatible Canon EX-series Speedlite external flash units. Setting 2 disables the beam of the built-in flash while allowing the beam of a compatible EX-series Speedlite to function normally.

Figure 11-5: You can disable the autofocus-assist beam.

6. **Press the Set button.**

   Your chosen setting affects all the advanced exposure modes. In fully automatic modes, the autofocus assist beam continues to light from the built-in flash when the camera deems it necessary.

Without the aid of the assist beam, the camera may have trouble autofocusing in dim lighting. The easiest solution is to simply focus manually; Chapter 1 shows you how.

Enabling Mirror Lockup

One of the components involved in the optical system of an SLR camera is a tiny mirror that moves when you press the shutter button. The small vibration caused by the movement of the mirror can result in slight blurring of the image when you use a very slow shutter speed, shoot with a long telephoto lens, or take extreme close-up shots. To eliminate the possibility, your camera offers a feature called *mirror lockup.* When you enable this feature, the mirror movement is completed well before the shot is recorded, thus preventing any camera shake.

To try out this feature, take these steps:

1. **Set the Mode dial to an advanced exposure mode.**

   Mirror lockup isn't available in the fully automatic exposure modes. So set that dial to P, Tv, Av, M, or A-DEP.

2. **Display Setup Menu 3, highlight Custom Functions, and press Set.**

3. **Press the right or left cross key to scroll to Custom Function 8.**

4. **Press Set to access the options shown in Figure 11-6.**

5. **Press the up or down cross key to highlight the Enable option, as shown in the figure.**

6. **Press the Set button.**

After you enable mirror lockup, you take a slightly different approach to picture-taking than usual. Use this technique:

Figure 11-6: Mirror lockup prevents camera shake caused by the movement of the optical system's mirror.

1. **Frame your shot.**

2. **If using autofocus, press and hold the shutter button halfway to lock focus.**

   Or, if you prefer manual focusing, twist the focusing ring as needed to focus the image.

3. **Press the shutter button all the way down to lock up the mirror. Then release the button.**

At this point, you can no longer see anything through the viewfinder. Don't panic — that's normal. The mirror's function is to enable you to see in the viewfinder the scene that the lens will capture, and mirror lockup prevents it from serving that purpose.

4. Press the shutter button all the way again.

The camera then takes the picture.

Using a tripod or other support is critical to getting a shake-free shot in situations that call for mirror lockup. For even more protection, set your camera to the 2-second self-timer mode, introduced in Chapter 2, and take your hands completely off the camera after you press the shutter button in Step 3. The picture is taken two seconds after the mirror lockup occurs. If you purchased the remote-control unit for your camera, you instead can trigger the shutter button using it.

Adding Cleaning Instructions to Images

You've no doubt noticed that your camera displays a message that says "Sensor Cleaning" every time you turn off the camera. And when you turn on the camera, a little "cleaning" icon flickers in the lower-right corner of the Shooting Settings display. These alerts tell you that the camera is performing a self-maintenance step that is designed to remove from the sensor any dust particles that may have made their way into the camera interior.

If you don't see these alerts, open Setup Menu 2, choose the Sensor Cleaning option, and then press Set. Next, set the Auto Cleaning option to Enable. (There's really no reason to disable this feature, although Canon gives you the choice to do so.)

The automated sensor cleaning normally is all that's necessary to keep the sensor dust-free. But if you notice that small spots are appearing consistently on your images, you may need to step in and take action on your own.

The best solution, of course, is to take your camera to a good repair shop and have the sensor professionally cleaned. I *do not* recommend that you take on this job yourself; it's a delicate procedure, and you can easily ruin your camera.

Until you can have the camera cleaned, however, you can use a feature on Shooting Menu 2 to create a custom dust-removal filter that you can apply in Digital Photo Professional, which is one of the free programs that ships with your camera.

The first step in creating the filter is to record a data file that maps the location of the dust spots on the sensor. To do this, you need a white piece of paper or other white surface and a lens that can achieve a focal length of 55mm or greater. (The kit lens on the Rebel XS/1000D qualifies.) Then take these steps:

1. **Set the lens focal length at 55mm or longer.**

   If you own the kit lens, just zoom in as far as possible, which sets the focal length at 55mm.

2. **Switch the camera to manual focusing.**

   On the kit lens, move the focus switch on the lens from AF to MF.

3. **Set focus at infinity.**

   Some lenses have a marking that indicates the infinity position — the symbol looks like a number 8 lying on its side. If your lens doesn't have the marking, hold the camera so that the lens is facing you and then turn the lens focusing ring clockwise until it stops.

4. **Set the camera to one of the advanced exposure modes (P, Tv, Av, M, or A-DEP).**

   You can create the dust data file only in these modes.

5. **Display Shooting Menu 2 and highlight Dust Delete Data, as shown on the left in Figure 11-7.**

Figure 11-7: You can record dust-removal data that can be read by Digital Photo Professional.

6. **Press the Set button.**

   Now you see the Dust Delete Data message shown on the right in Figure 11-7.

7. **Press the right cross key to highlight OK and then press Set.**

   The camera performs its normal automatic sensor-cleaning ritual, which takes a second or two. Then you see the instruction screen shown on the left in Figure 11-8.

Figure 11-8: The Dust Delete Data is recorded when you press the shutter button all the way.

8. **Position the camera so that it's about 8 to 12 inches from your white card or piece of paper.**

   Your card or paper needs to be large enough to completely fill the viewfinder at this distance.

9. **Press the shutter button all the way to record the Dust Delete Data.**

   No picture is taken; the camera just records the Dust Delete Data in its internal memory. If the process was successful, you see the congratulatory message shown on the right in Figure 11-8.

   If the camera tells you that it couldn't record the data, the lighting conditions are likely to blame. Make sure that the lighting is even across the entire surface of your white card or paper and that the paper is sufficiently illuminated and then try again.

10. **Press the Set button.**

    The current date now appears on the initial Dust Delete Data screen (shown on the right in Figure 11-7).

After you create your Dust Delete Data file, the camera attaches the data to every subsequent image, regardless of whether you shoot in the fully automatic or advanced exposure modes.

To clean a photo, open it in Digital Photo Professional and choose Start Stamp Tool from the Tools menu. Your photo then appears in an editing window; click the Apply Dust Delete Data button to start the automated dust-busting feature. The program's manual and Help system offer details about this process; look for the Help entry related to using the Copy Stamp tool.

Turning Off the Shooting Settings Screen

When you turn on your camera, the monitor automatically turns on and displays the Shooting Settings screen. At least, it does if you stick with the default setting selected for Custom Function 11, which bears the lengthy name LCD Display When Power On.

You can prevent the monitor from displaying the screen every time you power up the camera, if you choose. The monitor is one of the biggest drains on the camera battery, so limiting it to displaying information only when you need it can extend the time between battery charges.

As with other Custom Functions, this option works only when the camera is set to one of the advanced exposure modes — in other modes, the screen still appears automatically. Still, any battery savings can be helpful when you're running low on juice.

To take advantage of this feature, take these steps:

1. **Set the camera to P, Tv, Av, M, or A-DEP mode.**

2. **Display Setup Menu 3, highlight Custom Functions, and press Set.**

3. **Use the cross keys to select Custom Function 11 and then press Set.**

   You see the screen shown in Figure 11-9.

4. **Press the up or down cross key to highlight Retain Power Off Status.**

5. **Press Set.**

6. **Press the DISP button to turn off the monitor.**

7. **Turn off the camera.**

Figure 11-9: You can prevent the monitor from turning on automatically when you power up the camera.

When you turn on the camera again, the monitor will not automatically display the Shooting Settings screen — as long as the Mode dial is set to an advanced shooting mode, that is. Nor will the screen appear when you press the shutter button halfway, as it normally does.

To view the screen, press the DISP button; press the button again to return to monitor-off status. Alternatively, you can press the Set button to turn the monitor on and off, but only if you stick with the default setting for Custom Function 10, explained at the start of this chapter.

Note that if you turn off the camera while the Shooting Settings screen is displayed, it will appear again automatically the next time you power up the camera. So if you really want the monitor to retain its "power off status," be sure to press DISP (or Set) to shut off the monitor before you turn off the camera.

Creating Desktop Wallpaper

You can quickly turn an image on your camera memory card into *desktop wallpaper* — a background image that appears on your monitor, behind any icons or program windows. For example, I plastered my Windows desktop with a water lily image, as shown in Figure 11-10.

Figure 11-10: You can use a favorite image as your monitor background.

To decorate your monitor, follow these steps:

1. **Connect the camera to the computer, following the instructions in Chapter 8.**

   After a short time, the Direct Transfer screen appears on the camera monitor, as shown in Figure 11-11.

2. **Highlight Wallpaper and then press the Set button.**

   The camera monitor displays your most recent image.

3. **Press the right or left cross key to scroll to the image you want to use as wallpaper.**

4. **Press the Set button to start the transfer.**

Figure 11-11: Highlight Wallpaper and then press Set to select the image.

   The camera downloads the image to your hard drive and then saves a copy of it in the correct format to use for wallpaper. The wallpaper image then appears on the computer desktop.

If you prefer, you also can turn an image that's already on your computer's hard drive into wallpaper by using Canon ZoomBrowser EX (Windows) or ImageBrowser (Mac). See the Help system in those programs for instructions. Also note that because the images your Canon creates have an aspect ratio of 3:2, they won't fully cover the desktop of most monitors, which typically have an aspect ratio of either 4:3 or 16:9. If you want the image to fully fill the screen, you must edit it to the correct proportions and then use the Windows or Mac display customization tools to turn the edited file into wallpaper. Chapter 10 shows you how to crop to specific proportions.

Adding Original Decision Data

Now that photo editing has gone mainstream, determining whether a digital photo has been altered from its original state is difficult. However, through Custom Function 12, you now have a way to prove that a picture file hasn't been edited.

If you enable this Custom Function, as shown in Figure 11-12, the camera adds to the image file a tag that verifies the photo as original. There's a catch, though: To make use of that tag when the file is opened on your computer, you must use a special piece of software, the Original Data Decision Security Kit OSK-E3. You can buy that product for about $650.

If you want to know more about the whole issue, visit the Canon Web site.

Creating Your Very Own Camera Menu

Canon does a good job of making it easy to change the most commonly used camera settings. You can access many critical options by pressing the buttons on the camera body, and others require only a quick trip to the camera menus.

Figure 11-12: This Custom Function is relevant only if you buy a $650 accessory software kit.

To make things even simpler for you, the Rebel XS/1000D enables you to create your own, custom menu containing up to six items from the camera's other six menus. For example, I created a custom menu that contains the options shown in Figure 11-13. (The last item, My Menu Settings, is always on the menu; more about that later.) Logically enough, the custom menu goes by the name My Menu and is represented by the green star icon, as shown in the figure.

Figure 11-13: Group your favorite menu items together with the My Menu feature.

To create your menu, take these steps:

1. **Set the camera Mode dial to an advanced exposure mode.**

   Sadly, you can create and order from your custom menu only in P, Tv, Av, M, and A-DEP exposure modes.

2. **Press the Menu button and display the My Menu screen, shown on the left in Figure 11-14.**

3. **Highlight My Menu Settings, as shown in the figure, and press Set.**

   Now you see the second screen in Figure 11-14.

4. **Highlight Register and press Set.**

   You're presented with a scrolling list that contains each and every item found on the camera's other six menus, as shown on the left in Figure 11-15.

Figure 11-14: To add items to your menu, select Register and press Set.

Figure 11-15: Highlight an item to put on your menu and press Set.

5. **Highlight the first item that you want to include on your custom menu.**

   If you want to add a specific Custom Function to your menu, scroll *past* the item named Custom Functions to find and highlight the individual function. (The item named Custom Functions simply puts the Custom Functions menu item on your menu, and you still have to wade through the multiple levels of steps to get to your function.)

6. **Press Set.**

   You see a confirmation screen like the one shown on the right in Figure 11-15.

7. **Highlight OK and press Set.**

   You return to the list of menu options. The option you just added to your menu is dimmed in the list.

8. **Repeat Steps 5 through 7 to add up to five additional items to your menu.**

9. **Press the Menu button.**

    You then see the My Menu screen, where the items you added to the menu should appear.

After creating your menu, you can further customize and manage it as follows:

✔ **Give your menu priority.** You can tell the camera that you want it to automatically display your menu anytime you press the Menu button. To do so, select My Menu Settings on the main My Menu screen and then press Set. You see the screen shown on the right in Figure 11-14. Highlight Display from My Menu and press Set. Highlight Enable and press Set again.

✔ **Change the order of the list of menu items.** Once again, highlight My Menu Settings and press Set. Then highlight the Sort option (refer to the right screen in Figure 11-14) and press Set. Highlight a menu item, press Set, and then use the up or down cross keys to move the item up or down in the list. Press Set to glue the menu item in its new position. Press Menu to return to the My Menu Settings screen; press again to return to your custom menu.

✔ **Delete menu items.** Display your menu, highlight My Menu Settings, and press Set. Then, to delete a single item, highlight Delete and press Set. Highlight the menu item you want to remove and press Set again. Highlight OK and press Set again to confirm your decision. To remove all items from your custom menu, choose Delete All Items, press Set, highlight OK, and press Set again.

Getting Free Help and Creative Ideas

Okay, so this last tip is a bit of a cheat: It isn't actually found on your camera, but it will help you better understand the features that are. I speak of the Canon Web site, which you can access at www.canon.com.

If you haven't yet visited the site, I encourage you to do so. In the Support section of the site, you can get free technical support for camera problems and even download an electronic copy of your camera manual, should you happen to misplace the one that shipped in the camera box. Most importantly, check periodically to make sure that your camera is running the latest *firmware,* which is the geekspeak term for the camera's internal software.

Be sure to also check out the Learning Center section of the site. There, you can find loads of tutorials and other great instructional offerings not only about your camera but also about the software that ships with it.

Index